NATO:
LOST OR FOUND

SPEECHES ARTICLES
AND STUFF VERBATIM
1991 – 2021

MATJAŽ ŠINKOVEC

NATO: LOST OR FOUND
SPEECHES ARTICLES AND STUFF VERBATIM 1991 – 2021

iUniverse books may be ordered through booksellers or by contacting:

iUniverse
1663 Liberty Drive
Bloomington, IN 47403
www.iuniverse.com
844-349-9409

Because of the dynamic nature of the Internet, any web addresses or links contained in this book may have changed since publication and may no longer be valid. The views expressed in this work are solely those of the author and do not necessarily reflect the views of the publisher, and the publisher hereby disclaims any responsibility for them.

Any people depicted in stock imagery provided by Getty Images are models, and such images are being used for illustrative purposes only.
Certain stock imagery © Getty Images.

Author's e-mail: ambassadorsinkovec@yahoo.com

Front cover: photo of the author with Slovenian troops, in the vicinity of Kabul.

ISBN: 978-1-6632-3426-1 (sc)
ISBN: 978-1-6632-3427-8 (e)

Library of Congress Control Number: 2022900428

Print information available on the last page.

iUniverse rev. date: 01/04/2022

SELECTED OTHER WORKS
BY MATJAŽ ŠINKOVEC

A Night Lighted Tower, LMC Press 1974 (ed., a compilation of Kurt Vonnegut quotes)

Stardrive, LMC 1976, 1ˢᵗ Books 2002 (a collection of short stories) *in print*

Od Bradburyja do Vonneguta, Sekcija za spekulativno umetnost 1978 (ed., a collection of stories)

Peklenski dar, Sekcija za spekulativno umetnost 1981 (ed., a collection of stories)

Kako zmagati na volitvah, ČKZ 1990 (with Božidar Novak, a how-to-win elections handbook)

What a Waste Love Affairs, 1ˢᵗ Books 2002 (a collection of poems) *in print*

Love, iUniverse 2003 (a collection of short stories) *in print*

Goodbye NATO* - *Everything you wanted to know about it but were afraid to ask, Lulu 2006 (ed., with Barbara Žvokelj, a collection of farewell speeches of Ambassadors, Permanent Representatives on the North Atlantic Council, and its Chairman – Secretary General of NATO) *in print*

The Magic Mr. Sweeney, Lulu 2013 (a collection of short stories) *in print*

Toy Toy, Lulu 2013 (a collection of short stories in Lovenian) *in print*

1001 Laws of Survival, Lulu 2013 (a self-help book of rules of life) *in print*

The Book of Morian, Lulu 2013 (a short historic/religious novel) *in print*

The 2020 Vision for the Western Balkans, Lulu 2014 (a collection of speeches) *in print*

Čakajoč Samuela, Lulu 2014 (a collection of speeches and papers) *in print*

The Truth Is Our Most Powerful Weapon - Political Prisoners of Today and Yesterday, Lulu 2017 (ed., with Pia Luznar) *in print*

This book is dedicated to the members of my staff who supported me in various ways during my just about 8-year stint as Slovenia's Ambassador to the North Atlantic Treaty Organization; I only managed to name just a few in my farewell speech to the North Atlantic Council, included in this collection under the title Pearl Eleven. The same goes for my EU Political and Security Committee team between 2011 and 2017. I have deep appreciation for all the expert advice, often included in my speeches, as well as their patience when I diverged from their advice and did things on my own. The combination of both of these elements finally bore fruit – after we had dotted all the i's and crossed all the t's – with Slovenia's accession to the Alliance on 30 March 2004. Belatedly, I would also like to thank these same people for contributing tidbits to the speeches, included in my book The 2020 Vision for the Western Balkans, and to all those anonymous contributors at the relevant ministries at home, especially in the Ministry of Foreign Affairs and Ministry of Defense, who fed their pieces to my staff.

CONTENTS

WE NEED TO MAKE NATO GREAT AGAIN SINCE IN OUR CIVILIZATION OF CLASHES THERE IS NO PERMANENT VALLEY OF PEACE

Why this book now

This book is a compilation of my 70-odd NATO-related speeches, interventions, letters, interviews, articles, and you-name-it last minute thoughts that I have released upon the unsuspecting world from 1991 all the way to 2021, this year, when I turned 70. Some time back I decided it was high time to clear my desk of NATO-related stuff. If nothing else, it may serve as a historic document of the past three decades since Slovenia's independence and my endeavors since I first addressed the North Atlantic Assembly meeting in Madrid in September 1991 with my wish that Slovenia became a NATO member. Well, if anyone cares about Slovenia's recent history. Especially in Slovenia.

The title of the book "NATO – LOST OR FOUND" reflects both the uncertainty of NATO's future as well as my incomplete search for the texts of relevant statements I have made in the 30-year period. It seems I never accepted the nebulous belief that there might be life after NATO although I did perform many other jobs since my farewell from NATO HQ at the end of 2006. However, the record shows that I did dip into the subject occasionally. It must be in my blood, my DNA. I still believe that NATO is an Alliance of Values: peace, order, education, hard work, initiative, enterprise, creativity, cooperation, looking out for one another, looking out for the future of children, patriotism, fair play, and honesty. I believe that the wide spectrum of shared challenges requires NATO to retain awareness, flexibility, agility, and freedom of action to ensure it has the right forces in the right place at the right time – to protect or defend threatened Allies or contribute to crisis management outside NATO territory.

I am using the opportunity of this foreword to voice my concerns about NATO's future. What worries me most of all is its relationship with the European Union and the role of the most important Ally, the United States. In addition, generally – as far as I can see – the Allies have a cloudy vision of how this bastion of our values and our way of life can be preserved and empowered to carry out, using its tools in the form of missions and operations, wherever necessary around the globe.

I am certain we do have this single bedrock of stability and I believe we should stick to it. Everything else is a wet dream or a bad dream. NATO is still the only insurance against the unspeakable horrors of war, which could destroy civilization. There is still general complacency that the U.S. will always be there with its clout and resources. We need less talk about European Armies and strategic Autonomy. They are empty buzzwords meaning little. If talking about EU countries' contribution to defense it is necessary to emphasize ending duplication with NATO and inefficiency in defense budgets.

How the book is organized

Thank God (an agnostic speaking) this compilation is not complete as many speeches resembled each other *ad nauseam*, some were unfortunately lost or misplaced, some deemed inappropriate for their eventual sensitivity, while some other pieces are hoping to see the light of day in the long-planned books with the working titles, such as *Putting Slovenia on the Map* and *Slovenia's Contribution to the Formulation of EU's Common Foreign and Security Policy*. All confidential stuff is excluded.

Each piece is previewed with a short intro to set the scene. They go – using European-style dates, from the most recent to the most remote, except for the 2011–2017 "EU–NATO Medley" that I did not want to break up. They, as well as the intros, are presented without editing, exactly as they were written/delivered, with a mixture of U.S. and British spelling/misspelling, and in naturally flawed "*international English*," to have their authenticity preserved. While I was putting the texts together, Word kept correcting me incessantly. However, I wanted to remain true to history, without adding any attractive embellishments and updating. Only this introduction was slightly edited and/or commented on by my dear friends Christina Webber Ragsdale and Barbara Žvokelj.

I had intended to use asterisks in the table of contents to mark the pieces that I deemed important or interesting. The category of "important" included my briefest intervention to the Euro Atlantic Partnership Council the day after the 9/11 attack on the United States, dramatic words that I addressed to U.S. Defense Secretary William Cohen during the Kosovo crisis in 1999, my first intervention to the North Atlantic Assembly's Political Committee back in 1990 (being the first mention in any international organization of Slovenia's eventual future membership of NATO), and the quite visionary speech that I still love reading today, my contribution to the debate *Looking at NATO in 2015*, delivered at a North Atlantic Council's Away Day in 2005. I could include in that category also my probably never published article from 2014 and my 15th anniversary of membership speech from 2019. In the category of "interesting" I wanted to mention my "Women in Space" address to the WINE (Women in NATO Eating) lunch club, done in a somewhat relaxed atmosphere at the NATO HQ Staff Center, overflowing with my twisted sense of humor, including self-mockery. A former NAC colleague of mine called me in his farewell speech the "master of self-deprecation." I initially thought that highlighting just a dozen pieces would make it easier for the reader to get the gist of the book, but I finally decided not to take decision-making out of my gentle reader's hands.

My personal contribution

While everything that I said and did related to the Alliance in the past three decades was on behalf of Slovenia, I did it in my quite particular way that I hoped would help us achieve our objectives: first joining NATO and then becoming a top-notch Ally. As Slovenia's Ambassador to NATO, I was pushy enough to have my country take formal decisions on general security issues and its role within the Alliance. During my 8-year tenure I managed to develop on the one hand direct relations with the Prime Ministers, the two most involved Ministers (Foreign Affairs and Defense), Chiefs-of-Staff of the Slovenian Army, as well as Members of Parliament. I always recognized that my formal bosses were the President, Prime Minister, Minister of Foreign Affairs and Minister of Defense. However, as a strict individualist I saw myself as the person who should know best what Slovenia needed and I always remained staunchly loyal to my country, no matter who was in power at any particular time. This may sound preposterous but with all the changes of governments and personalities I am sure this stance served Slovenia well.

Not everything went smoothly: I did have battles both with Ministry of Defense and Ministry of Foreign Affairs officials to push through decisions, such as our troops being deployed to Herat, not Kandahar, NATO's solution for air policing Slovenia's section of NATO airspace, signing up to the Air to Ground Surveillance scheme, a 35 million US dollars grant for the upgrading of our military airfield at Cerklje, membership in the consortium that owns and operates 3 giant C-17 cargo airplanes. As far as the latter is concerned, I was even asked to propose how many flight hours per year we would need the aircraft for. The Slovenian Army was thinking of 30. I said 60 (4 Slovenian Army troop rotations annually, requiring 4 return flights by a C-17 to Afghanistan) and that was it. Simple. However, probably the most important battles were the following. First: the one that decided that it is the Government and not the Parliament that decides if and where to deploy our troops. Second: my lobbying to prevent before the national referendum on Slovenia's membership in NATO in 2003 the expected opposition by two large NGO's (WW2 National Liberation Combatants Union and the Trade Union Confederation). Not all of my suggestions fell on fertile ground, such as the one that Slovenia should pull its troops out of Afghanistan by September 11, 2011.

On the other hand, I developed sincere relations with my colleagues on the North Atlantic Council. After all, NATO's decision-making is based on consensus. The North Atlantic Council needs to be a closely-knit family to carry out sometimes quite difficult decisions. As the first Secretary General of NATO Lord Ismay said ages ago, "The Council had been like a large family and the international staff had seemed like our children." After all, most of the important decisions are taken by mere Ambassadors. When I came up in 2005 with the idea to have the next Defense Ministerial in Portorož on Slovenia's Riviera and cleared it with Prime Minister Janša and Defense Minister Erjavec I still had to sell it to my colleagues. I managed that and I feel we had in September 2006 the best NATO Defense Ministerial ever. The organization perfectly carried out by MOD people, including a great party next to the beach, with a grand view of the Bay of Piran and the high seas. And probably it is time to reveal the secret why I wanted it to take place at that particular time: on the day of the Ministerial my wife Magdalena and I were 100 years old together.

I should explain that NATO Ambassadors are extraordinarily pampered (if I forget about 12+ hour working days), as governments provide them with VIP transport whenever and wherever they decide to fly. It is not just dangerous places like Afghanistan where during Ambassadors' visit all the NATO forces there provided security. Once, when the North Atlantic Council was visiting the uber-dangerous Kandahar, its members were taken by a number of Black Hawks to "recce" its surroundings. Each Black Hawk carried about half a dozen Ambassadors, pilots, as well as two hopefully not too trigger-happy gunners on each side of the helicopter (HELO in NATO talk), following the movements of people on the ground. Each HELO was protected by two Apache attack helicopters, left and right. Awesome.

For the long trips, the U.S. provided either an enormous C-17 in sort-of-VIP configuration, including bunk beds, or an all-business class B-777. So did other members states; often Prime Ministers lending their "private" jets. For trips to safer destinations celebratory meetings, such as Ministerials or Summits, our spouses were also hosted; after all, NATO is a family affair, if we talk of values. My top three values, Freedom, Family, Country, had no problem with that.

MEGA

I first became fully aware of the growing threat of some EU forces seriously attempting to push NATO into irrelevance or obscurity, sitting at the informal EU Defense Ministerial in Bratislava on 27 September 2016, listening to several worrisome ministerial interventions. It became obvious to me that the unfortunate results of the kangaroo Brexit referendum had opened flood gates to the onslaught of proponents of the Defense Union, the fishy smelling PESCO ("Permanent Structured Cooperation"), the European Army, Permanent Operational HQ and the like, that had until then been kept in check mostly by the United Kingdom. The rhetoric of the ministers of three large EU member states, Germany, France and Italy, soon to be joined by Spain, was full of "not competition but complementarity with NATO, no duplication, a single set of forces, strong Europe - strong NATO" babble but the nonverbalized ambitions sort-of pointed elsewhere. I felt that EU's "call to arms" should concentrate only on forging a more integrated and competitive European defense industry and market but not create either "EU's strategic autonomy" or "defense sovereignty" of Europe.

While I trusted, also on the basis of reactions of quite a number of ministers who opposed more or less vehemently the big guys, that at the end of the day the political will to actually go all the way to the dark side would be lacking, I felt uncomfortable with the attempts to play dangerously with the North Atlantic Alliance, the sole guarantor of true European Defense, as I saw it both as a former hippie, former fighter for independent Slovenia and former Ambassador to NATO.

Usually, such ministerials are at best run-of-the-mill boring occasions, but this one was quite different. Sitting at the front table, having for some reason found an unassigned seat between my defense minister and the Portuguese one, I realized, looking around the packed Slovak Philharmonic Hall, that I was probably the person who had attended most defense ministerials – on NATO, the defunct Western European Union and EU sides. Perhaps it was time to quit. But could I? Having been the first Slovenian who proposed – while we were still part of Yugoslavia – that

Slovenia should join NATO I felt that it was my personal mission to help carry on the baton.

Later on, I even got a bit involved in the process of the drafting of the EU-NATO Joint Declaration that was to be issued just before the 2016 Warsaw Summit. As an EU Political and Security Committee Ambassador on the European Union side I was consulted in a couple of rounds by the European Council drafters. On the other hand, I had the opportunity to contribute my intimate thoughts – with which I have always been at least transparent if not pushy – to NATO drafters who approached me on account of yours truly being a rare specimen of someone who had served as Ambassador on both sides of the major but unseen divide, that I call the River, that separates the EU and NATO in Brussels. I still feel strongly about improving the pathetic and naturally quite schizophrenic state of relations between the two organizations, in my time there sharing 22 Member States.

On both occasions I expressed my firm belief that NATO should be recognized as Europe's sole defense organization and that everything possible should be done to build bridges between the EU and NATO and truly make them strategic partners if not true allies. In the backdrop of what I was saying remained my profound doubts about the current defense thinking in EU's institutions where Global Strategy appeared to me more like Global Stupidity. Faced with threats coming from the East and the South, and uncertainties inside, Europe seemed to be pushed by some of its most important players even closer to the slippery edge of no return. What lies beyond this edge is a Europe that would be moving away from its North Atlantic Allies, a Europe incapable of forming its collective defense, a Europe without having a nuclear deterrent, a Europe wide open to further aggression by Russia, for instance. As I see it, "a post-pandemic Europe hopefully without internal borders but unfortunately a Europe without balls." I apologize for this bit of *machismo*.

However, I am encouraged by the fact that we have had numerous failed attempts at developing a serious EU defense cooperation project in the past and that there still exist large conflicts around defense cultures and long-term priorities, as well as both technical and political obstacles to successfully implementing PESCO. Europe's defense momentum may not lead to much if anything at all. I guess when you are incapable of concentrating on what is desperately needed, such as the creation of a true European maritime and land external borders protection force, to counter irregular/illegal mass immigration and trafficking of who-knows-what, you start dreaming and wasting resources on unachievable ideas. All in all, I hope that there is a chance of making Europe Great Again by protecting EU's external borders. If/when that "level of ambition" is achieved we may look elsewhere.

MAGA

In Europe, we loved the fairy tale where the U.S. would be there for us forever. However, the worrying signals have not only been coming from Europe. The Transatlantic relationship has experienced turbulence since the Cold War ended, but populations and leaders have largely remained committed to the raison-d-être of the Trans-Atlantic strategic partnership. However, not only Trump but also Obama before him tried to redefine the U.S. global leadership. The debate seemed to be stuck, unable to update itself as the question of burden sharing and the articulation of different frameworks of European defense cooperation poisoned the discussions. It has proven exceedingly difficult to overcome the comfortable habits of the pre-1989 world.

With Biden's administration, we could initially see some constructive changes in the U.S. approach, such as not romancing or at least acquiescing world dictators, but I was not ecstatic either. Then the fiasco of the pullout from Afghanistan added to my doubts about U.S. leadership. Also, America's military strength has been rapidly deteriorating in the face of technological change and increasingly competitive rivals. We are in an uncertain period of transition, with U.S. dominance in the rearview mirror and a more anarchic order looming dimly beyond. A recalibration of the geopolitical landscape amid the coronavirus pandemic means that the world is wrought with new and resurgent challenges and disorders. It may be high time to realistically try to Make America Great Again.

Making NATO Great Again

It is evident that Europe and the United States will be facing daunting challenges that threaten our way of life: pandemics, economic recessions, almost hopelessly accelerating climate change, a rising China, Russian troll farms, collapse of INF treaty, "DPRK" and emerging security threats. The issues that transcend national borders can only be successfully dealt with together and there is no better mechanism than NATO.

Europe and the U.S. do need a renewed joint Trans-Atlantic agenda: reasserting NATO's free world values and principles. The main threats (China, Russia and the wider Middle East) should not be just seen as challenges but opportunities to raise the liberal order to a higher level, together with friends and allies worldwide. The strong Alliance needs to become stronger still. NATO is the only place that brings Europe and North America together, every day! We need the political will to work with others that share our basic values, such as Australia, New Zealand, Japan, South Korea, not forgetting the European "neutral/non-aligned" countries. Democracy and human rights need to be put at the top of NATO's agenda. The Alliance cannot be just an elite-driven relationship between politicians and business leaders; it needs to be much more inclusive. To quote Dwight Eisenhower, "When the world is in genuine danger from the 'extremes of the Far Left and the Far Right' we need a pragmatic course wide enough to accommodate all reasonable citizens, from the moderate conservative to the moderate social democrat. These are the people who get things done."

It is high time for the Alliance to attempt again forming a more stable and more productive relationship with Russia. It is evident that there are no shortcuts to restoring trust. Russia's actions in Ukraine fit into a larger pattern of aggression. It is true that to counter Putin's sabre rattling – as Russia will be forced to create and deploy new types of weapons, seeking to restore empire in the East and weaken and divide the West, using international NGOs as a tool for her projection of influence – NATO can respond both diplomatically and militarily. But as someone who back in 1999 opened on my own a face-to-face ad-hoc chat with the then Russian Ambassador to Belgium and NATO, Sergei Kisliyak, much later known as Russia's Number

One Spy in Washington, of eventual future membership of Russia in a wider NATO, I do see a glimmer of hope that there still are chances to improve the present stalemate. If we look at NATO and Russia from beyond Earth's orbit it is obvious that we should have more common interests than not. It is doubtful that Russia and China could evolve their "comprehensive strategic partnership" into a comprehensive alliance; however, our inactivity towards Russia could ease if not enable such a process.

I do not quite see that there is a clash of civilizations, but I do realize we live in a civilization of clashes. I am sure that there is no permanent *Valley of Peace*, referring to a post WW2 Slovenian movie the filming of which I witnessed at close range as a child. There are lots of areas where more could be done, as international arms control keeps eroding. Arms control needs to remain among NATO's priorities while it is hard to claim that it is in NATO's DNA. Nuclear testing is a nightmare that still plagues us all today. Comprehensive Nuclear-Test Treaty (CTBT) still awaits entry-into-force and full universalization. Dangerous military technologies are emerging and are unregulated. Dialogue between adversaries is constrained, adding to instability. Failure to act is likely to result in a new nuclear arms race.

More needs to be done to improve interaction with China. In NATO's pivot to Asia China should be at the center of our concerns. There is a host of challenges associated with China's Rise (remember 1620!) and its implications for Transatlantic security. If we do not have the tools, we need to create new ones to counter China's global ambitions. And we should get even more aware of Outer Space. Deterrence in space is an extension of terrestrial deterrence policy, but the use of space to support nuclear and other high-end systems makes deterrence failure much more consequential. Cyber threats are more than just a buzzword. Let us not pussy foot around. The Alliance is still far from being able to face cyber threats in a relevant way.

There are many other issues that should or will concern NATO. One being the "Turkish question" as Ankara is obviously a destabilizing factor with its reckless trajectory vis-à-vis the Kurds and Syria. A decade ago, there were democratic hopefuls of international liberal order (Brazil,

India, Indonesia, South Africa, Turkey…), however expectations have been sobered by autocratization and regression. And, as I have devoted quite a bit of thinking to my country's neighborhood to the South East, the Western Balkans, security in that once "powder keg" region is intrinsically linked to stability in the EU as whole. Eventual land swaps are extremely dangerous. The WB is not a jigsaw puzzle but a Rubik's cube. Any move produces unexpected changes elsewhere. I had argued, unsuccessfully, for a "big bang" entry of the countries of that region into the EU and NATO. However, the "regatta" principle has prevailed. I believe this has made the integration of this part of the Continent into a "Europe Whole and Free and in Peace" more difficult. For Slovenia this is not an academic question. Not only that we border on Croatia, but even Bosnia-Herzegovina is only 25 miles from Slovenia's border, as the crow flies.

SLOGA

Finally, Slovenia. I will not repeat what I said at the celebration of 15 years of my country in NATO; do read that. The state of affairs in Slovenia, particularly regarding our involvement in the Alliance, seemed to deteriorate with anti-NATO forces gaining ground until the latest change of Government early 2020. For ages, most Slovenian politicians in charge were paying lip service to the "Two Percent" while the country experienced a continuous fall of the percentage of GDP spent on defense. With the new people in charge, namely Prime Minister Janša and Defense Minister Tonin, we saw then an upturn of activities to not only raise the spending but also revitalize the armed forces. I do hope their tenure is long enough for results to show. I felt a glimmer of hope in March of this year when, finally, after 17 years of Slovenia's membership in NATO, I was honored to raise NATO's flag at the MFA, together with Minister of Foreign Affairs Dr. Anže Logar. I do hope it will keep proudly flying there.

The deep division between the Left and the Right, stemming from the times of WW2 resistance to the Nazis and post-war massacres, demands that sensible leaders dedicate themselves to national reconciliation, or at least try to find at least concordance (sloga in Slovenian) if not unity on a handful of vital national issues. Let us try to make Slovenia Great Again.

15 YEARS OF SLOVENIA'S MEMBERSHIP IN NATO

Slovenia organized on 20 March 2019 a formal celebration of its 15 years in the Alliance with an event at the Brdo Convention Center, in the grounds of Brdo Castle, in the olden days used by the Hapsburgs, Karađorđevićs and Marshall Tito. The MFA, not knowing how to get in touch with former Secretary General Lord Robertson, asked for my assistance. I was glad he agreed to come in spite of having to use a low cost flight to Ljubljana and back to London. I was sort-of elated I was included in the panel discussion after the main event with Presidential and Prime Minister level speakers. I followed George who was, as always, brilliant. I had my usual 5 plus minute song and dance and was later asked twice to add some thoughts. In the text below, I have integrated the three interventions. I sort-of forced my Minister Dr. Miro Cerar, who was in the audience, to publicly agree there and then that I could say whatever I wanted, in spite of not following the official line. If you have nothing better to do – and I cannot quite imagine that – there is a video of the panel on YouTube. https://www.youtube.com/watch?v=LEVbgzqmyBQ

Thank you very much, Chair, and, really, it's good to have you back here, George, after quite a while.

I also want to use this opportunity to acknowledge what Lord Robertson and the British Labor Government did for us two decades ago.

In 1997 they – namely Defense Secretary George Robertson and Foreign Secretary Robin Cook – proposed to include Slovenia on the list of invitees to join NATO. Instead of a "small" enlargement with Poland, the Czech Republic and Hungary, it would have been a "smallish" enlargement, 3 plus 1. Unfortunately, the U.S. did not support this idea.

I also want to thank the Slovenian Army Big Band for having played in my garden 13 years ago. They had a wonderful concert there. And I think when they sang a few minutes ago their "ra-ta-ta:" you could see that NATO is fun and not as serious as it sometimes sounds.

As I was asked by the Chair about history, let me start with a very original quote, not from any Secretary General of NATO, but from the Oscars ceremony, by Lady Gaga: "If you have a dream – fight for it!" Not very original, but she's pretty influential, as they say.

My dream was – and I first expressed it in the Slovenian Parliament -- back in 1991 – before our recognition – for Slovenia to be in NATO. I wanted Slovenia to sit at the top table, in the Alliance of Values that won the Cold War!

A year after the 1997 NATO Summit Fiasco I was sent by the late Prime Minister Drnovšek to Brussels and then got stuck there for just about 8 years as Slovenia's Ambassador to NATO and the first Permanent Representative on the North Atlantic Council, NAC in short.

It was not easy to shape up Slovenia in the five accession chapters (political, economic, military, security, legal) even though we actually had already become a de-facto Ally during NATO's Allied Force Campaign over Serbia, don't forget that, by providing both our airspace and intelligence.

Still, we managed: I believe we became a good rookie Ally, played a constructive role in the consensus-based NAC's decision-making, sent troops to Afghanistan, Kosovo and Iraq, opted for NATO's no-cost air policing of our airspace, became even a co-owner of 3 giant C-17 strategic transport airplanes (that nobody in Slovenia knows anything about), and entered the Air-Ground Surveillance scheme. We opted for fully professional Armed Forces and now spend almost zilch on defense in comparison with what we had to pay for the so-called defense of the former federation. When I left NATO in October 2006 Slovenia had more troops in NATO's operations than any other Ally, on the per capita basis of course. That was before all U.S. troops came under NATO command, and then we were Number 2. Well done, Slovenia.

Where do we go from here? Back in 2005, I presented a Science Fiction sounding scenario, at a NAC Away Day discussion, talking about NATO in 2015. Among the elements threatening us, that I predicted, were the following: 1: Spread of more violent Islamic extremism. 2: Mass migrations. 3: Militarization of China. 4: Rise of authoritarian Russia. 5: Effects of Global Warming. That was 14 years ago: and where are we today?

Relevance of NATO has been discussed for decades. It reminds me of questions if the Rolling Stones in their Seventies are still relevant today. I feel they both are. As I see it, 70 years ago the Democratic community probably faced a less uncertain security environment than we do today. Even the threats mostly in our minds today could be just "small fry" in comparison with the magnitude of the threats we could – and probably will – face in the future. Perhaps the public perception is that this very moment we do not need NATO that bad. But defense planning is not something that produces results overnight. It takes years. And coalitions of the willing are not the right answer to long term threats. We need to maintain and develop the Alliance, train it in operations, and find new ways of defending ourselves against new threats.

NATO needs to acquire maximum awareness, it needs to be able to act truly globally, it needs to be more agile and flexible, it needs more common assets and more common funding. I proposed a formula a decade ago that every NATO Ally should be able to have permanently 200 troops per million population in missions and operations. Slovenia has proven that it is possible. To gain a better image and more public support NATO should get involved very visibly in more natural or manmade disaster relief. Finally, there is no NATO without nuclear deterrent and there is no NATO without consensus decision-making and Article Five.

NATO and the EU need to overcome the still pathetic relationship between the two and work together much better. I do hope that one day, perhaps in ten or twenty years, when facing the international crises, they can have common strategies, division of labor and coordination on the ground. Being a PESCO and Defense Union skeptic I would hope that the EU could prove itself at least in successful protection of EU's external borders against irregular migrations and trafficking of people, arms and drugs. But there is no chance at all that Europe could replace NATO in collective defense. I've been following the relationship between the two for quite a while. It's good that finally NAC and the PSC are meeting semi-regularly, sometimes twice in two weeks and sometimes with a two year hiatus.

The current rocky relationship with our largest Ally should be a wakeup call for the Europeans. We need to pay for our own defense – and sensibly, not just for salaries of troops in the barracks and in retirement, but for up-to-date capabilities, training and participation in missions and operations. The U.S. will be fully back in the fold in no time, I expect. But let us walk the walk, not just talk the talk.

Five final brief points on Slovenia:

First, Slovenia needs a small force of well-trained, well-equipped troops that we can send wherever we decide to and rotate. Let us have more teeth and less tail. I feel we have disregarded tactical air transport capabilities, and being a maritime nation we are very shy proving this reality in our sea and the high seas.

Second, can we be proud of evading paying our fair share for our own defense that we have been promising for ages? Does one for all – all for one – mean that someone else has to step up if we do not deliver? Let us not be complacent.

Third, membership in NATO ensures that there will be no militarization of our society, as we had known it in the past. It also keeps us sitting at the top global table. Do we want to crawl back into obscurity?

Fourth, to me, personally, NATO, just like the EU, is not a religion, it's not a burden; it is a tool for maintaining our territorial integrity, security, peace, development, prosperity, freedom, rule of law, our way of life.

Finally, in our global civilization of clashes there will be no permanent Euro-Atlantic valley of peace, if we do not continuously work on maintaining it.

Thank you.

TEN YEARS AFTER: NATO, DON'T GO HOME!

I wrote this article at the request of the Ministry of Defense of Slovenia for an upcoming book supposedly to be published in order to mark the 10th anniversary of Slovenia's membership in NATO. After it had been submitted I was asked to add footnotes and all the rest of the stuff to satisfy the PAIS International. Reluctantly I did that and sent the "improved" text back in the evening of 20 September, 2014. I received the lady editor's confirmation of receipt and then there was silence. I have not bothered since to check whether the book got published with or without my masterpiece or at all. The version below is the original text. I felt all along that the MOD people preferred an academic text, not the real down to earth stuff that I usually do. I had no interest in catering to their aversion to the truth. And aversion to fun!

* * *

I'm goin' home, I'm goin' home
I'm goin' home, I'm goin' home
Hoo, hoo......, right where I belong
Alvin Lee, frontman of the Ten Years After rock band, 1944 - 2013

A VIGNETTE OF A FOREWORD

Over the 2013/2014 Holiday Season I put together two books of old addresses, speeches, lectures, interviews and the like to be published this year.

One is in English – well, the sort of English that non-native diplomat speakers use – and represents an almost integral collection of what I said in various fora from 1999 to 2011 about the Western Balkans. The bulk of it cannot escape dealing with NATO. The other one, in Slovenian, is more eclectic and represents more or less a collection of things I wrote or said in my spare time between 2008 and 2011. That was the period when I was formally the Foreign Minister's Special Envoy for Slovenia's Security Council bid. There is a handful of texts that deal with NATO in depth. What I am driving at are the two different styles of relating what I wanted or was supposed to say. There is the more subdued, static, bureaucratic, professional style that was the result of following too closely the drafts provided by my collaborators, usually because of lack of time on my part. And there is the other one – passionate, flamboyant, egocentric, common sense – where I did more or less my own thing, not following any official line or draft prepared by others.

Well, here we are. On NATO I will do what I have always done or attempted to do: present a very personal view. This should be tolerated of someone who is on record as the first Slovenian who said publicly that Slovenia should become a member of NATO. Yes, this does not even sound preposterous or boastful, but actually boring and uninteresting today. But in the late Eighties, early Nineties, when democratic Slovenia was disentangling itself from a totalitarian multinational state, that sounded just about insane. While talk about joining the European Community was kind of wishful thinking, talking about joining NATO was Science Fiction if not Fantasy. As I was a former minor SF author, perhaps the proposal was seen in that light.

Now, that we have been a full-fledged NATO member for a decade, one is expected to more or less write reminiscences on how this historic step of our nation was made ... and the rest was supposed to be history.

But lo and behold: follow the Slovenian media that in many cases dissected brutally our ten years in the Alliance and open your eyes to what is happening not that far from our borders! We may not be back to square one, but we seem to be getting close to an irreversible situation. It is high time to get serious about NATO again.

Now, before I jump to discussing what should be done about NATO and about ensuring Slovenia's active Allied role in it, let me look back at the past, say a few things about the present time, and then try to gaze over the horizon.

AFTER THE BIG BANG AND THE DINOSAURS

Why did I want Slovenia to be in NATO? It is true I often like to play an *agent provocateur* and devil's advocate. But that was not the case during the period of Slovenia's democratization and independence. I did not only have great *hopes* for Slovenia. It was more: it was a *vision* of Slovenia being a sovereign state on par with other sovereign states: independent, recognized, appreciated and respected. And a Western nation. I was tired of living in a non-aligned nation, living in a country led by an amalgamation of a single party and the military. To become a state like that, membership in the North Atlantic Treaty Organization, the Alliance, was a *sine qua non*.

I believed Slovenians deserved better. And the best of that would be as a member of the Western Alliance. As a Slovenian patriot I also believed that Slovenia should be the first of all eventual members from the territory of the former federation. In such a case we would have the decisive voice on the rest joining or not. I saw this as a powerful tool to solve our bilateral relations with our former compatriots. I also wanted to have the cheapest and most effective defense you can buy. I wanted Slovenia to sit at the top table. And, as we all say, I wanted Slovenia to become part of the family of democratic nations that share values…

It is true that during the first free election campaign in Slovenia, the one in early 1990, I was more tightly lipped. My name was pulled out of the hat, so to say, to be the first representative of any political party to appear on the TV program that presented parties' statements on their electoral programs. It was Monday night, I believe, and I did my song and dance on what kind of Slovenia the party that I was one of the founders of, wanted to have. I believe I compared my vision with the images of Austria and Sweden. Of course, both neutral, but I believed that sounded proper to the audience and I was toeing the then party line.

In the years that followed I was involved bilaterally and multilaterally in NATO business. First as chairman of the Parliamentary Foreign Affairs Committee, then ambassador to the United Kingdom, followed by a short stint as State Undersecretary for NATO & the Western European Union, and then 1999 – 2006 as Slovenia's ambassador to NATO.

I am sure there will be others who will relate in detail our arduous way into the Alliance. But I will spare you and not venture down this road.

Let me just list some of the valuable things I initiated and/or was directly involved in: a. Slovenia becoming a de facto Ally in the Allied Force campaign, b. Slovenia's successful participation in ISAF in Afghanistan, c. Slovenia taking part in NTM-I in Iraq, d. Slovenia's highest number of personnel on the par capita basis in Allied operations in 2006, e. Slovenia acquiring the Russian-built ship Triglav as part of the Russian debt to us, f. Slovenia's participation in the Alliance Ground Surveillance, g. Slovenia's membership in the Strategic Airlift Capability consortium (that owns and operates 3 giant C-17 aircraft, of which the Slovenian defense system is more or less silent), h. Slovenia organizing a NATO Defense Ministerial in Portorož in 2006.

USERS OR LOSERS?

Have our expectations as far as NATO is concerned come true? Or has NATO lost relevance as it has been claimed on and off, *ad nauseam*, since the Fall of the Wall and the disappearance of the Warsaw Pact? Have our dreams and hopes as far as Slovenia is concerned come true? Or have the independence and integration skeptics been vindicated?

When I was leaving NATO, almost 6 years ago at the time of the writing of this article, I was invited together with two other colleagues whose time at the top of the Alliance was also running out, to deliver our valedictory speeches to the NATO College in Rome.

The title of mine was NATO: A Bigger Bang. I took the title from the title of the current Rolling Stones world tour. Not just the title but also its *fil rouge*. Having just attended the impressive and uplifting Stones concert, together with my wife, in Vienna, I tried to compare the relevance of the Rolling Stones rock band and the North Atlantic Alliance. Both were in their 60's and questions about their relevance had been popping up time and time again.

I believe I successfully defended the claim - the thesis - that they both remained highly relevant. I wrote the text both under the heady impressions from the concert as well as my deep belief that we, the Western Civilization, need - and will need even more in the trying times to come, the North Atlantic Treaty Organization. The Stones proved their relevance by selling tens of thousands of tickets in minutes. And I found enough reasons to evaluate NATO – in that post 9/11 time – as relevant as ever. And I pleaded for better and more usable capabilities, a Bigger Bang.

But let me not repeat the thesis that was worked out in detail - and sprinkled with a jest here and there, which comes naturally to me. I need to present a bit of an antithesis now, namely: the true relevance of NATO and the Stones do diverge. Perhaps I missed that at the time or consciously evaded it. The Stones do not really need to adapt to the new times and could - theoretically - play the same songs over and over again for the next hundred years; we actually WANT to hear that old stuff! We do not need new tunes.

On the other hand, for NATO it is not enough to rehearse and repeat well the tunes we have heard before. It needs to learn new ones. It has to adapt not just to the new times, the new security threats, but try to look beyond the present time into the future. A rock tune can be composed in a few hours if not minutes. But the adaptation of the military needs a lot more time – years on end – as NATO defense planners know all too well. Also, while a rock band is a small outfit that can decide fast, the Alliance is made up of 28 quite different sovereign nations that need to find consensus on just about every single issue. While NATO needs to reinvent itself time and again, the needed consensus, even with strong leadership, is difficult to come by. What is needed, are the incentives or precursors, of which I will speak later.

So where do we stand now? How is NATO holding up as far as its capability development is concerned? Not well, if we look at the majority of the Allied nations. It is easy to say that the main reason is still the impact of the financial crisis that began in 2008 on the defense budgets. Especially the disproportionate toll that the defense area suffered in relation to the general decline in public spending.

On the other hand not many Allies used the pressures of financial stringency to rationalize and streamline both their forces and the command structures. I have always believed that there are ways of achieving better results when faced with fewer resources. In the times of plenty there is no incentive to cut the fat. And there is still plenty of fat. In spite of talk of smart defense the results are lacking.

As I see it there is still wide belief in many Allied nations that they need to provide foremost for the territorial defense and only later for what the Alliance actually needs. It is no wonder that many an Ally still calls its Defense Ministry - the Ministry of National Defense. How can they then align their thinking with the idea of Collective Defense?

Well, I am not fair to everyone. There are Allies that have concentrated the available resources on more operational outputs. And, after all, the Defense Ministers are not the masters of their budgets. It is the Finance Ministers that are attracted to the defense savings and suck the savings into the overall budgets. How can you then go right?

Also, in spite of all the talk of Smart Defense, all decisions are more or less taken without looking at the overall Alliance picture. This is resulting in a serious lack of certain capabilities in the Alliance, as many Allies have reduced the same capabilities. The lack of vision as far as the possibility of large scale high-intensity conflicts in Europe has contributed to this to a large extent. I cannot go into listing the areas, having been only an interested outsider since 2006. But I am concerned, especially in this Ukraine crisis period. Both NATO and the European Union have invested in establishing stable, long-term partnership and cooperation with Russia, while the latter on the other hand deployed its military forces twice in the past half a dozen years in NATO partner countries.

All in all, we are left with a NATO that can hardly respond to any serious conventional threat on its territory. Also, the ability to project into out-of-area theaters has been, I believe, in spite of all the rhetoric to the contrary, diminished. NATO's ability to act in the spirit of the mightiest military alliance ever has suffered because of the serious problems in its Partnership, as well as the Allies dragging their feet in inviting into membership the countries willing and capable of carrying the responsibility of membership.

The bottom line is that – in spite of the non-US Allies formally providing the bulk of land forces and even "minor" naval forces, i.e. excluding the aircraft carriers, nuclear submarines and destroyers, as well as combat aircraft – when push comes to shove we all have to run to Uncle Sam to help us out. It is incomprehensible that in spite of all that talk in the European Union how "defense matters," the only stable things are the negative trends in funding and the resulting capabilities, training and... you name it.

As far as Slovenia is concerned the situation is also far from rosy. The people who believe in NATO's and Slovenia's Allied role in it seem to be between a rock and a hard place. On the one hand skepticism towards NATO is growing and on the other one the financial resources earmarked for defense can not do much more than provide for salaries and other basic things. The drop in the defense budget is among the highest in the Alliance.

2019 A SPACE ODYSSEY

When I toiled as Slovenia's Ambassador to NATO and consequently its Permanent Representative on the North Atlantic Council, all together just about 8 years, I had a number of speeches in numerous Public Diplomacy events on various subjects. One of my favorites was preaching about why we need NATO, exactly the way other Permanent Representatives preach when they do the rounds.

However, in my farewell NAC speech in the Fall of 2006, a part of which I will try to incorporate here, I tackled this subject slightly differently. I stated that the threats we were experiencing then – and now I can more or less say the same thing – were still "small fry" in comparison with the magnitude of the threat we could – and probably will – face in the future.

In other words, perhaps the 28 Allies do not really need NATO today that badly. At first glance this brief statement goes hand in hand with the foaming-at-mouth statements of Natophobes globally, including those in Slovenia. But there is a "yes, but" addition, especially if you consider the previous paragraph.

Here it is: if we do not keep maintaining the Alliance, and building it, training it in operations, and finding new ways of defending ourselves against new threats, we will be left up some sort of an unsavory creek without a paddle when we are in dire need. And we would not be able to put Humpty Dumpty back together, I am certain. As I have said before, defense planning is long term business. Nothing happens overnight. Nation states will not be able to deal with the new threats on their own. Even successful coalitions can only be feasible if they are based within an alliance such as NATO.

In my speech I reminded my colleagues of the story of a graffiti "Remember Pearl Harbor" somewhere in the U.S. back in the Thirties. There had been ample warnings of the looming Japanese threat. Similarly, 9/11 was not unexpected either. There was intelligence that was ignored for some reason or other.

I tried to impress upon my colleagues that with a bit of vision, and unfortunately even more realism, we could imagine that out there in the future there are threats to our civilization, our way of life, the ramifications of which were hardly comprehensible at that point in time. Eight years have gone by since then and perhaps my concerns can be grasped with more ease as the phenomenon of climate change has been accepted widely.

I called this future threat "Pearl Eleven." Not very imaginative, I agree. I actually even considered "Pearl Eleven" not as only a single phenomenon but a series of destructive events that could hit us separately, consequentially or even simultaneously.

Let me quote what I said then: "As we are faced with the growing reality of nations to the East arming disproportionately to their defense needs, the radicalization of Islam, natural and manmade disasters, global warming effects, mass migrations, dwindling energy resources, combined with terrorism becoming almost a way of life – the combined threats will be more global, more long lasting and perhaps almost cataclysmic."

Well, the international situation is somewhat different now but not that much. In the meantime additional worrying elements have been added, such as the growing assertiveness of Russia that we worked so hard to pull closer as a very close partner.

I then continued: "How will we deal with it when it comes?
Are we ready militarily? NO.
Are our intelligence and security services ready? NO.
Are our emergency civil services ready? NO.
Is the general public concerned? NO."

I closed my "Pearl Eleven" song and dance with a plea to my colleagues on the North Atlantic Council, made up of people whose job it is to be alert and concerned and have vision, that they should see the need for a NATO, a mighty military Alliance of Values and Action, even disproportionate to the current needs. I asked them to support involvement in operations with the understanding that we were training for what our forefathers invented the Alliance for. And I also asked that Allies should get involved more heavily in humanitarian and disaster relief, also to score points with the taxpayers who will in the end decide if NATO members' militaries are worth financing or not. I added that there should be more common assets and more common funding.

I was more or less aware – as I am now – that what I said was a lot of wishful thinking at best although there are more graphic ways of describing that. It is true; we are not used to doing things in such a way. We just respond to what occurs; a sort of a knee-jerk reaction. Can we start thinking more long term? Sometimes it seems that NATO is driven by wake-up calls.

Sometimes the wake-up call, the impetus for keeping NATO strong comes from unexpected sources. The crises in the Arab world have provided NATO nations with much needed exercises in the case of Libya, not just the usual virtual ones. There was the missed opportunity in Syria to help stop the carnage by forcibly grounding the regime's aircraft. The growing Russian assertiveness seems to be another precursor for taking defense more seriously.

Now, trying to wind up my contribution, I am about to suggests a few cornerstones of Slovenia's future direction as far as NATO's – and our own – future is concerned. This is not an exhaustive list and there is no specific order to it.

1. Europe needs a collective defense organization if we want to continue living in peace, security and relative prosperity. It has been said that if there was no NATO we would have to invent one. In spite of its deficiencies NATO is our best chance to achieve our legitimate interests at no one else's expense. However, its capabilities should not fall victim to the overall financial problems, but be used in a better and more cooperative way. I furthermore believe that Europe and the broader international community need NATO, perhaps not as the "world cop" but at least a "world fireman." If not tackled, sometimes seemingly innocent crises in the world can blow out of control. NATO should be capable of projecting its power globally.

2. There are occasional dilemmas about the overall purpose of the Alliance. They often pop up once a decade when a "need" arises to concoct a new Strategic Concept. My skepticism in Strategic Concepts has arisen from the fact that most of them if not all poorly warned us of what was about to happen. I believe we have to stick to the Washington Treaty and its preamble which states that the Allies are determined to safeguard the freedom, common heritage and civilization of their peoples, founded on the principles of democracy, individual liberty and the rule of law and that they are resolved to unite their efforts for collective defense and for the preservation of peace and security. I believe this suffices. Full stop.

3. The Transatlantic link, where the security of North America is permanently tied to that of Europe must be preserved. It is of utmost importance that the European members, most of which are members of the European Union, finally face the responsibility of contributing its fair share to – after all – their own defense. As I see it, European Defense needs to remain Transatlantic Defense. The Transatlantic link would also be helped by Europe becoming independent of any single or overarching imported energy source, including Russian gas.

4. The gist of the Washington Treaty remains in Article 5. "All for one and one for all" is the *sine qua non* of the Alliance. Without it the NATO that Slovenia needs does not exist. It is true that ad-hoc coalitions may be the way of dealing with some security issues but they should not threaten Article 5. At the same time Slovenia needs to act fully like an Ally, not a partner, taking into account that every decision of the Alliance is our decision.

5. We should not allow any debate about the rule of consensus. I believe that for any Ally – small like Slovenia or large like the United States – decision making by consensus is in its national interest.

6. I have not tackled the following issue before but it is vital that it is mentioned. Nuclear deterrence capability is crucial to our long term survival. As long as the bad guys have nuclear weapons – or are working hard to acquire them – the nuclear Allies need to keep them and be ready to use them if necessary. I am aware

this sounds like barbaric warmongering to just about any person. Unfortunately it is the only way to keep the really bad guys at bay. And their number is not diminishing.

7. The Open Door Policy must remain within the framework of the Washington Treaty, without any limitation. This means that the North Atlantic Council can invite to accession talks any European country, willing and capable of fulfilling the Treaty as well as NATO's acquis. Slovenia should be in the forefront of supporters for the issuing of an invitation to Montenegro at the NATO Summit in Wales, and also support the candidacies of Moldova and Georgia. Against the backdrop of the Ukraine crisis we should also look more seriously at the possibility of bringing into the fold our "brothers-in-arms," Finland and Sweden.

8. It is also time to make serious attempts to move beyond the frigid relationship between NATO and the European Union. Meetings at the level of Secretary General and the HR/VP, staff to staff contacts and very informal NAC-PSC meetings once in the blue moon do not reflect the fact that both organizations should consider each other as its foremost strategic Partner and Ally. They each have complementary tools and they should work on finding common strategies, division of work and coordination.

9. NATO should not shy away from but actually be capable of providing disaster relief globally. Its forces should be of dual use, to the extent it is feasible. The same goes for the Slovenian Armed Forces. Humanitarian crises can easily grow into more complex ones and turn overnight into security issues for all of us. At the same time it is the right thing to do for a political Alliance equipped with military tools, such as sizeable airlift and maritime capabilities. And last but not least, that is the way to gain public understanding and hopefully support of the taxpayers. There is no better Public Diplomacy than helping people in need.

10. Finally, I am definitely not pleading for larger armed forces. They should be lean and truly usable. They should have short tails and long teeth. They should be capable of acting globally. They should be well trained and well equipped. Although while serving as Slovenia's ambassador to NATO I had excellent relations with

my defense and military advisers, there was one area where we did not quite agree. I pleaded for much smaller armed forces but ones with all the characteristics just listed. My numbers were usually half of what they imagined. My last figure that I presented in a debate in July 2009 at the Ministry of Foreign Affairs in the presence of Ministry of Defense people was 4000 troops. The figure incorporated the civilian and military personnel, including navy/coast guard and air components (tactical transport and HELO gunships). I even ventured as far as proposing a formula for Allied nations' participation in operations abroad: 200 troops per million of population at any given time. As far as Slovenia is concerned this has been proven as achievable.

After all, the European NATO members have profited enormously in the "dividends of peace," while taking NATO for granted and simultaneously disregarding their militaries. Now is the high time for all European NATO member states to take seriously the wake-up calls and focus on revitalizing the Alliance, the only guarantee of our security. Now is the time for Slovenia to refocus on being an Ally. This is not the time to tell NATO to go home.

To end on a lighter note I was going to use a quote by Sun Tzu but then I decided that I should instead repeat my proposal from a few years ago. Here it is: let us have the 70th anniversary NATO Summit in 2019 in Slovenia.

Perhaps we need such an incentive to do our homework. Slovenians are excellent at carrying our clear-cut projects, as was the one that ended a decade ago with Slovenia joining the Alliance. It should not have been an end to it but a new beginning. Let us now find an incentive for a new beginning.

THE PSC—NAC MEDLEY 2012-2017

The history of joint meetings between European Union's Political and Security Committee and the North Atlantic Council is – if we are looking for a single word – sad. Formally it can only discuss issues dealing with Berlin Plus operations (please Google that). Even in the early days of this relationship EU's High Rep for CFSP Javier Solana – who chaired the joint meetings – would abruptly end the session if someone proposed another discussion theme. What is probably odd – if not schizophrenic – but what I enjoyed very much was the markedly different views that the EU and NATO ambassadors from the same country would express. In our case it was especially the view about the Russian activities in Ukraine, where I was, I believe, on the right side. My song and dance on EU/NATO relationship was in line with Slovenia's policy but I always pulled out all the stops and probably sounded corny if anyone remembered my previous interventions. Ambassador Alexander Vershbow, "Sandy," Deputy Secretary General of NATO and my former colleague on the North Atlantic Council, commented to me after the PSC/NAC meeting on 28/9/2015 that he heard more buzzwords per minute in my intervention than anywhere ever before. Yes, although speaking seriously and with lots of concern, I still wanted to have some fun. And most of the time I tried to intervene early, to underline our/my major interest in the subject; the order of my place in the interventions is clearly demonstrated in the figures (e.g. #3/16).

1. PSC-NAC, NATO HQ, 20/3/2012 (#3/16)

Thank you, Olof. Good to see you, Sandy, back in Brussels.

It is good that the PSC and NAC are finally meeting. It's a shame we have not been able to do this sooner. We should find ways for informal or formal meetings for the EU and NATO to work together better. Ideally – when we face crises – we should formulate a common strategy and have a division of work as well as coordination.

It's good to talk about Bosnia: one of the few things we are allowed to talk about together. Slovenia is very much concerned about BiH, in spite of some steps forward… Slovenia is the top investor in the BiH economy – on the par capita basis. We are also investing in BiH security and we are ready to do more. However, we have always been discussing the Western Balkans in a piecemeal manner. Not in a comprehensive manner.

There is one thing I would like to mention. There is unfinished business.

In late June 1991 Europe started discussing the region. NATO did that a bit later when things got really nasty. Both got involved substantially and we have seen results. But have we done enough?

I believe we should have the future of the Western Balkans on top of the agendas of both the EU &NATO. If we want to have long-term peace, stability and prosperity not just in the Western Balkans but wider, if we still want to have Europe Whole and Free, both the EU and NATO should do their utmost to help European and Euro-Atlantic integration of all the seven countries of the Western Balkans, meaning into the EU and NATO. Into both organizations, not just one or the other.This should not be a pick and choose exercise. If tey do not end up as members of both, we will also end up with more problems in the EU-NATO relationship.

Thank you.

2. PSC ON EU-NATO, 4/3/2014 (#1/18)

Thank you, Walter; and good to see you here, Sandy.

I more or less have just one point. The PSC and NAC should at least informally meet, as we used to do years ago on a more or less regular basis, when I was still on the other side of town. I support your proposal in this respect. At least we should find a way for the members of the two bodies to meet informally and discuss issues of common concern.

Perhaps the situation in Ukraine could represent the breakthrough in having the two bodies meet.

Thank you.

3. PSC-NAC, JUSTUS LIPSIUS, 5/3/2014 (#5/28)

Thank you Walter, Sandy,

Let me express satisfaction at having the PSC and NAC meet so fast, without any unnecessary fuss. May I thank all those that have contributed to that.

I have three brief points.

First, as a former permrep on the other side of town, I am a firm believer – not only in the value but actually sheer necessity of such meetings, as most of the time the two organizations deal with the same issues, the same crises. The situation in Ukraine is a wakeup call and I hope it will represent a breakthrough, so that the two bodies meet on a more regular basis. Ideally, when we face crises, common assessments by the EU and NATO, possibly common strategies, division of labor and coordination would result in a multiplying effect of our efforts.

Also, in this dramatic situation, without precedence in the post-Cold War period, there is even more reason to look closely at the December European Council Conclusions on CSDP, that affect both organizations.

Second, we have strongly condemned the clear violation of Ukrainian sovereignty and territorial integrity. We have commended the measured response demonstrated by Ukraine and we are ready to assist Ukraine. It's good to see that here we both share assessment of the situation in Ukraine. Slovenia has been a staunch supporter of Ukraine's way forward since early days. We have expressed belief in its European identity and a decade ago we were one of the first supporters of the Membership Action Plan to be offered to Ukraine. Of course, it takes two to tango – and we expect a lot of homework from the Ukrainian side – but we should do as much as we can on our side and I believe also go further in our indications of what the final goals in our cooperation with Ukraine, beyond Association and DCFTA, might be.

And last but not least, both the EU and NATO have been in the business of helping "Europe Whole and Free" in various ways, including the enlargement of both organizations. The enlargement perspective and the Open Door Policy should not fall victims of the situation in Ukraine. Quite the opposite, we should find ways to reinvigorate these processes, especially with the countries that are investing most in their reforms.

Thank you.

4. PSC ON EU-NATO, 10/6/2014 (#22/24)

Thank you, Walter; and thank you, Terry, Maciej and Gunnar.

I'm glad to see there is a high level of cohesion in our views here today. Well, there's no time for me to get into details. But let me just say that there can be no business as usual with Russia, as long as it occupies Crimea.

What I also want to say is that it seems that the EU and NATO need a serious crisis in pour common immediate neighborhood – a wakeup call – to start talking more frequently and more seriously to each other.

It would be useful if we could also find a common strategy, division of labor and coordination as far as the Ukraine crisis is concerned.

I have been a fan of PSC/NAC meetings since my NAC days and I believe that we should also find the time to exchange information and views on other issues of common interest, such as – for instance – the Western Balkans, if we want to see one day Europe Whole and Free, at Peace, and, I hope, integrated into both organizations.

Thank you.

5. PSC ON EU-NATO, 3/7/2014 (#10/14)

Thank you, Walter; and thank you, Terry, for briefing us on the NATO Summit in Casnewydd as, I believe, Newport is called in Welsh.

Just two points: first, to Slovenia enhancing the relationship between the EU and NATO is of utmost importance and we hope the Summit will be an impetus to go forward with it.

Second, we are sorry than an invitation will not be issued to Montenegro. As we always say: if we really want to make Europe whole and Free and at Peace, bringing the Western Balkan countries – that are ready – into NATO is the way to go.

Thank you.

6. PSC ON EU-NATO, 7/10/2014 (#1/14)

Thank you, Walter; and thank you, Sandy, for this.

I did not want to be the first one, but I'll be brief: I am happy to see that both the EU and NATO seem to be looking seriously at how they can do more and better in the area of defense.

Also, what is happening on the ground in various crises, such as Ukraine, ISIS, perhaps Ebola, should prompt both organizations to get more serious about their relationship.

Now, after a long summer, we are looking forward to have a PSC/NAC meeting ASAP.

Thank you.

7. PSC ON EU-NATO, 16/12/2014 (1/11)

Thank you, Walter; and thank you, Sandy. Good to see you here.

I have just one point. And I can only repeat what I say ever time when you come here to brief us on what's happening on the other side of town which – of course – is very useful to us.

It is unsettling that the PSC and NAC still cannot sit down together. Hybrid warfare sounds a good theme to discuss together.

If formal or informal meetings of the two bodies are not feasible perhaps we could sort-of use the PSC-UN Security Council meetings formula as we practice in New York and have meetings of members of the PSC and members of the NAC. I do not see any formal reason why we should not meet in such a format. I believe it is very important to meet together.

Thank you.

8. PSC-NAC, NATO HQ, 8/6/2015 (#3/27)

Thank you, Sandy; good to see you.

As a former member of this Club I'm always happy to be back here. Although the EU is EU and NATO is NATO, it looks like that the twain shall keep meeting. I guess we need a crisis or two to do that.

Now, let me touch briefly upon Libya. Its instability poses a direct threat most of all to Europe – through an upsurge of illegal immigration – which can serve also as a conduit for the trafficking of arms, terrorism, you name it.

This relates directly to the growing ability and determination of ISIS/ DASH to consolidate its influence across Libya and expand its presence in the region.

And this is all happening not just in our backyard but – literally on our doorstep. It is not too farfetched to imagine that Libya could turn into an ISIS/DASH base from which it could launch terrorist attacks in Europe. This should concern both of us, the EU and NATO.

And when the going gets tough, the tough get going, I hope. As I see it, there are things that the EU and NATO do best when they work together. One more thing: Slovenia supports a rapid launch of the EU NAVFOR MED operation and intends to participate in it. We are looking forward to an UNSC Resolution and hoping that Bernardino Leon will broker an agreement, as this could make our lives much easier.

Once – hopefully – a National Unity Government is formed there will be plenty of work for all of us in Libya, for instance helping with Border Management and Security Sector Reform. This could contribute a great deal to limiting the arms and human trafficking and minimize terrorist threat against Europe.

Thank you.

9. PSC-NAC, JUSTUS LIPSIUS, 28/9/2015 (#1/20)

Thank you, Walter; and thank you, Maciej and Luis Felipe. And good to see you, Sandy and James.

It seems that when the PSC and NAC do manage to meet, here or at NATO, I cannot but repeat my usual song and dance: how things in the world would be better if the EU and NATO finally built a sturdy bridge across the river that divides us in this town, and worked together in tackling various crises in our neighborhoods.

But let me try to turn this belief sort-of upside down. As I see it, the crises that we are facing today, are also closely related to the inactivity of both organizations – and the inability to work closely together – not only in reacting to actual crises but also not having dealt properly with their root causes, resulting also in mass migration that the EU and NATO member states are facing today. But let's not cry over spilt milk. When the going gets tough – the tough should get going.

We are currently faced with an unprecedented frequency, complexity and diversity of security challenges – if we look to the south or the east – coupled with a high probability of huge spillover effects. The indiscriminate and far-reaching nature of the security threats demands – especially in times of continuing austerity – a serious goal-oriented joint EU-NATO self-reflection, both in terms of comprehensive policy planning and in combining political, military and economic capacities and capabilities of both organizations. Joint strategies, division of labor and coordination would be ideal, of course.

Now that the European Union is embarking upon the formulation of its Global Strategy – and NATO is preparing for its Warsaw Summit – it is high time to find solutions to the problems preventing us from acting together. It is high time that we finally sit down together and do our best to see what we can do together – and how – when facing the unstable neighborhoods. The push has come to shove. We are not just looking at crises in our neighborhoods. The crisis has reached us.

I do hope that the EU and NATO will react to this wakeup call and will not sit idly by and leave the attempts of resolution of the acute crisis in Syria and the deteriorating situation in Iraq to various coalitions of the willing that seem to be popping up. This would not bode well for either organization and for Europe's long term security.

And – last but not least – the EU and NATO must continue to support Ukraine's independence, territorial integrity and sovereignty.

Let me pass the floor now to my colleague, Jelko Kacin.

Thank you.

10. PSC ON EU-NATO, 23/2/2016 (#7/9)

Thank you, Walter and thank you, Pedro.

We have always been in favor of increased EU-NATO cooperation. Full support, period. Hopefully this cooperation will help limit the number of migrants entering Slovenia on a daily basis.

Thank you.

11. PSC ON EU-NATO, 16/6/2016 (#2/24)

Thank you, Walter. Thank you, Pedro; and good to see and listen to you, Sandy.

I have been intervening on EU-NATO relations for ages – on both sides of the apparent river that separates the two organizations in this town.

I have hoped all along that the twain shall meet one day and become true strategic partners and more: true Allies, if possible, where we could have common strategies, division of labor and coordination when dealing with various crises that we both face together.

I have, I do and I will see NATO as Europe's defense organization – when push comes ton shove.

This has not happened but any, any move forward is welcome and I am happy to see that we are finally about to make such a step.

This is not just personal. For Slovenia, EU and NATO are natural and strategic partners; they share the same values and face similar challenges. Combined, they possess an invaluably wide spectrum of tools and capabilities that can complement each other to a tremendous effect. In a rapidly changing and unprecedented tense security environment, it is unreasonable and dangerous not to do everything to make the best use of this relationship.

In the context of the upcoming European Council and NATO'S Warsaw Summit we therefore strongly support sending a highly visible and credible message, acknowledging both our common threats as well as developing the EU-NATO relationship.

However, our message can only be as strong as the substance of our work together and the impact of our actions.

Thank you.

12. PSC ON EU-NATO, 22/11/2016 (#7/26)

Thank you, Walter; and thank you, Pedro and your team.

I guess, I've talked too much in favor of greater cooperation between the EU and NATO for the past decade and longer, as I see the two organizations as natural strategic partners, so I'll be very brief this time.

First, it looks like we have achieved the maximum we can at this point. Hopefully more can be done in the future.

Second, Slovenia will support the proposals on the table on stepping up both formal and informal cooperation at all levels and we'd be happy to endorse the document.

Finally, perhaps just one point more on Councuil Conclusions. We feel that regular progress reporting on implementation should be done at least twice a year.

Thank you.

13. PSC ON EU-NATO 5/12/2016 (#12/12)

Thank you, Walter.

The wording of the Draft Council Conclusions is the bare minimum for us. We'd wish for more, at least in line with Danius' proposal on reinforcing Trans-Atlantic solidarity.

But let's move forward and endorse the document.

Thank you.

14. PSC ON EU-NATO, 14/3/2017 (#1/17)

Thank you, Walter; and gracias, Pedro, Diego y Jorge.

I am happy to hear things have finally begun to take off on the practical implementation part. We are well aware of the need for realistic expectations – but even more of the risks of not cooperating fully and pragmatically on the issues that are vital to our security in these volatile times.

Exchange of information, mutual invitations to seminars, exercises, or any other forms of cooperation should – above all – not be one-off events. The aim should be a systemic, self-sustainable long-term cooperation, leading to a mutually reinforcing strategic partnership. That's what Slovenia has been advocating all along.

We strongly support recharging PSC-NAC meetings with substance, especially on topics of practical mutual concern, where our combined tools, instruments and approaches could result in value added. One case in point is definitely Bosnia and Herzegovina and the Western Balkans in general, not forgetting maritime security and SSR.

Thank you.

15. PSC AOB ON EU-NATO, 23/3/2017 (#1/1)

Thank you, Walter.

I have a question related to tomorrow's PSC-NAC meeting.

I know there's no fool like an old fool and I apologize for not listening closely in the morning when you mentioned tomorrow's PSC-NAC meeting. Did you say that it was decided that Montenegro cannot participate?

If I heard that correctly – could you just let me know who decided on that?

Thanks.

16. PSC-NAC, JUSTUS LIPSIUS, 24/3/2017 (#1/28)

Thank you, Walter, for giving me the floor that I would like to share with Ambassador Kacin.

Deputy Secretary General, I'm happy we're meeting here today after quite a while. Its been too long. Missing Montenegro, but I hope it will be able to join us ASAP. I did hope – naïvely – when on the NAC a decade ago that by 2020 all of the 7 Western Balkans countries could join the EU and NATO but we are unfortunately still far from making Europe Whole and Free.

As someone who has spent almost 14 years on the two sides of the mighty river that divides our two organizations I was happy to participate last year in the building of the bridges between the EU and NATO. The step ahead in our relationship in Warsaw was obviously the maximum we could achieve, while at the same time the bare minimum to me personally. I hope that we do move forward towards achieving a true strategic partnership. NATO is the natural ally and cannot be compared to any other partnership that the EU has. I feel that in the long term there is no EU without NATO's collective defense and perhaps no NATO without the EU. Hopefully last year's words on paper will be translated into facts on the ground so that we will not be just talking the talk.

Just a couple of brief thoughts on today's agenda items: When talking of *resilience*: the inclement weather on both sides of the Atlantic – facing and adversely affecting both of our organizations – demands that both the

EU and NATO – and their member states – dedicate themselves first to their own resilience to be able to also assist our wider neighborhoods. On *hybrid and cyber*: our bright future that we used to expect will be chock full of even brighter hybrid and cyber capable adversaries of one kind or another. It's time to get down to serious business together.

Thank you. Jelko…

17. PSC-NAC, NATO HQ, 16/5/2017 (#10/20)

Thank you, Chair, for giving me the floor, also this being the last opportunity for me to address the two august bodies together.

Also, it has been too long since we had such a gathering. Although an obvious topic for a formal meeting, we believe deeply that the Western Balkans deserves a broader discussion, especially considering the following:

First, fragile societies are more vulnerable to focused, complex and multi-faceted security challenges and threats. This is why, from the point of view of sustainable resilience: in Bosnia and Herzegovina employment and youth opportunities, law enforcement and civil society need to be strengthened.

Second, security and development are mutually dependent and there is hardly a stronger and closer case of the need for EU-NATO working closely together than in the Western Balkans. This has been an exemplary case, which we will likely need to build upon, and upgrade in the future.

And last, we expect nothing less than a true strategic long-haul partnership enabling us to tackle – in an orderly, systematic, planned and pragmatic manner – common security challenges, with a uniquely wide array of tools, policies and concepts. If I may add: hopefully the EU and NATO will also adopt common strategies, division of labor and coordination of activities when dealing with issues of common concern.

It is in light of these issues that we are looking forward to a comprehensive review of Althea, where Slovenia continues to support its executive mandate. We are also looking forward to the report on the implementation and further work on the common set of proposals for EU-NATO cooperation.

And, Chair, may I pass the floor now to Jelko.

Thank you.

SLOVENIA – THE 4TH BALTIC STATE

I was invited by the Lithuanian Government to attend events in Vilnius on 12 Jan 2011, commemorating the slaughter of Lithuanian patriots by the Soviet military in January 1991. The story is in the text below, so I won't repeat it here. One of the events was a Round Table at the Ministry of Foreign Affairs with a long heading: "Battle for the Freedom of Nations: Breakthrough in the Baltics: 1990-1991 Geopolitical Changes and the Relevance of Their Outcome Today." My contribution had the title that you see in the heading. I was treated with utmost respect and friendliness, even decorated with the Gold Diplomatic Medal by the MFA, presented to me by my friend from the Lithuanian revolutionary days State Secretary Asta Skaisgirytė Liauškienė. I was also taken to their Baltic Way Memorial Freedom Wall by another friend, Ambassador to Slovenia Rimutis Klevečka, and shown the brick with my name on it. I was humbled; it did not feel like it was just "Another Brick in the Wall…" When I got back to Ljubljana, I was asked to prepare a short text for the MFA website. When the text appeared the words "Soviet military" was missing from my mentioning of the slaughter…

Excellencies, ladies and gentlemen, friends,

Let me try and add something at least half-sensible to this discussion here today from my side. I'll try to touch upon the Past, the Present and perhaps the Future and relate how some of us in the 4th Baltic State – Slovenia – see things at this point in time. Beware – it will be a bit emotional.

1. **The Past**. Twenty years ago it was pretty hard to see much if
   any resemblance in the position of our states. While on one side
   Lithuania, Latvia and Estonia – "as we saw it back home:"
   – seemed to be immerged forever in a nasty totalitarian Soviet
     Warsaw Pact quagmire, enslaved nations of non-free people,
     slowly but surely being russified, with state ownership of just
     about everything, plan economy,
   – on the other hand Slovenians lived in a semi-workers' heaven
     of open borders, Yugoslav Non-Alignment, mixed economy,
     run-over by Western tourists, with semi-critical media, semi-
     affluence at the level of lesser developed European Community
     member states, geographically between Venice and Vienna,
     and with the capital Ljubljana lying further West than 4
     European Community capitals…
   – What a Continent – if not world of difference!

You can imagine that perhaps an ordinary Slovenian of the late Eighties
or early Nineties could not see many parallels.

It is not easy to explain why some of us did see not only parallels –
and you know that parallels never touch – but common points, common
interests, common values, common strife, and – eventually common future.

Why the hell did we have the guts to start our Slovenian Spring in
1988? If we had been the only nation waking up in Communist Europe of
this or that kind, asking both for democracy and for national freedom, we
would have probably been sent packing by Belgrade very early in the game.

However, with the backdrop of peoples demanding freedom not only
in our near vicinity in what became later the V-4 countries, but also in
the Baltic States, this fact gave both additional courage and impetus to us
until it was too late for our Yugo masters to put us down.

It felt so natural – but at the same time baffling - that one of the first
acts of the first Slovenian democratic parliament in May 1990 was the
adoption of a resolution in support of the aspirations and demands of the
three Baltic states. Somehow I found myself as one of the proponents of
the resolution.

Then in September 1990 I traveled semi-officially to Tallinn, Riga and
Vilnius and met just about everyone involved in the freedom movements.

Although I was chair of the Parliamentary Foreign Affairs Committee my contacts with the Baltic states did not make everyone back home very happy.

At some point the then Slovenian Foreign Minister publicly expressed concern that my trips to the Baltic States could hurt Slovenian-Soviet relations. What a nice statement. Slovenian-Soviet... Can you imagine anyone saying something as insane as that today?

The Slovenian parliament reacted strongly to the January 1991 massacre and sent a delegation to Vilnius that I was very proud to lead. You fought against a totalitarian force not dissimilar to the one that was getting ready to conquer us. Those were very emotional times. I remember even making a 6 minute speech in Lithuanian in your Parliament. A tape of it still exists.

Your struggle gave a lot of inspiration to us. You were faced with a bigger foe than we were. And we needed it. A day after declaring our independence in late June 1991, Slovenia was invaded by a 20,000 strong Yugoslav military force that was defeated militarily, politically and diplomatically in 10 days. And the rest is history.

And it gave me a lot of satisfaction that our Lithuanian friends were the first to formally recognize Slovenia. With friends such as Vytautas Landsbergis, Emanuelis Zingeris and many, many others it felt so natural.

2. **So where are we now?** As ordinary people see it, not all the differences in the outlook of the Baltic States and Slovenia have disappeared, but there are lots more similarities than differences. We almost live in what we hoped for then: Europe Whole and Free, equals in NATO and the European Union.

Personally I see one big difference. You guys really have moved forward 20 years in so many aspects. And you know them better that I ever will. So I will not get into details.

On the other hand Slovenia has had a different ride. All right, on the outside - apart from the effects of the current global crises – things seem to be fine. We were the first former Communist country to adopt the Euro, the first to be in the U.S. visa-waiver, we were the first to have the European Union Presidency, we seem to be well off enough even to help economically better off EU countries such as Greece and Ireland and who knows who else, we have less than two people per passenger car, with only a tiny agriculture we have more tractors per capita than any other nation in the world, and so on.

But in spite of this there is some sort of Yugo-nostalgia around, with quite a few people only remembering the good days when they were 20 years younger. Tens of thousands of Slovenians spend the New Year's Eve partying in Belgrade. Tito is an icon.

On the domestic front to call someone an "independist" is almost a dirty word. There is a much bigger divide by the two political sides in Slovenia than we had when we started our democracy and independence.

All the wrong moves of the past are coming to fruition and the public is daily presented with new cases of things going wrong so that no institution seems to be trusted any more: the government, the parliament, the courts, the banks, the big business, the doctors, the lawyers… no one.

And nobody seems quite sure what we need: is it just new elections, is it a "2nd Republic", a new Constitution, a Re-setting of Slovenia, a new Messiah, as proposed by some people.

3. **So what should I say about the future?** Well let me stop here and listen to you guys.

You were inspirational to us two decades ago.
Do it again!

Thank you. It's great to be back.

6 YEARS LATER: WHERE ARE WE NOW?

I was invited to address a gathering called the "Harvard Black Sea Seminar." As far as I understand, it was part of the Harvard Black Sea Security Program that started that year in Ljubljana and then moved on, I believe, to Sofia, Bulgaria. In Ljubljana the co-organizer was the Ministry of Defense. The MOD supposedly published a special issue of the Bulletin of Slovenian Armed Forces with a focus on security issues both in South East Europe and Wider Black Sea region. The Defense Minister Ljubica Jelušič was sitting in the front row and after I had finished my piece, actually thanked me. The event took place at the City Hotel in Ljubljana on 14 April 2010. Here it goes:

Minister, Ladies and Gentlemen,

I wanted to start my piece today with a joke.

For two reasons – firstly, I am sure you will hear the serious stuff from the rest of the speakers at the seminar.

And secondly: you are not the typical Slovenian audience which does not expect jokes when they expect discussion of vital issues of the state.

But life is full of surprises and shows us so often another side of the coin than the one we are used to.

Just like the case of Ruben Enajo, who has just survived his 24th time being nailed to a cross. Not here – but in the Philippines, it is true.

But have you heard about the Slovenian kamikaze pilot who flew 24 successful missions?

Sorry – that was a joke.

*

But, seriously folks:

Former NATO Sec Gen Lord Robertson liked to tell his 5 Famous Lies, such as:

»The check is in the mail. «

Or »I am from the Government and I want to help you. «

Or »I will respect you even more in the morning."

May I add my own lie: »I will be humble."

I want to use this opportunity this morning to discuss issues pertaining to Slovenia's drive towards membership in NATO, where we are today and where things might go in the future.

A couple of weeks ago I was asked for the title of my speech. I decided on »Six Years Later: Where Are We Now«. It reminded me of a 60's British rock band called Ten Years After. Probably you are all too young to remember their major track called Going Home by Alvin Lee with some of the best guitar work ever.

I once had a speech at the NATO Defense College in Rome, titled »NATO: A Bigger Bang«, after the title of a Rolling Stones world tour. I tried to compare the relevance of the Stones and NATO in their Fifties.

So, let's rock'n'roll.

*

During your stay in Slovenia you will have a chance to hear everything you ever wanted to know about Slovenia's membership in NATO – and other fora – and perhaps more than you ever wanted to hear.

As always, I will try to do my own song and dance – a very personal one, especially dedicated to those of you who come from NATO aspiring countries – such as Georgia and Ukraine.

I am not sure how much of what I can tell you, has anything to do with Black Sea security. I've been there, I keep flying over it, but I am no expert.

However, regional fora – if you look at the big picture – are an excellent litmus test of good neighborly relations between immediate neighbors and slightly removed neighbors.

Anyway, good neighborly relations and the related stuff is one of more or less formal prerequisites for getting into NATO.

And what counts for the Alliance when deciding your destiny – is not paying just lip service to values – but hard facts on the ground. And the closer to home the more it matters, I believe. The more you do in your own backyard, I believe, the more brownie points you should win.

Not just far away with troops on the ground in Afghanistan or elsewhere.

*

Slovenia managed to resolve its border issues with the neighboring countries before joining the EU and NATO. Unfortunately, one of them later on backed out of a border agreement.

Slovenia also managed to get actively involved in a great number of regional initiatives, starting with the Alps Adria Community when it was still a Communist state. I will not list them here, because the meaning of some of the acronyms escapes me by now.

So there is plenty of homework to do. At the same time, international organizations that some of you want to join – should not just stand by and watch you emotionlessly. They have to extend a helping hand. They have to create mechanisms to help others help themselves. Such as the MAP, for instance.

When at NATO I thought that MAP was perhaps good enough for the Central European states, but perhaps more was needed for the Western Balkans states and wider. Instead of a mere Road Map to the distant NATO Open Door, something like a GPS was needed that would persistently and insistently coach the aspirants to NATO Heaven. I mean Haven, of course.

I can almost hear the usual high pitched electronic voice of a car road navigation system, insisting: "Make a U turn and spend 2% of GDP on defense," or: "Turn left at the next intersection and make your forces 60% usable…" and so on.

Seriously, there should be better mechanisms that would prevent countries from veering off the road.

However, on the other hand, when a country does everything it was expected to do, via all the 14 Stations of the Cross, the so-called »political decision« should be more or less automatic.

*

I led an EU troika once in talks with the Russians. My counterpart, a vice foreign minister, asked »Why is Georgia rushing to join NATO?"

Don't worry; I am not divulging any secrets here. Such a question was so typical of the situation. And it was all happening in the midst of a crisis there two years ago. The question was expected.

I tried to explain that there was no chance that a country could rush into NATO, speaking from Slovenia's experience. It took Slovenia almost a decade and a half from the initial idea, and – let us be honest – Slovenia had it easy. I never said that back in the pre-accession times – when I was between a rock and a hard place, trying to help Slovenia get into NATO.

In the talks with the Russians I said that they should be happy of Georgia and other interested countries entering mechanisms, such as the MAP, as they force countries to solve possible open issues with their neighbors before joining up. Yes, I said, Russia should be happy to have neighbors join NATO as that would lead to more stability, more security. And so on.

Okay, it will take some time to convince them. But I firmly believed and still believe in what I said then.

*

If you by some odd chance remember the title of my speech you might think that I have veered off from the proposed subject matter. As everything else, it is open to interpretation...

But let me say something about Slovenia's drive to join NATO, the process, the membership and also how I see the future of NATO – and Slovenia's membership.

It is claimed that I came up with the proposal of Slovenia joining NATO when Slovenia was still part of the defunct communist federation, called

Yugoslavia. I chaired the Foreign Affairs Committee in the democratic parliament elected exactly 20 years ago and it is on record I said so.

But what was the reasoning behind it? Then and later on, when the political elite tried to sell the idea to the population, we especially liked to talk of ensuring Slovenia's security through membership in the Alliance.

I did myself quite a bit of NATO peddling, when I was ambassador to the Court of St James's, then Mr. NATO at the Slovenian MFA and later on – almost literally – as Slovenia's *Permanent* Representative to the Alliance. 8 years in Brussels was almost a permanent job.

But what was lurking in the background was not so much security – but national normalcy, if I can put it that way.

Although Slovenia is as old as any other nation in Europe – our first state established 14 hundred years ago – in modern terms we were born only in 1990/1991. We had to go through the growing years and trials of infancy, adolescence, towards our adulthood – which in the neighborhood that we live in – Central Europe – meant both membership in the European Union and NATO.

And we wanted to be a normal nation – not to be just left to ourselves – but to be able to be engaged regionally and wider in ensuring our long term stability, security, development.

We have achieved that. We have joined also other value-driven fora. We have become an involved nation that has contributed through its share of troops on the ground in a number of hot spots, with leading both the OSCE and the Council of Europe, as well as the UN Security Council very early in the game.

And most of all: two years ago we pulled off surprisingly well the difficult job of Presiding over the European Union, a task where our ability to be an honest broker, without any hidden agenda, helped resolve some European Union issues that had dragged on unresolved for years.

We made it and we wish all the other nations that are willing to transform their ways of doing things in accordance with Euro-Atlantic criteria to make it to.

*

It is no surprise for instance that Slovenia was one of the early supporters of Georgia achieving its goal of joining NATO. I did not write the song but I was the first to say to President Sakaashvili in the North Atlantic Council that I have "Georgia on My Mind". Our Prime Minister was the first who – in a NUC Summit – supported out loud Ukraine's President's request for Ukraine to enter the NATO Membership Action Plan.

The Washington Treaty is clear on who can accede. Slovenia will stand by it resolutely. For instance, we were an early supporter of all the Western Balkans nations joining both the EU and NATO once they fulfill the criteria. I sincerely hope that within this decade we can witness this happen. I believe Slovenia will do its utmost to help make it happen.

It will not be easy. A few years ago I had a series of speeches in Serbia on what Serbia had to do to be able to join NATO. I called my speech "A Dozen Dirty Truths." Yes it will not be easy. It is not just practical solutions. You have to change your mind set. You have to accept NATO's history as your own.

Not easy. But what else is there? What other future should the people of the Western Balkans want for their countries if they want to live in boring – but stable – run-of-the-mill European countries?

Slovenia has managed to fulfill its foreseeable destiny and now it is on the brink of new ventures. And the times that we live in demand just that.

We have all witnessed new challenges. The crises we are facing are and will be much more global than ever before imagined: economic, financial, climate, you name it. We will have to find new bold ways of tackling world problems.

And we should not waste time and energy and resources on half-hatched theories and schemes how to reverse the changes.

I don't want to go into the reasons, for instance, for climate change. Who knows? Who knows? Anyway, climate change is the rule, no the exception, it has always been around. Now – being more global than ever – we are more aware of it. And we are all in the same boat, no pun intended.

But we are not empty handed. We have magnificent tools at our hands. And they can be improved.

When I was leaving NATO three years ago I mentioned in my valedictory speech that when we are faced with great challenges, including climate change, possible mass migrations – and everything that comes along – terrorism, you name it - we have one organization that is capable of providing the security we need – if we build up its policy as well as its capabilities.

I have suffered listening for hours to complaints in the NAC by some Allies how much money they spent – for instance on providing transport for humanitarian aid to Pakistan after an earthquake there.

But what else is there for our forces to do? After Kosovo and Afghanistan – what are we going to do?

I believe all our capabilities should be of dual use: for hard security with all possible intensities of warfare, as well as for helping in man-made and natural disasters. We will see more of them.

With NATO's public image not in the best shape – we could overturn the public image of the Alliance – at home and internationally – almost overnight if we became a major provider of delivering aid in the Euro-Atlantic area – and wider – say, globally.

We say we are a value based Alliance!?

Let us demonstrate this clearly to the world. And to our taxpayers.

*

And let me tackle at the same time another issue. Russia.

Again, if we look at the big picture we are all in the same boat. Let us involve Russia as a major player in such a project as I have just mentioned.

They have the capabilities, and working together builds mutual trust. And that's not all.

Let us be bold and try to involve Russia in discussions on the necessity of building a Euro-Atlantic missile defense. Engagement works better then isolation.

Again, if we look at the big picture we'll be in the same boat for quite a while. We will be facing the same threats. Let me not name them but we know what or who they are.

As a State Secretary and Political Director during the Slovenian EU Presidency 2 years ago I was heavily involved in getting everyone in the EU aboard the idea that we should start negotiating a post PCA agreement with Russia. It was not easy. Concerns of some of our EU colleagues were great. I traveled to Vilnius. I traveled to Tbilisi. We pulled out all the stops. And we did it.

And I believe, especially in the present climate, we can make new giant leaps forward in getting Russia closer. This, in turn, I believe will lessen the concerns Russia has over some of the neighboring states getting closer to NATO.

And one last thought. Let us make our militaries – I am talking to NATO members and potential NATO members – truly Allied militaries. With more common assets and more common funding.

Let us forget about the National Defense, the Territorial Defense. If we trust each other, if we trust the Alliance – that we are building and leading together – we could have a truly Allied defense. Small (I believe 2000 highly trained, equipped and deployable troops per 1 million population would suffice), less expensive for the taxpayer (I believe below 1.5 percent GDP would suffice), and of dual use: lethal when necessary and with a helping hand most of the time.

Thank you. I hope you have enjoyed your quick hop to Slovenia.

And (I checked my watch), as Alvin Lee said: I'm Going Home.

EXPECTED AND IMAGINABLE

I prepared this intervention for one of the events where NATO's top honchos attempted to show their interest in involving as many Allies as possible to participate in the preparations of NATO's new Strategic Concept. It was held at Brdo in Slovenia on 13 November 2009. It was typical that I was not invited by my compatriot co-organizers, even though having been "Slovenia's Mr. NATO" for ages. When the top NATO people had realized I was not on the list of invitees they invited me themselves. The meeting was formally chaired or co-chaired by my former Latvian colleague on the NAC, Aivis Ronis, who had started his diplomatic carreer as, what was called, a Teenage Ambassador to the U.S., and attended by former U.S. Secretary of State Madeleine Albright. As far as I remember everything was running late and I managed to squeeze in – with some exasperation of the Slovenian civil servants present who kept silent – a shorter version of the text below in the form of a question to Secretary Albright. But I forget which one. She did react to the question briefly and after the end of the session came to me to thank me and discuss the matter. I was not sure she remembered my visit to her wonderful "time travel" office at the State Department a few years previously.

Aivis, Madame Secretary,

Watching the Fort Hood memorial service a few days ago, after the tragic slaughter of innocents there last week, I was startled by the words of the military commanders who spoke there. One called the dastardly act »unexpected« and the other one »unimaginable.«

Unfortunately, we have seen it all – almost all. In our global, multicultural, multi-value Civilization of Clashes just about everything should be expected and imagined to hit us in the future. It is still easy days. But it's gonna get really tough.

In my farewell speech to the North Atlantic Council three years ago I called the event which is going to hit us out of the blue a »Pearl Eleven«. In a way both Pearl Harbor and the events of 9/11 were expected and imagined. I described Pearl Eleven not even as an event but a series of events that could hit us separately, consequentially or even simultaneosly.

Today we are even more than then faced with the growing reality of some nations arming disproportionately to their defense needs, no abatement in the radicalization of Islam, more natural and manmade disasters, expected global warming effects, mass migrations, uncertain energy sources etc. All combined with terrorism that has almost become a way of life.

The combined threats of the future will be more global, more long lasting and perhaps almost cataclysmic.

How do we prepare to counteract the future threats? How do we prepare to defend ourselves? Well, we do not have to invent any new forum, any new organization. We got NATO. What I would like NATO especially to be is to be capable of – if not preventing or limiting the scope of damage – of being prepared for an aftermath of such an event.

Whatever anyone of us believes the reasons for global warming might be, the fact is that our planet has experienced throughout its history climate changes that have dramatically affected the life on Earth. And this seems to be expected in our future.

I therefore believe that NATO should get much more effectively involved in civil emergency and disaster relief. Our military capabilities should be of dual use, and so should our troops.

It is needless to add that such NATO's activity would also score points with Natoskeptics around the world, and the taxpayers back home. NATO is not at the height of its popularity neither there nor here. And let us make all our civil emergency units deployable – wherever we decide it is necessary.

Also, especially in the times of economic downturn, it is time to relegate most of territorial defense forces to the dustbin of history. I am afraid that the trend could be – and is in some member nations – quite the opposite – cutting the forces in crisis management operations. If we really believe in NATO defense, we should close the chapter of national defense.

Thank you, Aivis.

MAKE LOVE NOT WAR

For a Permanent Representative on the North Atlantic Council getting away from NATO is not as simple as it sounds. First you have your farewell speech in the Council, then the farewell dinner speech at some posh location where you receive a silver plated tray with the engraved signatures of the rest of the Ambassadors plus the Secretary General and Deputy Secretary General. So while I had bid my formal farewell to the NAC in July 2006, the dinner – when I had the little speech that follows – only took place in September. Farewell dinner speeches to NAC colleagues are supposed to be very informal, personal and, if possible, funny. I tried my best.

Colleagues, friends,

When Her Majesty's new ambassador arrived I knew it was time to leave. He was the 5th British ambassador to NATO that I have known since my arrival almost 8 years ago.

My father, a journalist, was sent to military exercises whenever he wrote something that did not conform to the current thinking of our Post World War II Communist leaders. My first memory of him is when I am two years old and my mother tells me the guy in the uniform, sitting in our kitchen, is my father.

My mother, a secretary, was imprisoned by Gestapo as a member of the Resistance, sent for hard labor to Bavaria, escaped to Slovenia, escaped the summary execution for allegedly being a Gestapo agent and then spent the next couple of years in the Resistance in the Slovenian forests.

As a high school kid I was questioned by the police twice, first when I protested prematurely the invasion of Czechoslovakia by the Warsaw Pact countries, well before our dear leader Marshall Tito decided the invasion was not a cool thing. And the other time I was questioned for distributing a leaflet that spoke in favor of political pluralism and Slovenian emancipation by turning Yugoslavia into a confederation.

So how could I not embrace the values enshrined in the Washington Treaty? As a onetime hippie, believing in Make Love Not War, I personally had to ensure we had good defense so we could all go about that much more interesting business.

Once I spoke to a group of NATO ladies who lunch together at the Staff Center, and it was about men and women and the thing that brings them together. I wish I could do this here but I'd better not.

As my mere existence was in the hands of Nazis and Commies even before my parents met, I have to take life with more than just a pinch of salt.

Just a few examples of what I have had to cope with in the past couple of decades, meeting the salt of the earth: diplomats and people from above our pay grade, as Toria called the Ministers (thank god this does not hold true in Slovenia).

- I remember the French Ambassador in London that I paid a *courtesy call* on. I was awaiting him in his ancient looking wood-panelled protocol office, with a burning gas fire, there were half a dozen coffee tables, laden with photographs of the Ambassador with Ministers, Prime Ministers, Presidents, the Pope, maybe an array of Popes, perhaps even Jesus, I cannot remember. Finally the Ambassador entered in a grandiose way, we shook hands and when he was just about to sit down across from me in an armchair, the phone rang. He walked to the desk and answered: "Oui Monsieur le President…" Very impressed I told the story at some point to another Ambassador colleague of mine. He said: "Wow, the very same thing happened to me when I went to meet him." So it goes.
- I remember the Carrington Conference in The Hague. The then Foreign Minister of the Netherlands Hans Van den Broek asked me: "Why is Slovenia separating when the rest of Europe

is integrating?" I replied without batting an eye: "Well, why then did the Netherlands separate from Spain?" And I was just a long-hair, still young-looking know-it-all too-big-for-my-britches guy, talking back at the great Dutch Foreign Minister. So it goes.

— And I remember the Istanbul Summit Heads of State or Government dinner at the Dolma Bahçe Palace – a great honor for Majda and me –when I was sitting in for my Prime Minister. I was placed between José Manuel Barroso, still Portugal's Prime Minister then, on my right, and Bulgarian Prime Minister and former King Simeon Saxecoburggotski (who kept addressing me – to my embarrassment – with *Your Excellency*) on my left. The British Prime Minister was sitting left of the PM/King. After we all had mostly finished with the food Laura Bush signaled President Bush it was time to go. We all got up and I stepped over to Tony Blair to give him the news of the result of the Serbian Presidential election that I had just received in a text message from my friend Bata Vukadinović in Belgrade. So I told Tony Blair that Tadić had won the election. The Prime Minister, feeling naked without any expert support, blankly looked at me and asked: "Is that good?" So it goes.

However, this is a serious occasion.

So, seriously folks, let me just quote briefly from an unpublished book of mine (hopefully out by the end of the year), called 1001 Laws of Survival, and please do not be offended:

— We demand comprehensive strategies when a silver bullet would do and shoot stray silver bullets when comprehensive strategies are needed.
— To understand something, you have to destroy it first.
— Intelligence, when talking about intelligence and security services, is an oxymoron.
— Admit it to yourself that you are the definite proof that there is no intelligent life on Earth.
— Women are more intelligent than men. However they are too stupid to realize that.

Thank you Jaap, thank you Jeannine, thank you Jurek and Iza.

When I look at you I see more faces than there are people physically present. I would like to mention everyone, and especially those that for some reason or other we had a special relationship with. Don't worry ladies ...

Thank you everyone for coping with me.

I know no one had a problem coping with Majda. But as she keeps making me better, one day I might be worthy of her and of you knowing me.

Cheers!

QUIZZING PRIME MINISTER OF UKRAINE

I have been an ardent supporter of Ukraine's NATO and EU ambitions. I remember starting an argument with Helga Schmid – who I did not know at the time (the year escapes me) – at a lunch in Kiev where I was on NATO business. She was telling the Ukrainians that it was "not the right time, it was premature to think of NATO." Of course I jumped on that – perhaps not in a very nice way – and told her that it was not for the EU to lecture the Ukrainians on their NATO aspirations. And, secondly, what she told the Ukrainians was exactly the same thing everybody in Europe was telling us at the time when Slovenia wanted to become independent. In the next few years I developed a friendly relationship with her; however I should not miss this opportunity to express my doubts in the usefulness of her and my friends and former NAC colleagues' Štefan Füle's and Toria Nuland's advice to Ukrainians a few years later. I believe they naïvely contributed to the present sordid situation in the country. The following address was delivered at NAC's meeting with the Ukrainian Prime Minister on 14 September 2006

Prime Minister,

Thank you for coming here with your delegation, especially our friend and colleague Ambassador Morozov.

Last night we were celebrating Ukraine's 15th anniversary of independence together and I still remember the heady days of the Orange Revolution.

It is also good to see here a driving force behind Ukraine's Euro-Atlantic aspirations – our friend Minister Volodymir Khandogyi. And I wish a speedy recovery to Minister Tarasyuk.

Slovenia has been very supportive of Ukraine's endeavors ever since President Yushchenko announced the wish to strengthen relations with NATO and for Ukraine to become a member of this Alliance. Being a strong supporter of offering the Membership Action Plan to Ukraine, I am sorry to hear it has been put on hold.

My question relates to an eventual referendum on membership: I understand that a possible final solution to join NATO would have to be based on the results of a referendum, which is to be conducted after the implementation of Ukraine of all required procedures. Do you believe that a referendum is necessary? What is the procedure to call a referendum and would the results be obligatory for the government?

Let me add that Slovenia did have such a referendum – and it was very successful, in spite of initial low public support. And here we are today.

Thank you, Secretary General.

DISCUSSING PARTNERSHIPS WITH PARTNER NATIONS

In comparison with the "brainstorming" on partnerships that NAC had behind closed doors in the beginning of the same year, this intervention, quite different, is from a very polite discussion in the Euro-Atlantic Partnership Council on 13 September 2006. The Allies hopefully closely listened to their Partners' opinions. Many of the Partners' interventions reminded me of the time when Slovenia (actually yours truly) was saying very similar things in the Council of the Western European Union. The language about "downstream" and "upstream" role of Partners in decision-making sounded very familiar. The two Ambassadors mentioned were Swedish and Finnish, representing countries that contributed a lot to NATO's operations and had better armed forces than probably most Allies had. I was sorry they remained formally neutral. I have no recollection who chaired the meeting as the text that I have on file just thanks an anonymous chairperson for the floor. Probably this was the last EAPC Council meeting I attended as my tour of duty – after almost 8 years – was about to end.

Thank you for the floor,

I would just like to say that Slovenia welcomes Partners' active involvement in the debate on possible changes in partnerships. I appreciate what Ambassador Anderman, Sierla and the Swiss representative have said.

I am sure that the Allies will try to incorporate your suggestions into our deliberations.

I remember how we were very eager to contribute to the discussions on the enhancement of Partnerships some years ago when we were still a Partner nation.

In our current discussions, we have supported the ideas on increased flexibility without diminishing the current structures, which we think are still very relevant; such as the monthly EAPC Ambassadorial.

As you might remember from our discussions last year we advocated strongly that the respect of the basic Partnership for Peace values is one of the crucial elements of our relations within the EAPC and wider.

This issue is featured in our current debate.

I hope we can reach the moment soon when we can discuss this topic together with you more in depth.

May I also, once again, express my disappointment that the seats of Uzbekistan and, if I see correctly, Belarus remain empty. This – not partner-like – situation should not continue indefinitely.

Thank you

LECTURING SERBIAN PRESIDENT

This intervention of 19 July 2006 at NATO HQ in Brussels when NATO Permanent Representatives were meeting with President Boris Tadić, and a few others in this book – related to the Western Balkans – should have been included in my book "The 2020 Vision for the Western Balkans." The simple fact is that a bunch of my addresses, interventions, speeches were temporarily missing at the time of putting that book together, on account of my family's moves from one job to another. Well… here it is. I first met Tadić in Belgrade when he was Defense Minister. It is quite emotional for me reading Ambassador Branko Milinković's name here. He was one of my rare Serbian friends and I co-dedicated the above-mentioned book to him. In private he felt he had to criticize me for a couple of my often expressed beliefs: first that Serbia will have to accept NATO's history also as its own history (including the bombing) and that Serbia could not join the European Union without fully recognizing Kosovo as a sovereign state. No one else seemed to be as clear as I had been on these issues; especially the EU representatives were feeding Serbia with one teaspoon of reality after another. They felt the naked truth would turn Serbia away from normalization of relations with Kosovo. Well, fairy tales are so much easier to swallow than the truth.

Secretary General,

I would also like to warmly welcome President Tadić with his delegation, especially our college and friend Ambassador Branko Milinković.

It is a year of great changes and a year of great expectations.

It is a year when the former Yugoslavia was finally put to rest and it is a year of rebirth of nations in the Western Balkans.

It should not be a year that Serbia will remember as a year of losses but more as a year of new beginnings.

Hopefully it is the year when all of the Western Balkans will embark upon the path of no return – towards permanent stability, development, prosperity and Euro-Atlantic integration.

Slovenia has always supported – here in the Council – a comprehensive, regional approach to the Western Balkans, instead of a piece-meal one, so typical of the International Community so far.

We believe the problems, the challenges, as well as their solutions, are so interlinked that they should be tackled simultaneously.

There is no way in stabilizing one part of the Balkans and leaving the rest to itself. It will never work. We believe that the International Community, especially NATO and the European Union, should commit themselves to bring all of the 7 entities of the Western Balkans both into NATO and the European Union in, say, next 10 to 15 years. We should invest our energy and resources into this project.

This is the only way to put the looming problems of today, problems with a long history, into perspective. Once all of the Western Balkans is part of normal, boring NATO Europe, with open borders, prosperity, people-friendly autonomies, high levels of protection of minorities, the highly charged problems can become academic ones.

No one in the Western Balkans should come out of the processes that are unraveling, as a loser. No one.

And everyone should look towards the future, not the past.

I hope this is the year when Serbia enters Partnership for Peace and finally takes its rightful place at the EAPC table. It has been too long. We look forward to working with Serbia more closely. As soon as you and we – in NATO itself – are ready.

And the Serbian Ambassador will sit just a seat away from us.

But it takes two to tango.

In the past couple of years I have been involved in 4 NATO Public Diplomacy stints in Serbia and I am sure the ball is still very much in Serbia's court, to tackle the well-known problems. And I will mention just two: Public support and the control of the Intelligence and Security services.

But there is a lot of good will on this side.

My wish is that Serbia becomes as boring as Slovenia...

Mr. President, I hope Serbia uses this opportunity well.

Thank you.

NATO: A BIGGER BANG

With my colleagues, NAC PermReps, Ambassador Dominique Struye de Swilande of Belgium, Ambassador Benoît d'Aboville of France and Ambassador Prat y Coll of Spain, all about to say farewell to the NAC, I travelled to the NATO Defense College in Rome to deliver a valedictory speech on July 17, 2006. This is one of my favorite speeches that I ever delivered: crisp, to the point, and a bit funny, but with a damn serious message. We were given 10 minutes each. My colleagues had no written texts at all. I admired them. Actually, Prat y Coll clocked 12 minutes, Struye de Swilande 11, yours truly 14, and d'Aboville even 16. After the speeches we had to indulge the crowd there by taking part in a plenary question-and-answer session and later in a seminar. There was no such thing as a free lunch, but we did earn it; it was pretty good, well, we were in Rome.

Commander, Colleagues, Ladies and Gentlemen,

Ambassador Struye de Swilande has granted me 4 minutes of his time. I'm the guy with a written text. Please bear with me.

Last Friday night I was in Vienna, at the "Greatest Show on Earth", namely a Rolling Stones concert. It was great to see that after 40 odd years together, the Stones were still doing a fine job; perhaps the finest ever. They call their tour **A Bigger Bang**, I believe.

A friend of mine, himself a Slovenian rock star, which I joined with my wife for the Stones World Tour concert, said the Stones looked better than half a dozen years ago when he had seen them last in a live appearance. I am no expert; I had only seen them live twice before.

But two things were very apparent to me. Sixty-some years old Jagger with his tuxedo Made in Slovenia and the post-palm-tree Richards have successfully gone through a transformation that keeps them still in the Greatest Show on Earth category. They have adapted well to the times and judging from the packed stadia they are still very much relevant today.

I remember well how years ago this was questioned time and time again: are the Stones still relevant in this world of asymmetric music tastes and fashions?

And the other thing that I felt was that in spite of all the adaptation, all the transformation, what they were doing was still very much on the basis of the same values.

They expressed it very clearly, without much brainstorming of their Public Diplomacy people. They sang: **I know it's only rock'n'roll but I like it, like it, yes, I do.**

*

But I am here to talk to you about NATO from my own experience, having spent almost eight years in Brussels, first as a Partner Ambassador, then an Invitee Ambassador, and for the past two years as the Permanent Representative of Slovenia…

Time and time again NATO's critics open the question of NATO's relevance and do their utmost to **paint it black**.

How do I personally see today's NATO, do we need it at all, and if we do, how do we make it really relevant?

(Relevance)

NATO's basic values, as enshrined in the Washington Treaty are as relevant as ever. There is no other organization not only devoted to the preservation of the basic values of the nations that make up the Alliance but also capable of preserving them. There is no other organization that would go as far as even using nuclear weapons to preserve the values held dear by the Slovenian people who only 15 years ago had to defend them, almost empty handed. I still fully subscribe to what has been said by others before me: If there were no NATO we would have to invent it.

As the North Atlantic Council, a collective body just like a rock band, could sing (and don't ask the 4 of us here to do it): **It's only Freedom but I like it like it...**

Beware; this is not the brief of the United Nations, not the European Union, not the Organization for European Security and Cooperation. This is what NATO is about.

Whatever NATO does or does not do today, well or not well, Article 5, which we seldom talk about, is at the heart of the Alliance. And NATO will be relevant as long as this is the case.

Look at what we in the free world enjoy today. And look at many other parts of the world where you see exactly the opposite.

While we often vehemently deny that NATO is a world cop, perhaps the world does need a world cop. Perhaps the international community, not only requesting NATO to do an odd job here helping in some natural disaster, and an odd job there transporting troops of another international organization to help stop a genocide in some hot spot or another, perhaps this international community should realize that the world does need a cop. The neighborhood watch can never perform well without an overarching national or local police.

(How good is NATO at the job?)

How good is NATO at the job? This is very hard to say. NATO did a fantastic job defending our civilization during the Cold War. It is true, we were never really tested, so do we truly know how good we were? But we did invest enormous financial and human resources to defend our way of life. And we won!

There are Slovenians who do not appreciate the role of NATO during the Cold War as they do not recognize that Slovenia would never have been able to develop relatively well in its liberal communist system, were it not for its next door neighbor: NATO. But we are all today reaping freedom's blessings that would not have been there without NATO.

We know that NATO was the only international organization capable of stopping the slaughter in the Balkans, first in Bosnia-Herzegovina and then in Kosovo, and stabilized the whole region that could have affected adversely the security of the Alliance.

And today we are tackling different jobs; stabilizing Kosovo that can still blow up any moment between today and the day Kosovo is part of the Euro-Atlantic Community, doing an important, perhaps not much appreciated job in Iraq, and putting our credibility on the line in Afghanistan. We keep saying we have to succeed in Afghanistan; we are increasing our troop numbers considerably, resuming responsibility for extremely difficult parts of the country.

We can fail miserably, as has been the case in the history with powers such as Britain or the Soviet Union, or we can succeed. We will either succeed or we can forget about NATO.

(Transformation)

There is so much hype about transformation. We are busily working towards Riga, the transformation Summit, without quite knowing what we will be able to deliver. Instead of putting all our energy into the standing up of the NATO Response Force, into the military side of transformation, it seems we are tackling a dozen initiatives, from those bearing strange, hard to understand acronyms, all the way to a major overhaul of Partnerships. Not concentrating on what I believe we should concentrate on, we are, I am afraid, already demonstrating doubts that we can do the main job, so we take on a number of smaller jobs, as if to make sure we can demonstrate to the public that we are delivering something.

Every time when we talk to ACT, Allied Command Transformation, the people sitting pretty mostly in Norfolk VA, we are faced with presentations that need an IQ twice the size that of an average NATO Ambassador. We become experts in the new acronyms, such as EBAO. No, not the E-bay, the place where you can buy the latest military gadgets our troops can only dream of, but something called the Effects Based Approach to Operations. As an amateur I would expect that all operations had an effects based approach anyway...

But what is this transformation all about? Is it this kind of transformation that would allow our Alliance to face the challenges of tomorrow, whatever they may be? Not quite! In a way we are just desperately trying to catch up with the challenges, with the threats of today.

(Vision)

What I see is a major lack of vision to look forward and get ready for the real challenges that will face our civilization in the future. I do not believe in a clash of civilizations. But I see a looming clash of non-civilization, countries with **Rough Justice**, countries not sharing our values, against our civilization. There's a big bad world out there – and it is not getting any better.

The stuff we are getting ready for is small fry. Even the NRF is only planned for small fry operations. A crisis here and there, challenging our security, yes. Wherever it happens the NRF will be able to go there and do its limited job. Even in spite of differences of opinion on the common funding, what we can do or not do, what sort of legal basis we need and so on. Well, the folklore of the North Atlantic Council.

But are we getting ready for the Big Stuff? I do not think so. We do not even discuss the Devil as if we had some **Sympathy for the Devil.**

Firstly, are we getting ready for the challenges from the extreme Islamist world, on a more major scale than the limited terrorist acts of today?

Secondly, are we getting ready for China in, say 2021 when it will pass 600 years since China was the single global power and its magnificent ships circled the world? Are we capable of defending our values in a possible conflict with an emerging global power?

Thirdly, are we getting ready for the eventual fall out of the Global warming, such as mass migrations of people towards our shores, or even bigger challenges perhaps of cataclysmic scale?

And fourthly, are we getting ready to do something about Energy Security? And I do not mean protecting the critical infrastructures and all the soft things we talk about today when we discuss energy security. That is still small fry. Are we getting ready to protect the sourcing of energy that we will desperately need as we keep driving our 10 cylinder SUV's and the rest of the world will want to do the same thing. There will be a lot of competition for the dwindling resources. Are we getting ready for that?

Well, my answer is simply: no.

Unfortunately, while we are still transforming to face the challenges of today or perhaps the next few years, we are not doing any strategic, contingency planning for the next decades.

(Selling to the public)

And are we trying to sell NATO and its spending to the public? Not really. Public Diplomacy probably does not actually stink, as mentioned somewhere by one of my colleagues, because there's not enough of it to register as a bad smell.

And Public Diplomacy is not something that the PD people can do on their own. It is for the Alliance to go all the way to show how the NATO nations' taxpayers and the entire world need us. For that reason our involvement in helping at the time of events such as the Tsunami, Katrina, Pakistan Earthquake, Darfur, are an initial step that should lead to more large scale involvement. Most of our capabilities should be of dual use.

If the Slovenian taxpayer saw NATO as the capable helping hand in such events, no one would question the raising of our contribution to the NATO budgets, even, say, a 100% up. But even if I said 10% or 5%, this is unimaginable today in NATO. The hit of the past few seasons has been something called ZRG – Zero Real Growth. Some nations are making it virtually impossible to even try matching our political ambitions (and I would say needs) with the funds we are providing. They do not want to hear about more common funding and more common assets. And sometimes it seems those same nations hinder the streamlining of the NATO HQ that would provide substantial savings.

Mind you, developing such capabilities is not just for the Public Diplomacy effect. It is not just to demonstrate we do not have a **Heart of Stone**. I firmly believe that such natural and humanitarian disaster capabilities will be needed to face the challenges and threats of tomorrow. Let us have finally some vision and get ready when there is still time.

While the Stones said that **Time is on my side**, I do not think this applies in this case.

(The Western Balkans)

One area where there is a major lack of vision is the Western Balkans. Anyone who looks at the map and studies for a minute the history of the region knows that for our own security this still existing powder keg in the middle of NATO territory has to be turned from an exciting part of

European landscape to a boring one and made part of NATO and the European Union.

Okay, anyone with a bit of brain would be busy formulating and executing a plan, a strategy, how to bring this about, and getting on board other international actors that have roles to play and capabilities at their disposal, especially the European Union, plus the UN, OSCE and so on.

But no! Firstly, even in NATO we are pussyfooting around on how to formulate a mere tasking we are giving to our underlings to develop a paper that might lead us in the right direction. The 26 member Global Alliance that represents almost a billion people of the most internationally responsible nations does not have the guts to formulate a simple plan.

Is this the NATO that won the Cold War? Is this the NATO that went to war to protect the people of the Balkans?

And, secondly, we cannot even talk to the other people in town. The European Union. Even though the two organizations share 19 member nations, we do not seem to be just on different planets, like Europeans and Americans, but in distant galaxies. We are still trying to find out actually if there is intelligent life in that other galaxy. We do not need to have NATO and the EU as **Sweethearts Together** but it is a shame we cannot sit down together and discuss things that concern us all.

You can imagine that **I Can Get No Satisfaction** being involved in all this.

(Closing)

Anyway, perhaps it is funny to you that you are being lectured by the Slovenian Permrep, representing a mere 2 million strong NATO nation, talking as if I am representing a super power. But I feel no embarrassment. We never negotiated our share of the financial burden to NATO. We just said yes. And we are not complaining. And our share of troops in NATO's operations has just put us at the top of the list on the per capita basis. To put it simply: we have one soldier per 8000 Slovenians in NATO's operations. No one is doing better. If everyone did the same there would be over 100 000 troops from Allied countries in NATO's operations.

And every NATO's nation is, because of the consensus rule, a superpower.

Finally, I believe in NATO and I believe NATO can do much better.

I believe we have to put our vision, our energy, our commitment, our perseverance to make a **NATO with a bigger bang**.

It is true NATO at the end of its 6ᵗʰ decade of life looks pretty good, it is relevant, and, especially we cannot do without it. But, I believe, we need **A Bigger Bang.** Otherwise this might be our last tour.

However: **You can't always get what you want… And if you try sometime… you find… You get what you need.**

Thank you.

PEARL ELEVEN

I have found two versions of my farewell speech to the North Atlantic Council on 16 July 2006. There is the one that was – slightly cleaned up – included in my published compendium of valedictory speeches of all the colleagues who left the NAC while I was a member, plus mine, as well as of a former Secretary General ("Goodbye NATO* - *everything you wanted to know about NATO but were afraid to ask.") And there is the other one, marked "draft," which may roughly be the speech delivered. I like this one better. Here it is. The first two lines relate tongue-in-cheek to the obligation – or expectancy – that NAC members should do at least part of the speech in French, one of the two NATO languages. The mentioned NAC committee refers to the intelligence one as I was about to become the Slovenian Spymaster.

Monsieur le President,

Okay, I got this out of the way. Thank you Mrs. Amf, my High School French teacher.

And thank you Secretary General, for your kind words. Usually to the point, but in my case exaggerated. I wrote my farewell speech before having heard you. So I hope it fits the situation.

Colleagues, friends,

I was just a kid trying to live free and safe and I thought Slovenia needed the same. Now, a few years older, I am glad I had read so much Science Fiction in my younger days that I was never afraid doing what I could to move things forward.

Now that I am being degraded to one of NAC's 300 odd committees, and having perused a score of farewell addresses of former colleagues on the Council, I have discovered two things:

Firstly, neither should I aspire to have the most brilliant and visionary farewell ever, as it has been done before by truly brilliant people, nor should I venture far from the usual length of my interventions in the Council, one of the last, when speaking on Georgia, very much to the point: "Same here." Unfortunately, there is this incessant urge to use all the lost minutes, and hours, I have generously granted to my 25 colleagues in the past and to reciprocate in kind!

Secondly, this should not be the moment to get all things off my chest, as I have been promising myself for the past 400 weeks here at NATO, that I would finally do. The last thing I want to be remembered for – well, as long as the Council memory lasts – say a week or so – is having this giant chip on my shoulder.

Actually, in my predecessors' speeches there were so many interesting things that should not be forgotten that I could not prevent myself, with the generous support of my main political advisor Barbara Žvokelj, from producing and publishing a little compendium of farewell speeches of those colleagues who left from the day I sat for the first time in the Council in June 2003. I was hoping I could circulate the book around this table today. As things usually go, it will take a bit longer to be delivered. But it will happen rather sooner than later.

But let me start with the niceties: I will remember the brilliant and incessant work of my two Secretaries General, George Robertson, and you, Jaap. I admire your capacity to deal with the mere Ambassadors who live in the belief that they are actually NATO's bosses and your courage when you ventured into my Château Sheen-Coates wine cellar in my village of Zgornje Pirniče. I will miss Alessandro, the best Deputy Secretary General I have known, and one day we will finally visit the Kobarid WWI museum that we have talked about so often. I appreciate what Secretary of the Council Bernie Goetze did to bring my Ministerial dream come true.

A number of great ASG's over the years, I cannot name you all, some who went from revered figures back in the aspirant times, to experts working for us after accession. Of the people in the IS I will remember most are our wiz kid ASG Marshall Billingslea, as well as my defense planning guru Frank Boland and my legal guru Baldwin de Vidts.

On the military side of the house I value highly the CMC General Henault, and I am glad it was at the end of the day left to me by my capital to decide who we should support in the closely run contest for his position.

I appreciate highly the people who lead our troops on the ground – the real strength of NATO – my three SACEUR's: generals Clark, Ralston and Jones. They advised the Council so well and then ran brilliantly the operations we decide on here.

And finally, on the NATO Staff, thank you very much translators into French for making sense out of my gibberish.

The Council: I cannot avoid mentioning you, my colleagues and your predecessors, about a hundred probably altogether, that I have known. We have a wonderful dean in Jurek Nowak and I have made a few good friends that I cannot expose here today. To be on the safe side I will mention just my next door neighbors who have managed to tolerate me, on the left Pablo Benavides, who can talk at length on any given subject, and on the right Igor Slobodnik who I shared many a joke with during our important discussions.

Je voudrais m'adresser à l'Ambassadeur de Belgique, Dominique Struye de Swielande, pour lui demander de transmettre à ses autorités ma reconnaissance et celle de ma famille pour tout ce qu'elles ont fait, sans relâche, pour contribuer à notre bonheur et à notre sécurité, ainsi que pour faciliter ma tâche diplomatique pendant huit ans de ma vie professionnelle. Majda, Boštjan, Aleš and Sox et moi regrettons vivement de quitter ce beau pays où nous avons passé tellement de belles années.

I am a control freak and I transformed the Slovenian Mission, one of two in NATO that are formally called missions, according to my vision how things should be. I managed to have enough influence - read luck - to get some of the best people in Slovenia for the particular jobs. The problem sometimes is there is no one they can really talk to back home. I would like to thank them all for enjoying this rollercoaster, almost everlasting ride. I say everlasting, as most have had their postings extended for years and years, quite unusual for the Slovenian diplomatic service. Thank you all in the Political, Defense and Military Sections of my integrated mission. Everyone who had to cope with me – especially Defense Department

Head Primož Šavc or my Milrep Brigadier Anton Turk, when I came up with such ideas as sending Slovenian troops to Herat or Iraq, or to have a Defense Ministerial in a symbolic spot, facing the Slovenian and High Seas.

I would like to thank my Deputy, Jurij Rifelj, who you will have to bear with here for a while, the 5th in the row of my deputies, and my personal secretary for all these years, a Samaritan called Renata Novak. And – who else but my Charlie's Angels, Barbara Žvokelj, Nina Bernot and Eliška Kersnič, who kept me on top of things and in a good mood most of the time.

And there is no one who shared my various moments and moods here with me more than my wife and ultimate boss, Majda, who got involved so much in the other NAC - Ladies' NAC. I am happy to have her here in this more somber NAC today – I almost said tonight – but who knows how long my speech will last…

Now to some substantial stuff, in line with one of Lord Robertson's famous 5 lies: "I am from NATO and I will be brief":

Firstly something about **THE PAST**:

As far as NATO is concerned I had two personal ambitions:

The first one from over a decade and a half ago: to have Slovenia enter the Alliance.

Check.

The second one from the Prague Summit: to help make Slovenia a good if not the best NATO Ally.

Check.

The first one took about 15 years since the initial idea, back in the heady days of the Slovenian Spring, when everything seemed possible, at least to me. It was fun to meddle in the history of my nation, but probably it would have happened anyway without my contribution.

The second one may take a long time to demonstrate. Last Spring I talked about troop contributions to operations. Coming from a small NATO nation I have learned that overall numbers do not mean much. There are better ways to assess individual nations' contributions. I believe I said last spring that my ambition was that by the time I left the Council Slovenia made it to Number One on the chart of troop contributors to NATO operations on the per capita basis. And here we are: Number One!

According to SHAPE's figures I received today we contribute 1 soldier per less than 8000 Slovenians (while our figures show us slightly lower which would put us in the Number Two position). If everyone did the same, today NATO would have over 100,000 troops at its disposal for operations. And as we intend to more than double the number of our troops early next year, if everyone did the same we could have over 200,000 NATO troops in operations!

Now something about **THE PRESENT**:

One of my hobby horses has been the Balkans, the area bordering Slovenia to the South East, where NATO has been involved successfully, but seems to shy away from having a more decisive role in finally making this region – not unimportant for NATO's security – a boring part of Europe. And, as I like to say, boring is good.

This has been an area of some frustration for me. On the one hand so much talk, on the other hand not much action.

To me NATO is an Alliance of Values and Actions, not an Alliance of Words.

I fear there is still wide non-comprehension of the area. So often harsh sounding but honest statements from the region are condemned as unhelpful while promises that could not and would not be delivered (starting with Milošević), were hailed as success. Only acts should count!

Let me just briefly repeat what I have been saying since the day a couple of years ago when the Council discussed at an Away Day "NATO in 10 years time": In spite of a gentle move forward in the past couple of months, we still are dealing with the Balkans in a piecemeal fashion and do not seem to be able to create a comprehensive strategy.

I called my vision of the Balkans a 2020 vision. I still believe that if we all pull together, NATO and the EU and the 7 Balkan countries/entities we might see by 2020 all of this area in NATO and the European Union. I do hope this is actually a 20/20 vision.

This needs courage and imagination and determination and energy. From the NATO side it will take abandoning the word "premature" when discussing one entity or another, being imaginative in creating ways in bringing all 7 closer to the Alliance, and making the MAP mechanism less voluntary and more tuned to making the aspirants capable of carrying out the responsibilities of membership.

Our comprehensive strategy should be both symmetric and asymmetric. Symmetric on the question of the basic values we want all the 7 to respect and asymmetric on the way different countries deal with their specificities – especially minorities, decentralization etc.

And while each should be judged on its own merits when we ponder eventual invitations, we should be careful not to create more instability by their separation. Let us make sure that the result of including one or other into the Alliance would not in turn result in a permanent exclusion of another Western Balkan country from NATO.

Now something about the **FUTURE**:

I have had speeches in some public diplomacy events, preaching about why we need NATO, exactly the way we all preach when we do the rounds. But let me tackle this slightly differently at the close.

As I see it, the threats we are experiencing today are still "small fry" in comparison with the magnitude of the threat we could – and probably will – face in the future.

In other words, perhaps the 26 do not really need NATO today that badly.

However, if we do not keep maintaining the Alliance, and building it, training it in operations, and finding new ways of defending ourselves against new threats, we will be left up a creek without a paddle when we are in dire need. And we could not put Humpty Dumpty back together.

There is this story of graffiti somewhere in the U.S. in the Thirties "Remember Pearl Harbor" and we know of people warning of the looming Japanese threat. Similarly, 9/11 was not unexpected either.

With a bit of vision, and unfortunately even more realism, we can imagine that out there in the future there are threats to our civilization, our way of life, the ramifications of which are hardly comprehensible at this point.

I call this future threat Pearl Eleven. Not very imaginative, I agree. Pearl Eleven is not even a single phenomenon but a series of destructive events that could hit us separately, consequentially or even simultaneously.

As we are faced with the growing reality of nations to the East arming disproportionately to their defense needs, the radicalization of Islam, natural and manmade disasters, global warming effects, mass migrations, dwindling energy resources, combined with terrorism becoming almost a way of "life" – the combined threats will be more global, more long lasting and perhaps almost cataclysmic.

How will we deal with it when it comes?

Are we ready militarily? NO

Are our intelligence and security services ready? NO

Are our emergency civil services ready? NO

Is the general public concerned? NO

The North Atlantic Council, made up of people who are concerned and who have vision – should see the need for NATO, a mighty military Alliance of Values and Action, even disproportionate to the needs of today. Let us get involved in operations knowing that we are training for what our forefathers invented this Alliance for. And let us get involved more heavily in humanitarian and disaster relief, also to score points with the taxpayers who will in the end decide if we are worth financing or not. Let us have more common assests and more common funding.

It is true, we are not used to doing things this way. We just react to what occurs. Can we start thinking more long term?

Two more things before I close: First: European Defense can only be Transatlantic Defense. Thank you, Transatlantic Allies, for sticking with us Europeans through thick and thin.

I was going to say Goodbye NATO when I was leaving here.

But being a bit superstitious I do not want to say Goodbye NATO. It sounds too ominous. We need NATO and I wish you all the best in making sure it is kept healthy so we do not have to say Goodbye NATO.

So, farewell NATO.

And just a quote before I go:

Sun Tzu said: "There is no NATO so we should invent it."

Farewell.

WOMEN IN SPACE

I prepared a draft and delivered this speech at a lunch of an informal club called Women in NATO Eating – WINE. Barbara Žvokelj, my »Ambassador's Pet«, as the closest NATO Ambassador's diplomatic staff member used to – or may still – be called, was a founding member of the club. I had noticed that the speakers at each lunch were only women, so I sort-of protested at such gender discrimination and offered myself as a speaker. Barbara suggested this to her international co-eaters and they – I do not know how reluctantly or enthusiastically – agreed. Therefore, this is what I said on 7 July 2006 at the NATO Staff Center, surrounded by a dozen or more women. Yes, at first glance, it sounds offensive to women, but the bottom line is quite the opposite: great respect and affection for them.

Ladies and … Ladies,

Why is a man allowed to talk to you here today? Well, I must have promised I would undergo a sex change right after the lunch.

The title of my address to you on this date, I mean day, that I was hoping would be hot – but is not – is Women in Space. I had to re-title it from the original one because of possible sensitivities. But if after my address anyone of you still feels offended, than you must have missed the gist of it.

Barbara saw my speaking notes and suggested I cross out all the interesting parts. Well, that would just leave Hello and Goodbye in it. So if anyone is really offended by what I say – being superficially offensive to women – you can take a rain check and I will pay for your lunch. There used to be a time when I had to watch my words, but that was during the time of totalitarianism. However, NATO is an alliance of values, including freedom of expression.

On the title: If there is such a thing as Women in Space – then why not Women in NATO?

Actually, I would be the last person to put women down.

In one of my books, dedicated to women, a book not widely available[1] if you are not even slightly inventive, I say the following thing about women: "I cannot get over you, women. You are the beginning and you are the end. And you are everything in between. You are everything that is worth living for. And you make us believe that. Women, who can figure you out? I will never (even) try…"

Gee, how pathetic! I must have been hard up when I wrote that.

Anyway, I will try to say something about women and something about NATO today.

Women have made tremendous progress since the day of the cavemen, sorry cavewomen, and dinosaurs, sorry, dinosaurettes.

In those days women were not regarded as equals to the male species. The men were the brain and the muscle, while the weak stupid women cooked, exchanged recipes, took kids to school and church and theme parks, and made themselves look pretty, so their husbands, hairy sweaty brutes, when they came back home, reeking of beer after having had slaughtered a pterodactyl or watched a stoneball world cup match, could have some relaxation and eventually impregnate them. In some of the early societies men actually had intimate relations with women only when they wanted to produce offspring. Otherwise men were much more fun.

Poor women. So unappreciated. So exploited.

But fortunately history moved on. Women became agricultural workers, teachers, nurses, railway workers, construction workers, miners, doctors, scientists, lawyers, business women, jailbirds… I mean how more equal could they get? They became even astronauts. And at some point they even started working at NATO!

While at the same time, men had to re-learn their role in life. We had to start **listening** to women. This is tough, and we are still working on it…

---

[1] Love….check Amazon.com.

And back in the 60's and 70's we had to learn about the women's bodies!

What the hell! We had known for ages what things were for.

But no! Women sprouted new, surprisingly hard to find and difficult to understand body parts and regions and spots and you name it.

Some sort of evolution occurred that only touched one half of the population. And it was all occurring in places harder to find than planets and galaxies millions of light years away from Earth.

And the concepts changed too. Women wanted enjoyment, they wanted to be appreciated just for the sake of being women, and they wanted to be wined and dined.

Mind you, not in restaurants! We had to learn to cook! Not just make an omelet but real stuff with fancy French names. And we had to look like we enjoyed it. And we had to learn how to use a fork and knife!

We also had to learn to drink wine out of glasses, not just suck on a bottle of beer as we had been doing since the olden times. We even had to learn to talk about wine. Distinguish between Bordeaux and Burgundies. We had to watch this Sideways movie time and time again, while sophistically appreciating Pinot Noir. And we had to light candles and look romantic. And all the time hoping that we would get what was by all rights ours!

So now we live in an equal world.

You women are free to choose whatever you want to do in life. All positions are open to you; not just secretaries, which men would prefer, but even more sophisticated servants of people: members of parliament, ministers, prime ministers and presidents. The only unachievable position ever is that of Secretary General of NATO. But there has to be a limit to everything.

So now you are free to work from dawn till dusk. Having a family is not obligatory any longer! There are actually more and more women who by their own choice shun the family bliss. But if you for some reason or other decide to have a partner and even children, maybe deep in the fourth decade of your life, you are the decision-maker in the family. You are the banker, the holiday planner, the chariot owner and the driver. You are the co-signatory of mortgages and car loans.

You have reached everything women for thousands of years have hoped and strived for.

And being so incredibly capable, full of energy, so fulfilled, and so generous, you also change the diapers, and cook, go to PTA meetings, change flat tires, dead batteries, mow the lawn, test the pool water and fix its acidity and add chlorine, and then fix yourself up at the end of the day, or say Saturday, and hope you will get what is rightfully yours!

Oh yes. How could we get along without you, women?

My three co-workers here know my deep appreciation for everything they do. Okay, I do not actually think of them as co-workers, but what in Slovenia we call "pucfleks," sort-of cleaning ladies with a university degree. But I never tell them that.

I have given Barbara, Nina and Eliška a nice collective name, in Slovenian "Tri gracije." I tell them – and just to spite the men at my Mission I do this in a transparent way – that they are much better at what they do than my male diplomats.

They are Honest, Hardworking, Handy and Hintelligent, the 4H's of what I want in people working for me.

And I see they have been joined here today by Eva and Mateja… ready to be offended and enjoy it.

As they are all women, still not quite believing that they have achieved equality, they will go all the way to provide the best there is. And I salute you for this.

In an unpublished book of mine – thank God – of 1001 Laws of Survival I now and then touch upon women.

One of the Laws says in the first sentence:

Women are more intelligent than men.

Unfortunately there also is the second sentence which says: However, they are too stupid to realize that.

I believe my three Graces are very close to realizing that too.

I have heard that the 4 of us… mmmmmm… sounds interesting… Okay, that here at NATO's HQ my three ladies are called Charlie's Angels. Cameron Diaz, Lucy Liu… and who was the third one? Drew Barrymore, thank you, Barbara! I think they like that. But I hope that they know that I, being Charlie, can "Chuck" them the moment I do not need them any longer.

Well, maybe they know that and they still like it... in a slightly masochistic sort-way way.

Not having any men around today, I can also talk about men.

The basic problem with men is (I had a Milrep a while back that I managed to get rid of, actually the 2nd one-star General in a row, who started everything he said with "The basic problem is...)." Yes, the basic problem with men is all that male insecurity...

Okay, the basic problem is that men either believe that the world started with a Big Bang or that there was a Divine intervention.

However, the true basic problem is that both of these facts are beyond their control. And men WANT to be in control. Why?

Because, except for one exception here, they are preoccupied every waking moment with the question if they will be able to perform, how long, with what results, will they be able to consult a cheat sheet to all the hidden things, is the guy's next door bigger (of course it is) and so on.

Every...waking...moment. This is terrifying!

And the people who invented all these terrifying subjects were actually men. Although men could blame you women, you had nothing to do with it. You had no idea what was deep down there until Sigmunds from Vienna and Alfreds from the States and authors of Joy of this and Joy of that invented the plethora of female Karst phenomena. It serves men right.

It is like inventing a nuclear bomb in the belief that it will power your home once the SUV's guzzle up all the Arab oil. And presto, someone gets the idea to drop it on someone else's unsuspecting head. The psychos stemming out of Vienna and spreading around the world have discovered a terrifying knowledge that is adversely affecting Mankind.

And watch out, I did not say Humankind.

Also, it was guys who invented an arsenal of gadgets and toys to make women even more liberated from them, very sophisticated ones, lacking at this point only artificial intelligence. But watch this space.

Gee, I have to wrap this up:

Okay, even in NATO men are affected by this. There has been more than one debate where, with smiles around the male dominated table, there is talk of **size matters**. Permreps love showing off how the **size** their troops in operations has **grown** or **increased**. They want to **insert** troops and love to discuss **exit** strategy. There is talk of **short fuses** and **staying power**.

When the NAC visited Kabul once, the Japanese Ambassador whose brief was the issue of election support kept talking about **erection support**.

When we condemned what the North Koreans did a couple of days ago, we were on familiar ground again, I thought. The little **toy boy** Kim Jong Il that likes to be called for some reason General (like some of our NATO people), little Kim, frustrated by his **size** (and women know about Asian guys anyway), shot 7 **phallic** shaped missiles high in the air. In a way he was giving the **finger** to the Free world.

No wonder his missiles are called either **Wangs** or **Dongs**.

And so on and so on.

Okay, so men are pathetic, while women do not just tolerate us, but actually – for some reason – still generally crave us and need us. Mmmm, how romantic.

I am glad I can end this on a romantic note.

There must be some moral here somewhere but it escapes me.

And I raise my glass to Women in NATO. I don't know why – but there must be a reason!

Cheers!

DEFENDING DEMOCRATIC SLOVENIA

My Mission received from Ljubljana an exhibition named "The War for Slovenia" to commemorate the events following Slovenia's declaration of independence on 25 June 1991. The exhibition seemed fine to me when I checked it out but I disliked the name. You see things differently when you are abroad than the people back home. The name implied that Slovenians went to war to secede Slovenia from the former federation... far from true. Therefore, I retitled it "Defending Democratic Slovenia 1991," without asking anyone back home for their opinion. I said the following at NATO HQ, just next to the ING Bank branch on 16 June 2006:

Colleagues, Ladies and gentlemen,

These days Slovenia is fifteen years young.

But dates, anniversaries are never simple. On June 25 we will celebrate the fifteenth anniversary of the official declaration of independence by the democratically elected Parliament and the 15th formal Anniversary of our Armed Forces.

However, the Parliament did nothing more than just implement the popular will of the citizens of Slovenia who in December 1990 overwhelmingly, with almost 90% of the electorate, supported dissociation of our Democratic state established in April of that year with the rest of the even by then defunct Totalitarian controlled Federation, with a very long and by now hard to understand name.

By some quaint chance I happened to be among those MP's who made it happen, not only formally, but who had also engaged in the Democratic movement in the late Eighties.

My Deputy has prepared a fine speech for me, listing in detail all the reasons why Slovenians wanted to be free.

But as we all live with this Alliance, based on common values, I believe there is no question why any nation, any people would not have the right to be free.

And we did it according to the rule of law, in a peaceful matter, expecting to negotiate all the bits and pieces that would make our dissociation with our 70 year old marriage partners as pleasant as possible.

Well, we soon knew de facto that the other party did not share our values, the values enshrined in the Washington Treaty.

In the early morning hours after the Independence party Slovenia was invaded by a 20,000 plus well-equipped armed force, strangely called the Something-or-Other People's Army.

Our response was firm and resolute. Within 10 days the YPA was in a shambles and was happy to negotiate – with the help of European mediators – a full exodus from Slovenia. By Mid October there was not one foreign soldier left on the Slovenian soil.

And the rest is history. And I will leave history to historians.

Today's exhibition shows the most critical days of the 10 Day War, as well as the overall context, for easier understanding. We did not have professional soldiers, but ordinary citizens who followed the call of their civic duty to stand for freedom and democracy, something that one half of Europe at that point in history had already enjoyed for almost half a century.

I would especially like to welcome here General Slapar, the CHOD of our armed forces who masterminded our military efforts in those crucial days. Besides that I would like to commend my colleagues from our Mission and military representatives from our EU Representation who in those days put their lives on the line.

We were victorious, which shows that the desire of people to be free is an unstoppable and unbreakable force.

The dividends of developing and strengthening democracy without any hindrance and pressure have brought some very tangible results. We have joined NATO and the EU and next year we are to join the Eurozone and the Schengen. Sounds pretty boring. But boring is good.

The years of development in democracy have also helped us become a security producer able and willing to contribute to the efforts of Euro-Atlantic community to safeguard its security and stability.

We are tiny, but serious. Our burden sharing in operations, if we look at the number of troops per capita, puts us into 6th or 7th place among the Allies. My personal ambition is that we climb to the 1st place within the next few months.

Let me conclude by repeating that in 1991 we were defending the values that represent the very foundation of the Atlantic Alliance.

We are as ready to do the same, but much more capable with our professional Armed Forces, if need be today, and we know that today we would not be alone any longer.

Learning of the importance of our common values through an armed conflict, and as a country firmly believing in the need of transatlantic security cooperation, we would not hesitate one single moment to provide our assistance to any ally that might face threats to its democracy, security and stability.

And I expect it is useful for the Alliance to have in its midst a country and an Armed Forces that in the past few decades not only fought a war but actually won it.

No wonder everyone from NATO wants to visit Slovenia these days. We've had the Military Committee visit, this week the DRC is there and in September we will host the Defense Ministerial. Welcome!

I hope you will enjoy the music provided by the Slovenian Armed Forces Band, as well as our wine.

Cheers.

SEEGROUP MINISTERIAL

SEEGROUP, or South East Europe Security Cooperation Steering Group, was a framework set up by NATO and consisted of a series of programs and initiatives aimed at promoting regional cooperation and long-term stability in the Balkans. As NATO SG Lord Robertson said: "*The region must be given a perspective of rejoining the European mainstream – because the clearest lesson of the past 50 years is that integration breeds trust, stability and prosperity.*" I have touched upon a bit of history on this issue in this book, as well as in my book *The 2020 Vision for the Western Balkans* that consists of over 30 speeches, interventions or statements on NATO and the Western Balkans. Soon after my taking over as Slovenia's first Ambassador to NATO early in 1999, I was faced with NATO's (read U.S.) concoction of a consultative body that would include all the Western Balkans aspirants for NATO membership, plus Slovenia, and be chaired by NATO. I expressed very vocally my displeasure with such a concept as I believed any such body should include also all the interested Allies. I was driven by a bit of paranoia that this framework could be a dead-end street for Slovenia, steering us away from the (more or less) direct track to membership. I learned via my Ministry that in Washington they called my position as the "Brussels Problem." I quickly gained support of my Minister Dr. Boris Frlec and continued my activities to find more appropriate ways how to of help the countries of the Western Balkans. Well, I did win. The framework was changed to something called the EAPC Open-ended Ad Hoc Working Group on

South East Europe and later to the Consultative Forum on Security Matters in South Eastern Europe. I cannot remember well when and how SEEGROUP was born… Anyway, this is my intervention at the SEEGROUP Ministerial on 11 June 2006. The bottom line is my penultimate sentence: Whoever expects solidarity of the Alliance should also demonstrate solidarity in the region.

Chair, Ambassador Alkalaj, and thank you Minister Ivanić for your address today.

It is great to see that the North Atlantic Council table can sit comfortably more than 26 members.

There is still about six months to go to the Riga Summit and I would like to appeal to all the Aspirants both for the PfP and NATO to use this time well.

The Alliance and the Partnership are based on common values. Democracy, rule of law, basic freedoms are not just mere words. Joining our Alliance and our Partnership is therefore not something requiring just a political promise but has to be based on hard facts and deeds.

As far as the region is concerned good neighborly relations especially, are of great importance. Much more can be done there,

Last time (and the first time) we met in this format I presented some slightly visionary ideas about the Balkans and its integration into NATO and the EU. I said I hoped to see all the missing jigsaw puzzle pieces in the Western Balkans both in NATO and the EU by Two Thousand and Twenty ("2020"). And I said we needed enhanced mechanisms to achieve that.

Since then, on the one hand things have moved on. Three MAP countries have progressed significantly towards fulfilling the criteria to join the Alliance. There are talks on Kosovo's future and there is more realism about the future status on both sides. Montenegro is poised to proclaim independence in the near future (July 13). Taboos are disappearing. We are closer to the reality of dealing with seven subjects in the region.

On the other hand, we are still stuck with the non-arrest of Mladić and Karadžić, preventing Bosnia-Herzegovina and Serbia from joining PfP and the EAPC. Also, both countries still have not formally become members of the Adriatic Charter. Solidarity in the region could be improved.

And finally, SEEGROUP is not a NATO body. It has regional ownership. And I hope the existing SEEGROUP members from the Western Balkans will have the vision to encompass new countries if and when they appear. Whoever expects solidarity of the Alliance should also demonstrate solidarity in the region. Challenges of the region should be seen as opportunities for the region.

Thank you and thank you for your excellent leadership of SEEGROUP.

LECTURING FUTURE CROATIAN PRESIDENT

Yes, another meeting with Croatians, this one on 29 May 2006, less than half a year before I left Brussels. The attitude of the Minister of Foreign Affairs, Kolinda Grabar-Kitarović, now Croatia's President, and minister of Defense Berislav Rončević towards Slovenia was clearly demonstrated at the close of the interventions of the NATO member countries when the ministers evaded reacting to the Slovenian questions. They did not quite believe that Slovenia was any factor in Croatia joining the Alliance. And, sadly, they were right. We did not use the power that the consensus rule gave us. When the proposal to issue invitations to the three MAP countries – Albania, Croatia and Macedonia – at the Bucurest NATO Summit in 2008, I was already out of NATO-related business, back in Ljubljana. I proposed to our people involved in the decision-making that Slovenia's position should be "Three or None." The Greeks managed to railroad Macedonia on account of its name (and let's not get into that...) while Slovenia supported the issuing of invitations to the other two. I felt that we could have ended with no candidates being invited, which would have probably worked in favor of more than rather less regional stability and good neighborly relations. It would have also left us with a useful lever to solve the border issue and check Croatia's territorial appetites. Later in life, I met Grabar-Kitarović a few times when she served as a NATO Assistant Secretary General and after that as Croatia's

Ambassador to the United States and the Organization of American States; I wished we had Slovenian politicians who could match her.

Thank you, Secretary General.

A warm welcome to you, Ministers, your delegation and especially our colleague and friend, Ambassador Božinović.

Let me be very clear: Slovenia supports Croatia's aspirations to join this Alliance. Being a country bordering the region, it is of great interest to us to extend the area of stability in the Western Balkans. As I said when we met your other MAP colleagues: it is not the question of "if" but "when.

Croatia has made considerable progress in implementing its MAP goals, and this is well reflected in the Progress Report.

We welcome Croatia's adoption of the Strategic defense Review and we are looking forward to the Long Term Development Plan to define the structure of your armed forces. In this regard, I would like to stress the importance of well-thought-out, realistic plans, in line with the available resources.

Membership in NATO is an enormous undertaking. It is not only a project of the Government, or the political parties. It has to be a national project, supported by the public. As mentioned by Secretary General at the outset, I would also like to express serious concern over very low public support for Croatia's ambition to join the Alliance. We advise against complacency and expect you to tackle this issue as a matter of priority.

May I also suggest that parallel to the campaign to raise this support, a transparent and comprehensive communication with the public is established, including the publication of official public opinion polls. As we've stated several times in the past, our offer to help in this area is still standing.

Whenever we meet with any of the three MAP countries, we underline the importance of other key MAP criteria, such as economic liberty and good neighborly relations. Given the fact that there is still potential for instability in the region of the Western Balkans, I would appreciate it if you could say a bit more about your relations with Bosnia-Herzegovina and Serbia and Montenegro.

In particular, we understand that a border agreement between Croatia and Bosnia-Herzegovina was signed in 1999, and Croatia has so far not ratified it yet. Could you give us a timeline for doing so?

Also, I understand that the agreements with Bosnia-Herzegovina on free navigation in and out of the Port of Ploče and the agreement on the unimpeded border crossing at Neum have also not been ratified by Croatia yet. Could you also give us a timeline for the ratification of these two agreements?

And, finally, I believe you should look with optimism towards the Riga Summit to receive a forward looking message.

Thank you, Secretary General.

MACEDONIA'S PROGRESS TOWARDS NATO MEMBERSHIP

The North Atlantic Council met with the Macedonian delegation, led by Minister of Foreign Affairs Ilinka Mitreva and Minister of Defense Jovan Manasijevski to discuss Macedonia's progress report on its participation in the Membership Action Plan on 22 May 2006, which happens to be my birthday and the official Slovenian Day of the Diplomat. As it is quite evident, I did not succumb to calling the country "the Former Yugoslav Republic of Macedonia" or "FYROM" as I will never call it either by its Greek-proscribed or recently newly adopted name North Macedonia. However, I used to advise Macedonians, including former Prime Minister Bučkovski, to accept whatever the Greeks were demanding. It would have been a litmus test if the Greeks had acted in earnest and dropped their objections to Macedonia's progress towards NATO and the EU (and disproved the saying "beware of Greeks bearing gifts.") I told the Macedonians that once they are in NATO and the EU, they can call their country whatever they want. Well, at the time of the meeting they still had not come to terms with that. (North) Macedonia finally became a full-fledged NATO member almost 14 years after this meeting, on 27 March 2020.

MATJAŽ ŠINKOVEC

Thank you, Secretary General,

I'm also very happy to welcome among us, again, Ministers Mitreva and Manasijevski. And a warm welcome to our friend and colleague, Ambassador Ružin, and to the whole Macedonian delegation.

First of all, let me reiterate Slovenia's firm support for Macedonia's membership in the Alliance: there is no "if", only "when" and that day is not too far away.

Second, let me welcome the impressive amount of work your country has done in the latest MAP cycle. I believe this progress is well reflected in the Progress Report.

The reforms you've undertaken in the legislative area, in the area of rule of law, in the implementation of the Ohrid framework are well on track. We hope you'll keep up the pace in the period ahead. We particularly expect the reform of the police to be a priority after the election.

We can only commend you for your work in the defense sector. Your plans are well thought-out, realistic and affordable. Their implementation will help you increase your role of a security provider and will make it possible to contribute even more to our operations.

I am glad to see that Macedonia has not played down the challenges still lying ahead. It takes willpower, money and political courage to deliver what has been promised, not just to the Alliance, but moreover to the Macedonian public. Speaking of the public, may I congratulate you on the incredible public support for NATO membership, quite uncharacteristic of the region. Well done.

Slovenia welcomes the adoption of the new electoral legislation, and we expect that the parliamentary elections will prove that Macedonia's democratic progress is indeed irreversible.

The cornerstone of NATO is our common values. This is why the standards listed in the Membership Action Plan set the bar pretty high.

It is not just the internal reforms that a candidate for membership must implement; its relations with the neighboring states are also of crucial importance. In this area, Macedonia can contribute greatly to stability in the region.

Today, on the eve of the re-establishment of two independent states in the Western Balkans – Montenegro and Serbia – we can have new hopes for more stability – not less stability – in the region.

Minister Mitreva, I would like to hear a bit more about relations with Kosovo, particularly about the issue of border demarcation. Slovenia firmly believes that in this context borders between republics and provinces of the former Federation as of 25 June 1991 must be respected.

In conclusion, let me say that we are looking forward to a time, not very far away, when we can welcome you at this table as a *de iure* member of the Alliance.

Thank you.

NATO & RUSSIA: TOGETHER!

I somehow got an invitation to participate as a speaker in an event called "NATO Rally," organized on 15 May 2006 in Samara, Russia, by NATO's office in Moscow. I gave my address the title "Together: Euro-Atlantic Security Yesterday, Today and Tomorrow." Even before the conference got to a start, there was a lively protest organized by the Communist Party of the Russian Federation, waving red (and one czarist) flags. A female Communist member of the regional parliament interrupted my speech and was then given the floor after my song and dance. As I read later on in our Moscow embassy's reporting, the embassy seemed to be happy with my reply to the slander, where I praised her use of the freedom of expression and pointed out to the nonsense she said about my dear NATO. After reading the text below, you will find it quite natural for people in the audience to react. I managed to handle the Q and A fairly well, by answering some pertinent questions. Note: from the corrected speaking notes it is not quite clear if I used the contents of the paragraph below which appears in italics. I was aware even at the time of delivering the speech, that it was naïve hoping that Russians may come to their senses. Most of my talks have been with Ambassador Sergei Kisliyak, starting in Brussels back in 1999, when I expressed to him my view that his country could join NATO one day if it went in the right direction with democratization, rule of law, respect of human right, etc. In my various jobs I did meet him later on in faraway places, such as Rekyavik, London, Tokyo, Kyoto, Lima, you name it. A couple of years

ago Kisliyak became notorious in the media as the top Russian spy in Washington. As far as I am concerned, a Slovenian daily newspaper in 2007 claimed that I had told the former Slovenian "resident" in Moscow that Russians were Slovenia's enemies. Anyway, let bygones be bygones; at least I put an appropriate musical backdrop to the speech below, as you will see at its end. I was aware all the time it was a bit naïve but I meant well. I wish I could relate the story of the night after the conference that I spent on the 50-meter long boat cruising up and down the Volga, owned by a local billionare, however...

Chairman, Rector, Excellencies, Ladies and Gentlemen,

It is nice to be here in Samara. Half a century of my life had to pass before I managed to visit this beautiful historic city on the Volga River.

This does not mean that I have not been to Russia before. I first crossed this country from the Pacific to Ukraine over 30 years ago, on a train, and discovered the great open heart and friendship of the Russian people.

This friendship had been confirmed during World War 2 when Slovenians and Russians were Allies, fighting the Nazis, each in their way, and in their part of the world. And we were in close touch. There was a Russian Military Mission at the Slovenian Partisan Headquarters. Along with the British and American missions. We confronted together the threat that the International Community faced 6 or 7 decades ago.

Today it is May 15. And that is the day World War 2 ended in Slovenia in 1945. Not on May 9; battles with the German troops lasted for another week. In 1941 Slovenia was not only occupied by and partitioned among our neighbors, but actually formally annexed to their countries. Hitler, Mussolini and their cronies wanted to wipe the Slovenian people off the map.

I am sure that you Russians, who suffered so much during the Great Patriotic War, understand such suffering of other people.

But the Slovenian people rose against the occupiers, created the largest liberated territory in occupied Europe and then, together with our Allies, liberated the country.

We learned early what it meant to be alone against a much more powerful foe, actually three of them, and then we learned what it meant to stand shoulder to shoulder with Allies that shared our values of freedom.

We learned what »one for all, all for one« meant. And that is why being in NATO is so natural to us.

And now that we face again a common threat: terrorism, spread of weapons of mass destruction and other asymmetric threats, I hope we can face it together again. Both us in NATO and Russia. Together.

It is a pleasure and honor to represent here today the North Atlantic Alliance and its highest decision-making body, the North Atlantic Council that I am a member of; here in the framework of the so ably organized NATO Rally. I would like to thank the Russian authorities, our NATO staff here in Russia for the splendid job and the French, Luxembourgish and Slovenian embassies in Russia especially for this event in Samara.

Slovenia, a country of 2 million people, encompassing 20.000 square kilometers, became just over 2 years ago an equal member of the Alliance as all NATO's decisions are made on the basis of consensus. No NATO's decision can be taken without explicit agreement of Slovenia, or Luxembourg, or Iceland or Estonia, even smaller NATO members than Slovenia on the basis of population.

As far as NATO's relations with Russia are concerned, Slovenia has a special, peculiar position. It is the only member country which during the Cold War years was neither confronting the Soviet Union, nor was it either its part or controlled by it.

So when Slovenia participates in NATO's discussions of relations with Russia, we have no hang ups, no historic grievances. Our only interest is in making the relationship between NATO and Russia develop further so that we can face common threats together. I believe this is a mutual interest of all the 27 nations participating in the NATO-Russia Council, another important body I happen to be a member of.

But do not misunderstand me. I am not putting any question mark under the existence or actions of NATO in all of its incarnations so far.

Quite the opposite, I firmly believe in its positive, indispensable role from its inception in 1949, throughout the Cold War, during the Balkan crises and now in the 21st century facing the new threats, new insecurities, wherever they come from.

If we look at the big picture we know why we have the freedom of today. Why both Slovenians and Russians are free people, living in democratic countries. It is great to see people demonstrating outside of this hall, freely expressing their beliefs. I wish we could have them here with us, so we could have a lively exchange of views.

Why is it so? It is because of the Democratic West countering for decades both the ideological and the military challenge posed by the Undemocratic Communist Bloc. The Alliance formed by Western democracies in 1949 was not just a regional military Alliance dealing with the regional threat. It was also a strong European and Transatlantic community based on common values.

The North Atlantic Alliance is the clearest expression of a lasting bond between the democracies of Europe and North America.

NATO is an organization that protects the values that our societies are based on: freedom, common heritage and civilization, democracy, individual liberty and the rule of law, as well as desire to live in peace with all peoples and all governments.

NATO has been successfully defending these values, initially with 12 members and now with 26. And there is a host of other nations who claim they believe in the same values and either want to join us to defend them together or work closely with us in defending them.

And in defending these values we are ready to go wherever we have to go outside NATO's borders. And as it has been demonstrated in Bosnia-Herzegovina, in Kosovo, in the Mediterranean, in Afghanistan, and in Iraq, we are contributing to peace and security in the areas affected and wider in the world.

What we should learn from NATO's existence, and the existence of the European Union that grew under the Alliance's umbrella, was that wars in Europe, among European states, could only be prevented through European and Euro Atlantic integration.

NATO's enlargement itself, both in 1999 with three new members, and in 2004 with 7 new members, did not only strengthen the Alliance – which after all is a performance-based organization and not a debating club – but also enlarged the area of security. The closer non-member countries are to NATO's borders the safer they should feel. And further enlargement – when the 26 member countries decide so – will result in exactly the same: enlargement of wider security.

Let us be realistic. As we are faced with globalized insecurity we have to counter it with the globalized security. To achieve that, a Global Partnership seems to be needed between NATO and a host of partners.

Today's security environment bears almost no resemblance to the Cold War. In those days deterrence took care of the West's security needs. The Alliance's solidarity was never ever tested in operations. The only element that remains is our collective capability of deterrence. Otherwise our Alliance would be considered by our foes as perhaps just a paper tiger in spite of all the operations we might be involved in.

Our Alliance, our NATO, has proven to be an Alliance that does NOT need to reinvent itself, it just needs to continue doing what it was set up to do, but in ways adapted to the new times.

From a sleepy giant of the Cold War, it has grown into a very active and indispensable collective member of the International Community.

Truly, as corny as it sounds, if there was no NATO we would have to invent it.

If we examine NATO's role today it is clear that Collective Defense remains the cornerstone of this Alliance. There is no stronger promise of solidarity sovereign nations can give each other than Article 5.

Let me briefly paraphrase from the Washington Treaty: "an armed attack against a member nation shall be considered an attack against them all and each of them will assist the attacked member nation, including the use of force, to restore and maintain the security of the North Atlantic Area."

But defense means more than just Article 5. The bulk of NATO's post Cold War missions and operations are actually non Article 5 missions. NATO has demonstrated it is the best crisis manager and peace keeper there is. These operations in turn provide also defense for NATO's members.

Although NATO is the single global military Alliance, it does not achieve its purpose solely or largely through military means. We are using a strategy that includes such elements as:

- Engagement, where we tackle the challenges to our security when and where they emerge, or they will end up on our doorstep.

- Multi-dimensionality, where multi-dimensional challenges require multi-dimensional responses. This means that political, economic, military and reconstruction and development cooperation instruments have to be applied in a concerted way.
- Patience. No job is done overnight, this has been clearly demonstrated in the Balkans. NATO cannot leave before the job is done, otherwise we will have failed as an Alliance.
- Solidarity. No nation can do much on its own. And we cannot expect others to do something that we could do. We cannot just pay lip service to solidarity.

Now let me say something about Partnerships.

First. More than we have done so far we should work together with other international organizations that are complimentary: foremost the European Union, the United Nations, the OSCE. When possible we should have common strategies to crises areas, a division of labor and coordination.

Second: We have learned that our Partnerships are indispensable when facing our common global threats: There are 20 non-NATO member countries in the so called Partnership for Peace and the Euro-Atlantic Partnership Council, covering more or less the rest of "OSCE Europe". By engaging them we are trying to promote the values they formally subscribed to when they joined the Partnership.

We are engaging Russia in the NATO-Russia Council. We are engaging Ukraine in the NATO Ukraine Commission, again with a lot of stress on the values, as Ukraine wants to proceed towards membership in the Alliance. We are engaging 7 Mediterranean Dialogue countries, bringing them closer to our values, as well as the Gulf countries in the newly established Istanbul Cooperation Initiative. And we are working closely together with a large number of the so-called Contact Countries, some of them already sharing our values, such as Australia, New Zealand and Japan.

Since the Rome Summit, almost 4 years ago, the NATO-Russia Council has developed into an effective forum both for political dialogue and practical cooperation. In the political dialogue we have gone far, including also controversial issues. Work on interoperability among the

NATO-Russia member states has grown to the extent that we can have joint action in military and civil emergency response operations.

Among the activities let me list just a few. The Council has devoted a lot of time, political will as well as resources to develop cooperation against the terrorist threat, with significant results. Actually one of these activities, an expert conference, took place in Slovenia almost a year ago.

We have taken great strides forward in enhancing cooperation in crisis management. We have put forward recommendations how to strengthen existing non-proliferation arrangements. Other areas tackled include Arms control and Confidence and Security Building Measures, nuclear consultations and theatre missile defense cooperation, search and rescue at sea, military-to-military cooperation and defense reform and so on.

Who would have thought a few years ago that NATO and Russia could do so much together!

But on the other hand, why not?

NATO nations share values with democratic Russia.

NATO nations and Russia are faced with similar or same threats.

NATO nations and Russia realize we can be more successful if we work together.

And finally, NATO nations and Russia both understand the responsibility for wider international security, not just that on our borders.

I appreciate very much the latest statements by President Putin in Sochi, expressing his unwavering interest in building good relations with the West.

And I remember watching the Live 8 concert from Moscow's Red Square last year. The Pet Shop Boys singing their song "Together." How appropriate: this is what we are discussing here today: Together.

I hope the NATO Rallies in Russia will both help a better public understanding of NATO as it is, meaning the values it is based on and the operations it is involved in, and be an impetus for even more work together.

I believe the international situation, as it is, requires that NATO and Russia combine their assets, their capabilities, their will and their energy to face their common threats together.

Together.

Thank you.

FIRST TIME ON BELARUS

On 12 April 2006, I could not hold my tongue in an EAPC Ambassadorial and actually tackled, first time ever, Belarus – that became much more present in my interventions 5 years later as Ambassador to the Political and Security Committee of the European Union. Lo and behold, nothing much has changed until this time. In addition, I did not expect President Lukashenka would still be in power and that I would ever have the opportunity to lecture him on human rights and death penalty.

Thank you, Secretary General,

I have been sitting at this table for over 7 years and I cannot but speak out – perhaps too often and not to everyone's taste – on the question of values.

NATO is not just an Alliance based on values, but an Alliance of Values.

So I believe is the Partnership. Every Partner has signed on to respecting certain common values.

To Slovenia and me personally the question of values is not academic. My parents fought in World War 2 for their freedom and other basic values. For expressing my democratic views freely I was questioned by the police in the Sixties and the Seventies, and in the Eighties I was in the streets of Ljubljana together with thousands, demanding basic human rights, including free and fair elections.

And in 1990 I was elected to the Parliament in the first Slovenian free and fair elections. So I cannot evade speaking out in support of the statement of Secretary General, the OSCE and the EU.

I deplore the use of force by any authorities against civilian demonstrators, who peacefully demonstrate against the violation of their right to a democratic election process. These principles are not just empty words. It is important to keep this issue on NATO and EAPC agenda as a regular item and not just if or when we are faced with violations of the basic values that we've all sworn to protect.

And lastly, I hope that representatives of Belarus do not follow the sad example of Uzbekistan at this table. Let us keep talking.

Thank you.

NATO IN AFRICA!

The North Atlantic Council flew on 6 April 2006 on an Airbus A-310 (and our support staff on a C-130 in VIP configuration), both provided by Spain, to Rabat for a 2-day High-Level Event with Mediterranean Dialogue Countries. NAC always travelled in style, with member country governments falling over each other to transport us effortlessly to European, American, Asian or African destinations, you name it. Sometimes our wives/partners travelled with us. I had to intervene in the meeting, after all Slovenia is also a Mediterranean, not just an Alpine country. This event was a breakthrough in NATO's relations with the so-called Mediterranean Dialogue Countries, the framework initiated in 1994. Their representatives, Ambassadors of Algeria, Egypt, Israel, Jordan, Mauritania and Tunisia even flew with us from Brussels. The Moroccans were already there, naturally. Let me just point out that the countries that I mention below – and felt were missing from the table – were Lebanon and Palestine. The offer at the end of my address to organize a NATO-Med Dialogue Defense Ministers meeting in Slovenia was purely my own. Having managed to persuade both my Government as well as the North Atlantic Council to have a NATO Defense Ministerial in Slovenia in September of 2006, I was sure I had enough clout to manage the addition of another eventual meeting to the Ministerial. Speaking of NATO in Africa: later in the summer, NATO did execute a very successful training mission, Called Steadfast Jaguar 2006, in Cape Verde where we met

the NATO-friendliest people ever, waving NATO flags when the NAC Ambassadors and our troops drove through Mindelo, São Vicente.

Thank you, Chairman.

Let me first thank the Moroccan authorities for the warm welcome and excellently organized historic event. We can have a slightly different view of this gathering today. We mostly talk of NATO meeting with the Mediterranean Dialogue countries. But at the same time we have here at this table two other groups: Mediterranean countries, including Slovenia, and 19 non-Mediterranean ones.

We treasure very much this relationship, this Partnership between our Alliance and the Med Dialogue countries. We see many chances of enhancing it and, hopefully, enlarging it with new Med Dialogue members so that both sides of the Mediterranean could profit more fully from this joint venture.

Now I will omit substantial parts of my contribution to make it shorter. Let me just say that there was no initiative given here today that we would not support.

We can do more in the practical dimension of our cooperation, especially in achieving a certain degree of interoperability.

Regarding the issue of terrorism, we should seek to weigh the comparative advantages of our partnership and we should avoid duplicating work with other international organizations.

We would like to see our cooperation to be result-oriented and to exercise our practical cooperation effectively. To do this we have to improve even further our exchange of information and intelligence,

We also believe that there is a lot of room for improving and expanding our cooperation in the area of consequence management, especially in managing the consequences of terrorist attacks, and that an exchange of views on national practices and policies would lead to an advantageous joint end product.

But let me just add this: we support the initiative to draft a political statement or declaration. The Istanbul discussions and priorities we set should be the basis in drafting such a statement.

We believe that it should be placed on the agenda of a meeting of Foreign Ministers but that we should give ample time to a working group to prepare a solid text which we could all agree on. We also believe it would be useful to have more regular meetings of both Foreign and Defense Ministers.

If so agreed, Slovenia would be happy to host a meeting of Defense Ministers.

Thank you.

NATO'S TRANSFORMATION

On 2 March 2006, the North Atlantic Council tackled one of its regular themes, Transformation, during its "Away Day" somewhere not too far from the Brussels HQ. In my intervention, I followed closely the advice of my defense people, headed by Primož Šavc, as the matter was a bit too technical for me. My colleagues also had many brilliant ideas, but there were no silver bullets.

Thank you Jaap.

Toria, may I extend condolences at the death of the U.S. diplomat in Pakistan.

I am speaking early in the discussion, because if I wait too long, everything will have already been said by others.

We believe the transformation package should be the focal point of Riga. Not partnerships, not Enlargement but Transformation.

Jaap, thank you for the document that provides a useful basis for our discussion.

Looking at it, I am, as far as Para 2 is concerned, in favor of a single Transformational Report and a single Transformation Declaration. Such a single transformation report can stand on its own in terms of what NATO has done and is doing in the area of transformation. It adds strength to the CPG in terms of making it operational – it would actually mean that the CPG is in action. If we stick to the line of "big packages" to be delivered at Riga, the puzzle might never be completed.

On Para 3: the CPG is a stand-alone document, but I agree that its role should be emphasized also in the Transformational Report.

Para 4: I understand that the Transformation Report would essentially have two sides: the ongoing work of the Alliance and the forward-looking one. Guidance on future work is very welcome, but I do not believe that inconclusive guidance or partial conclusions have a place in such a document. We both agree in full or not at all – and leave the subject out.

I believe that what we require is a good working map to outline the way forward in all the different areas – and how to coordinate them. That should reduce the number of doubts and uncertainties on what will or will not mature to a deliverable for Riga relatively early in the process.

On possible new initiatives or a major push for the ongoing work, mentioned in Para 5, let me say that each of the Washington, Prague and Istanbul Summits had a major drive engine in terms of pushing the work forward. I do believe that the one for Riga could be developed from the field of preparing NATO for its future tasks, *read*: operations.

Let me end with Para 6: In terms of capabilities for effective conduct of future operations I support the inclusion of the idea captured in Point 16i of the CPG: the ability to bring military support to stabilization operations and reconstruction efforts across all phases of crises. Here I would support the ideas outlined under "training initiatives" and "planning improvements."

On other considerations I would like to strongly emphasize the necessity to harmonize our activities with the EU and to do it in a transparent manner – we have stated that clearly in the CPG. But moreover, it derives from the realities of our day-to-day work; and that will be even more the case in the future.

Thank you.

SPOTLIGHT ON THE
WESTERN BALKANS

My contribution to the above subject matter is below. It was prepared for some sort of NATO Ambassadors' restricted brainstorming on 1 March 2006. On the original text that I have found there are some deletions and some explanations in an unfamiliar handwriting in pencil. I gather that I was absent from the discussion for some reason and it was delivered by my (by then 5th in a row) Deputy Head of Mission Jurij Rifelj, a rare youngish pro-NATO hardliner. In what exact form it was done, I do not know. I am sure that he, mentioning that it was my personal view, cut it short, knowing well the diplomatic phrase: "Deputies are to be seen, not heard," and excluded at least some of my inanities. I can see lots of my I's changed into We's, as mere deputies are not supposed to express their own views in front of a gathering of Ambassadors. While retyping the text, lacking any electronic file, I had a slight urge to prettify it but then stayed true to my resolution to present all the texts in this book as they were created and/or delivered, as my family's and my Alma Mater's motto states: *Viam Veritatis Elegi.* No corrected grammar, no exclusion of flamboyancy, no re-writing of history. The people, mentioned in the text: Jaap de Hoop Scheffer, NATO Secretary General, Robert Badinter, Head of the Arbitration Commission of the Conference on Yugoslavia, Igor Slobodnik, the Slovak Ambassador to NATO, Franjo Tudjman, President of Croatia, Slobodan Milošević, President of Serbia, Vuk Drašković, Foreign Minister of Serbia. Lastly, Karl

May, a prolific 19th century German author of adventure novels that I, as a kid, had read all available in the Slovenian language.

Thank you, Jaap, for putting this on the agenda.

I apologize for wanting to say more than I usually do. I sat down last night and wrote a little lamentation, without checking the things prepared for me by my political advisors. I know I'll be in trouble with them.

And thank you for the paper that I only saw after having had prepared my speaking notes. I can mostly go along with it. I am glad it contains mentioning together for the first time 7 countries and that is a step forward from the so far piecemeal approach, in the direction of a comprehensive strategy and through closer cooperation with the EU – this has been the gist of what I usually say on the Balkans.

What happens in the Western Balkans is of vital interest to Slovenia. Slovenia spent 7 decades politically in the Balkans. I like to joke that that it is our backyard. Okay, a pretty big backyard…

More appropriately – the Western Balkans is the Backyard of NATO and of the EU. Okay, so there are other areas of concern to us: Afghanistan, the Mediterranean, the Middle East, the Caucuses, Central Asia. But if we are realistic, this **should** be both to NATO and the EU, collectively, the most important region.

As far as NATO and the EU are concerned, this actually is our own little Mediterranean. Why a Mediterranean? It is the only major spot of Europe engulfed by NATO and EU countries – okay, with some exceptions that confirm the rule. This is a yet to be tamed Sea of Seven Islands, too long known for its sharks and the carnage caused in storms there. Now that most of the sharks either are safely in the Hague/Scheveningen or buried, both NATO and the EU should deal very seriously with this region, with the end result of all of the Seven Islands being both in NATO and the EU.

We need vision, determination and energy. And they should be encompassed in a Comprehensive Strategy for the Western Balkans. I like to call this my 20/20 vision. If we do the right thing both in our own interest and the interest of the Western Balkans, by 2020 we could have (and I believe should have) all of the Western Balkans in NATO and the

EU. This is – contrary to what it sounds – a very short period. But I believe it could be done.

Why Seven Islands? If we are realistic – and realism is what we most of all need – we will be dealing – maybe not this year as yet – but soon with 7 units, countries, independent states. I am not advocating independence for Kosovo and Montenegro – but what else is there in their future?

Why Islands? It is because we treat most of them in that way. We deal with B-H, then deal with FRY or SAM (since 1945 Serbians had to call their country 6 different names), and then Kosovo, and we deal with Macedonia, and with Croatia, and with Albania. This piecemeal approach does not recognize the fact that just about all the **problems** of the Western Balkans are so intermingled that they require a common approach. Even the paper, that is quite visionary, still deals with individual or groups of countries, not really with the whole region.

I mentioned realism. When we had a discussion on Montenegro (at the lunch hosted by Igor), I had a *déjà vu*. Back in 1991 in The Hague, I was behind a table like this with the European Community representatives, and Tudjman, Milošević and the rest of the gang, and there was this discussion on "why in Yugoslavia there was separation when the rest of Europe was dealing with integration." Of course, Milošević was playing the integrationist card, he was the Good Guy, and I was the Bad Guy, representing secessionist Slovenia). So let us not get into lamenting why, why, why, but try to do our best to help bring these seven missing jigsaw puzzle pieces into the NATO and EU frameworks.

I have now mentioned a dozen times the EU. If there is any region that NATO and the EU should discuss together at all, it definitely should be the Western Balkans. The Backyard we share. If a Common Strategy is too farfetched – and I have been a Science Fiction fan for almost half a century – could we at least have an informal discussion on how we see the future of the Western Balkans? There are some worrying messages coming from the other side of the divide – of some in the EU **not** seeing the Western Balkans countries as future members. I feel it is very shortsighted thinking of Exclusion, not Inclusion. The past decade and a half since the Fall of the Wall we have seen that Inclusion works.

Both NATO and the EU should not only offer a Euro-Atlantic perspective to these countries, but something even more solid. A cooperative mechanism that would integrate the region both regionally, using tools developed on the basis of Dayton, Ohrid, and Badinter, and mechanisms to speed up the Seven to carry out the reforms necessary to fulfill the requirements of NATO and EU memberships.

A few words on the Membership Action Plan: I'm one of those guys who have seen this mechanism from both sides. I believe it has an inherent flaw. It was invented – I believe – by our former colleague Emyr Jones-Parry – to prepare Central European countries for NATO membership. I am not so sure this works as well for the countries of the Western Balkans. I believe we should reform it to the extent that the aspirants involved would have more guidance and less free hand at choosing what they do and what they don't do. When we had a meeting of the SEEGROUP at Ambassadorial level last year I called such an enhanced mechanism a sort-of-a GPS that would prevent Aspirants from veering off the right direction. Anyway, GPS sounds more Transatlantic than Galileo…

Almost lastly, on Invitations. I have said that there was not much time left until 2020. However, there is enough time not to rush into things. Let us keep NATO as a Performance Based Alliance. If an invitation is just a political decision, then we can invite just about everyone just about any time. But if we try to stick to what we have said, then let us seriously look at the performance. Generally I think that the Three (Macedonia, Albania, Croatia) are as ready as the seven latest members were around 1996; if we are realistic and check out all the 5 Chapters of MAP. They all have some good points, and they have some bad points. Some have a total lack of public support, some overflow with it, some are economy-wise basically sound, some barely scrape together 10% of Slovenia's GDP per capita, some excel in good neighborly relations and some seem to attempt to do quite the opposite, some are getting close to realistic defense planning, while some would have to raise the share of GDP for Defense to 10% (Okay, I'm slightly exaggerating) to deliver what has been promised.

What we should especially strive for in the Western Balkans is not to divide them more but help bring them closer together. Let us have more balance than less balance. Premature invitations for purely political reasons could further destabilize the region. Let us show that what we say on Performance is valid and that results will be rewarded. If we act out of a mere whim, the rest will see that what we preach is out of synch with reality. What we do with the three MAP countries (Macedonia and Albania in it for 6.5 years and Croatia for 3.5) will also influence very much the performance of the rest: B-H, Serbia, Montenegro, Kosovo. Drašković keeps repeating that he has been promised NATO membership next year. If we admit countries without them fulfilling pretty basic criteria, we can forget about any serious reforms in the whole region.

Lastly, yes this is the Western Balkans. The Balkans! We seem to forget that in the Western Balkans only performance matters, forget the promises. As a kid in The Fifties I read a book by Karl May on the Balkans. And when I travel there, I see that nothing much has changed in the thinking of the region since the 19th century. But we should not step away. We should get even more involved. Otherwise things could get out of hand again. We have seen a lot of that in the past hundred years since the 1st Balkan War. Let's take a break and do the right thing.

On the conclusions:

- A clear message on the necessity of further reforms and that eventual invitations will be considered at the 2008 Summit.
- A more dynamic relationship should mean an improved MAP mechanism.
- An increased political role in the Western Balkans for NATO.
- As soon as possible a dialogue with the EU on regional security and integration.

Thank you.

LECTURING PRIME
MINISTER OF CROATIA

On January 31 2006 the North Atlantic Council met with the Croatian Prime Minister Ivo Sanader, a few years later a fugitive from the law. He presented Croatia's case for joining the Alliance. It was the usual thing for leaders of the so-called Aspirant Countries to address NATO's decision-making body. He talked about the reforms under way in the different expected areas (no need to list them as lots of my speeches in this book do that) while at the same time surprisingly claiming that Croatia by its full cooperation with the International Crime Tribunal for the Former Yugoslavia simultaneously fulfilled all criteria for NATO membership. Presto! I admit I have never been a fan of Croatia's policies, especially its disregard of good neighborly relations. In March 1991 – three months before Slovenia's proclamation of independence - I proposed to the Slovenian Parliament the conclusion of an agreement with Croatia that would encompass the border, defense, economic, you name it issues, but to no avail. I was even accused of warmongering by a lady colleague of mine, representing the Hungarian minority in the Parliament. I believed and believe that Croatia should have solved all its open issues with the neighbors, especially Slovenia, before it could be admitted into NATO and the EU. I managed to oppose successfully Croatia achieving the exchange of radar picture with NATO for years, on account of its publishing maps with the state border with Slovenia drawn in the middle of the Bay of Piran that had always been considered part of

Slovenia. Also, at no point in history Croatia has shown any gesture of friendship towards Slovenia, while we – naïvely – have helped it when it was attacked in the early 1990's and later agreed to admit it both into NATO and the EU. My Ministry, knowing my stance, asked me to send them my written text beforehand. They faxed back the "corrected" version that crossed out the two probably most important paragraphs that appear in the following text in italics. Did I obey the instruction from Ljubljana or not?

Thank you, Secretary General.

Prime Minister, a warm welcome to you and your delegation, especially to our colleague Ambassador Božinović.

We appreciate your visiting the Council again this year and expressing views aimed at strengthening Euro-Atlantic security, as well as presenting your country's ambitions of adhesion to the Alliance.

We understand very well the enormous undertaking a country has to do to join the Alliance. We had to go through it ourselves. We found out there were no quick fixes, no back doors, but on the other hand a lot of hard work carrying out reforms in a great number of areas.

Often it is thought that the main thing is the reform of the armed forces and ensuring adequate funding for defense budgets. It is true NATO is a military Alliance, but it is also much more. So the Membership Action Plan chapters on Political, Economic, security and Legal issues are as important as the Defense & Military chapter.

And most of all it is an Alliance of values.

What we especially learned was that it was not only the technical work of preparing plans, not even just delivering what we promised, but especially aligning our thinking with the thinking of the Alliance.

In this vein we expect of the candidates for membership to demonstrate they accept and share Euro-Atlantic values. And let me list just a few: good neighborly relations, non-adoption of unilateral measures that adversely affect Allies, non-discrimination of Allies in Foreign Direct Investment and access to the financial markets, fulfilling of agreements, etc.

Slovenia is a staunch supporter of the Open Door Policy and sees Croatia as a future Ally. We fully understand your aspirations, as we had to go through a similar process in the past, including disappointments at the 1997 and 1999 Summits.

We stand ready to assist Croatia especially in the areas where we are strong. Noting the problem with the public support for NATO membership we are ready to share our expertise, as we are doing, for instance for Serbia and Montenegro. Candidature for membership in NATO needs clear public support.

We hope Croatia will use the opportunity for a more in-depth dialogue on the issues we noted in the questions put to your delegation at the SPC(R) last October and invite your authorities to fully reply to them. It is important to work with all Allies, not just "key Allies," as Croatia announced in the current Annual National Program.

All in all, we urge Croatia to seriously tackle the reforms before it and also increase endeavors for security and stability in its neighborhood as well as in the region, especially within the Adriatic Charter, where, for instance, full inclusion of Bosnia and Herzegovina and Serbia and Montenegro would demonstrate the solidarity that the Alliance not only treasures but practices daily.

Regional stability depends also upon a balanced relationship the Alliance has with the candidate countries and the rest of the Western Balkans. The success of each country depends upon the success of all. While each country – as the saying goes – will be judged individually, future enlargements of the Alliance also have to be in service of greater stability and not on the other hands cause imbalance and instability.

Let me close by saying that small countries can become good Allies, often they even punch above their weight. We are looking forward to the time when we could welcome Croatia in our midst.

Thank you.

THE FUTURE OF PARTNERSHIPS

On 27 January 2006, NAC had another "brainstorming" on its partnerships of different types or classes. It have noted on my speaking notes it was Agenda Item II, I have no idea what Agenda Item I was. It was another attempt to push slowly forward the agenda of relations and cooperation that are more substantial with countries that we saw eye to eye on many issues but for one reason or another were not members of the Alliance.

Thank you Jaap,

When talking of Partnerships, we agree it is true that PFP/EAPC is to a certain extend in trouble and needs to be revitalized. Both the latest Ministerial and the latest Ambassadorial showed that very clearly. I see the main reason for this development in the fact that the PfP has largely served its purpose as a vehicle for membership. We still have some aspirant nations, but at the same time the majority of partners – while interested in certain aspects of cooperation – are not motivated to be the driving force of partnership.

The idea of having different 26+n formats is very attractive. We were actually proposing something of the kind when still an aspirant partner, but it was too early. Self-differentiation was taboo! However, like Igor and some other colleagues I feel we need to seriously consider what such formats would mean for our meeting load.

We have always seen both Partnership and NATO as fora based on values. Any new NATO policy should retain that. Our common values should not be subject to so-called differentiation between individual countries.

And, last but not least, we like Herman's Partnership for Security proposal.

On Enlargement: Okay, let's not beat around the bush. Let's call a spade a spade. At present, if we honestly take MAP performance as criteria for membership, I do not see the three current aspirants as ready to receive invitations this year. We should have such a debate ASAP.

I am not sure how the suggestion to "keep options open" is helping the MAP countries; I think it would be better for all if we gave them a clear indication what we intend to do on the Open Door Policy. I already mentioned the Madrid Summit today. Perhaps we could make a step ahead by mentioning the 3 MAP aspirant countries in the same way the Madrid Declaration mentioned Romania and Slovenia and list the others, such as Ukraine and Georgia.

We'll be under less pressure; and the MAP countries will be able to better manage the expectations regarding the Summit outcome (the MFA of Croatia has recently publicly said in the Parliament that Croatia expects an invitation in Riga).

The other aspect to consider when talking about enlargement is regional stability. Countries of the Western Balkans have to be assessed on individual merits, but any future enlargement has to mean greater regional stability and not cause additional rifts in the region.

Thank you.

DEFENDING NATO'S VALUES

I was invited by the Institute of Strategic Studies in Ljubljana to speak at their seminar: Defending NATO's values Beyond Europe, on 24 November 2005, together with my NAC colleague, Canadian ambassador Jean-Pierre Juneau, and an official from NATO Staff, Knut Kirste, whose brief included Slovenia. The three of us were on a sort-of a Slovenian NATO tour.

Chairman, Ladies and Gentlemen, Colleagues,

May I first warmly thank you for hosting this seminar and inviting my Colleagues Ambassador Jean-Pierre Juneau, Mr Knut Kirste and myself to take part in it.

It is a timely kick off of a series of public diplomacy events before the NATO informal Defense Ministerial next fall in Slovenia. There is no more important thing than working with the public to understand Slovenia's role in the Alliance.

When we entered NATO on March 29 last year, it was not just my Mission in Brussels that entered, not just the Foreign and Defense Ministries, not just the Government, but all of the country.

Very soon it will be 3 years since the heated debate about Slovenia's membership in NATO when two opposing views clashed, and, fortunately, as far as I am concerned, the right and historic decision was reached in a referendum.

The title of your seminar reminds me of what one of our colleagues said about a document we have been working on for a long time in the

Alliance, called the Comprehensive Political Guidance. He said it has to be Comprehensive, Political and Guidance.

In the same vein we should perhaps dissect the meaning of the title of this seminar, and talk about Defending, talk about Values and talk about Europe.

I. Talking about **DEFENDING**: If we examine NATO's role today it is clear that Collective Defence remains the cornerstone of this Alliance. There is no stronger promise of solidarity sovereign nations can give each other than Article V. And just for the sake of it let me briefly paraphrase from the Washington Treaty: "An armed attack against a member nation shall be considered an attack against them all and each of them will assist the attacked member nation, including the use of force, to restore and maintain the security of the North Atlantic Area."

In an uncertain world, when we are faced with asymmetric threats, such as terrorism and the spread of Weapons of Mass Destruction, Collective Defence is an asset we must preserve and defend.

But defense means more than just Article V. The bulk of NATO's post Cold War missions and operations are actually non-Article 5 missions. NATO has demonstrated it is the best crisis manager and peace keeper there is. These operations in turn provide also defense for NATO's members.

II. Talking about **VALUES**: The North Atlantic Alliance is the clearest expression of a lasting bond between the democracies of Europe and North America. I am so glad that my colleague, the Canadian Ambassador Juneau is here with us. Too often we forget that there are two Trans-Atlantic nations, but if we examine Canada's contribution to operations world-wide it is clear that we could not do without them.

But let me get back to the values. When the former Secretary General of NATO Lord Robertson was taking over his job a number of years ago he mentioned he had three priorities: Capabilities, Capabilities and Capabilities. Far from disputing the importance of capabilities – and I would like to say something about the Slovenian capabilities later – I would say, after my over a decade and a half long belief that Slovenia should be a part of this Alliance – that NATO is about Values, Values and Values.

NATO is an organization that protects the values that our societies are based on: freedom, common heritage and civilisation, democracy, individual liberty and the rule of law, as well as desire to live in peace with all peoples and all governments. NATO has been successfully defending these values, initially with 12 members and now with 26. And there is a host of other nations who claim they believe in the same values and either want to join us to defend them together or work closely with us in defending them.

III. And lastly, talking about **EUROPE and beyond Europe**. I would prefer to say, beyond NATO's borders. What we used to call "out of area."

a) As far as our missions and operations are concerned, as you know, we are not talking about "out of area" any longer, especially after 9/11. Our resolve is to go wherever we have to go outside NATO's borders to protect ourselves inside NATO's borders. And as it has been demonstrated, for instance on the example of Afghanistan, thus contributing to peace and security in the areas affected and wider in the world.

b) When we are talking about defending NATO's values beyond NATO's borders we cannot talk just about missions and operations. We should talk about Partnerships. NATO has a vast network of them. There are 20 non-NATO member countries in the so called Partnership for Peace and the Euro-Atlantic Partnership Council, covering more or less the rest of "OSCE Europe," if you will. By engaging them we are trying to promote the values they formally subscribed to when they joined the Partnership. We are engaging Russia and Ukraine also individually, again with a lot of stress on the values, especially with the latter as Ukraine wants to proceed towards membership in the Alliance. We are engaging 7 Mediterranean Dialogue countries, bringing them closer to our values, as well as the Gulf countries in the newly established Istanbul Cooperation Initiative. And we are working closely together with a large number of so-called Contact Countries, some of them already sharing our values, such as Australia, New Zealand and Japan.

Let me now say something more general on how we see we can achieve best the goal of defending our values beyond our borders.

Although NATO is the single global military Alliance, it does not achieve its purpose solely or largely through military means. We are using a **strategy** that includes such elements as:

a) **Engagement,** where we tackle the challenges to our security when and where they emerge, or they will end up on our doorstep, say Slovenian borders.

b) **Multi-dimensionality,** where multi-dimensional challenges require multi-dimensional responses. This means that political, economic, military and reconstruction and development cooperation instruments have to be applied in a concerted way.

c) **Working together with other international players.** No single country or international organisation has at its disposal all the means for effective security environment. We, first of all, have to find ways how to work better with the EU, UN and OSCE.

d) **Patience.** No job is done overnight, this has been clearly demonstrated in the Balkans. NATO cannot leave before the job is done, otherwise we will have failed as an Alliance. And our patience will be tested in Afghanistan, where I believe we should be prepared to stay a decade or so.

At the close let me **touch upon Slovenia.**

Just a couple of elements:

a) First, over a year and a half ago Slovenia found itself in the position where every NATO's decision is also HER decision. NATO's history is her history and NATO's future is her future.

This is not just rhetoric.

When I sit in the North Atlantic Council, NATO's decision-making body, day by day, the stories of the overwhelming power of one or other member country disperse. Every nation acts according to its national interest, and so do we. No decision is made without Slovenia or, say, Iceland.

I am saying this because it is important that we are all aware of both the power and the responsibility of such a position, when we are dealing with defending our values, our way of life, far from our own borders.

b) Second, that is why it is vital that there is a larger understanding and involvement of the society, not just the Government.

Also, when Slovenia gets engaged in missions and operations abroad we should not just expect our soldiers to do the job. This does not mean that they are not doing a fine job. I regularly visit our troops in NATO's operations, be it Kosovo or Afghanistan, and they are doing an extraordinary job for their country and the Alliance.

But as I have mentioned previously, our engagement should be multifaceted. If we have done and our doing a lot in the Western Balkans, we have not really looked seriously what we, as the whole Slovenian society, can do for Afghanistan, for instance. There are great needs in the Provincial reconstruction teams, and the clearest option is the one in Herat where the bulk of our military contribution is stationed.

I would like to see Slovenian civilian project in the areas of reconstruction and development there: water supply, agriculture, small business, schools, universities. There is a host of Slovenian institutions, especially including the Non-Governmental Organizations that could lend a hand there. In the campaign leading to the NATO referendum back in 2003 a lot was said by them about soft security and solidarity. Where are they now when they can put their money where their mouth is?

c) And finallyy, solidarity is a well-established Slovenian value. It is clear to us we cannot just be the consumers but must also be the producers of security.

In order to transform obsolete territorially based units of the Slovenian Armed Forces to expeditionary forces, adopting the Robertson formula of 40% of usable forces and 8% of forces at any time in operation, we still have an enormous task to perform. And there are analogue processes going on in the other Allied nations.

However, at the same time while we will be providing forces that are well trained, well equipped, deployable anywhere in the world, and capable of rotation, thus acting in accordance with our proclaimed Allied responsibility and solidarity, we will also be acting in accordance with the interests of the Slovenian taxpayers. In mere numbers these troops will be a far cry from the Cold War tens and tens of thousands of troops. But they will be usable.

A few thousand usable forces can do the job that Slovenia and the Alliance's need today. And in the long run this will also bring the cost of defense down.

And saving a Tolar - or better a Euro or two - is also a Slovenian value.

Thank you.

GPS FOR THE WESTERN BALKANS

From my speaking notes I gather that my intervention was delivered on 17 October 2005 at a "NAC PLUS" that included also a number of non-NATO countries. I may have had one of the first interventions. I have a few scribbled remarks: the colleagues supporting me: Macedonian Ambassador Nano Ružin, Bulgarian Ambassador Lubomir Ivanov, United States Ambassador Nick Burns, Serbian Ambassador Branko Milinković, Polish Ambassador Jerzy Nowak, as well as diplomats of Romania, Turkey and Austria. The Italian Ambassador Maurizio Moreno supported a "comprehensive approach" to the region and the Spanish Ambassador Pablo Benavides stated that organized crime was the basis of all problems of the region. Acting SG Alessandro Minuto Rizzo might have chaired the meeting. As usual, I was speaking of my own beliefs and ideas.

Secretary General,

I'm encouraged by this discussion on the long and winding road. What I will present here is a very personal approach that I already touched upon at the NAC Away Day when we discussed NATO in Ten Years.

The way I see it the International Community has been dealing with the Western Balkans too much in a piecemeal fashion. It dealt with one problem, then moved to another. I am not sure this is the right approach as situations can untangle again if not dealt with on a permanent basis.

The problems of the Western Balkans are so interconnected, so intermingled, the success of each case depending on the success of the others, that the International Community should have a common, comprehensive regional approach to the whole area.

Also, some schemes that have been invented to bring countries into the fold – say NATO with its Membership Action Plan – leave too much uncertainty, too much self-reliance, as all decisions are national decisions, the countries identifying the areas themselves. They do not assure the countries of the Western Balkans that they are on the right track and that there is "light at the end of the tunnel."

Perhaps we need a clear 20/20 vision for this region (and I am not just talking about eyesight):

1. There should be a joint comprehensive approach or strategy of International Organizations, such as NATO, the EU, OSCE and UN.

2. The countries, entities of the region, say, Albania, Croatia, Macedonia, Serbia, Montenegro, Kosovo, Bosnia-Herzegovina, should have a clear perspective that at the end of the process they will be members both of NATO and the European Union.

3. There should be a clear... not just Road MAP... that allows countries to veer off and get lost on the way to their intended goal, but a sort of a GPS Navigation that leads each of them along the fastest and safest route to their final destination. A GPS that reminds these countries clearly when they have veered off the route and directs them back to their final destination.

4. Each case in the Western Balkans is different from each other and at the same time the areas of concern are similar: minority protection, inclusion of ethnic groups in the decision-making process, decentralization, borders.

5. So while there should be a **symmetric** approach with the same set of values for the whole region, and as far as values are concerned we do not have to invent anything new – they are clear basic Euro Atlantic values, garnished with the well tried solutions on this continent as far as minority groups' emancipation is concerned. Aat the same time it should be **asymmetric** so that the most appropriate solutions are adopted for each case.

6. As far as the time scale is concerned there does not need to be a common end date for all, but a clear commitment of all involved that they would not block the entrance of other nations if they get in first.

7. This *Grand Political Scheme*, building upon the documents such as Dayton, Ohrid, MAP and other successful instruments dealing with the region, would need a general agreement of every country or entity, wanting to be involved, while at the same time a host of regional, inter-state, cross-border and local arrangements, and definitely, a clear EU and NATO perspective for all the Seven.

8. If we all pull together, in 2020 the region would lose the sense of being a region – it would just be a run-of-the-mill area of the EU and NATO.

Thank you.

UNWELCOME OR WELCOME STATEMENTS

Norwegian Ambassador Kai Eide, our former colleague on the North Atlantic Council, addressed the NAC on 20 July 2005 in his new position of United Nations Secretary General's Special Envoy to Kosovo. There is some doubt if Secretary General Jaap de Hoopp Schaeffer actually chaired the meeting, as I have question mark next to his name. Anyway, here is what I felt I had to say, as usually either on my own or disregarding any instruction from home.

Thank you Jaap,

Kai, nice to see you back in the Council.

I will be brief as I know you had a useful exchange of views with CIO/OSCE Rupel.

I appreciate your clarity. You are not beating around the bush. I have also concerns that Kosovo is running out of Serbs, so that soon decentralization might become pointless, and that Kosovo is light years away from the Rule of Law.

I appreciate also that you are meeting with the widest possible array of people. I hope you will hear how these various people actually see things. Too often we hear only what we want to hear. A couple of recent statements by Kosumi and Čović have been labeled as "unwelcome."

I would – on the other hand – say that they are in a way "welcome" if we really want to know what Kosovo Albanians and Serbs think on the minorities. Better know it, than be surprised by events. I believe it would be dangerously wrong for this Alliance and the International Community not to recognize such statements for what they reflect, which is very likely the majority of the public opinion.

I'd also like to ask one question: can you tell us more about the pace of transfer of authority to the PISG, especially in the economic field, which is my song and dance whenever we visit Kosovo, as I see it potentially as a rare bright spot in Kosovo.

Thank you.

THE TEN NATO COMMANDMENTS

I delivered this speech at a "SEEGROUP Seminar on the PfP/PARP Experience," in Belgrade on 10 May 2005. It is one of the texts that I only found a couple of years after the publication of "The 2020 Vision for the Western Balkans" book. It is clearly the father of my 2006 speech, also in Belgrade, with the juicy title "The Dirty Dozen Truths About NATO…" included in the above-mentioned book. It also seems to be the prototype of texts I used when preaching to different audiences in the Western Balkans where "my commandments, truths or rules" varied from 9 up to 13, a "baker's dozen."

Ladies and Gentlemen,

I visited Belgrade about a year and a half ago, after a 13-year absence, and took part in a NATO seminar on Democratic Oversight of the Armed Forces, that Slovenia organized for Serbia and Montenegro, together with the United Kingdom and Austria.

At the time representing an Invitee nation that still had in front of it about half a year of hard work before formally joining, I was struck by the statements I heard here in Belgrade that SAM was interested in joining the Partnership for Peace but not NATO itself.

Coming from a nation that is not very much geographically removed, and which spent 70 years of its history in a marriage with your country, I was hoping that you would see that PfP for a country in your position is just a way station, an anteroom, a reform tool to get into the North Atlantic

Alliance. And I clearly commented on that, at the same time accepting your recent history.

I was happy to find out that things have moved on since then and the Defense Strategy document, adopted at the end of 2004, clearly states that SAM's strategic goal is NATO membership. Even better, a recent Faktor Plus opinion poll shows that 43.8 percent of Serbs supported NATO accession (and 68.4 PfP accession). Having spoken recently to your foreign and defense ministers Drašković and Davinić, as well as your excellent Ambassador to NATO Milinković, I am glad that both the political elite and the wider population see eye to eye on the future direction of your country.

Congratulations, and we, NATO and Slovenia, are here to help.

Although Slovenia is a small nation, it is a great Ally. And you can do the same. Our way to membership was not easy. But it worked, and I will try to present here some practical ideas how you can make this way easier.

As I am supposed to be the person who first gave the idea that Slovenia should join NATO, at the time when it was still part of Yugoslavia, and was then involved in our accession process for the next decade and a half in various ways and places, perhaps some of my pointers could come in handy.

When I sat down a week ago in Brussels to prepare my address, I came up, not intentionally with 10 Rules, not quite Commandments, that perhaps a country should follow, based upon my own experience, if it wants to make its road towards NATO membership successful.

Number 1: You are enrolling the whole country in NATO, not just the Ambassador and his Mission in Brussels, not just the NATO departments in the MFA and the MOD, not just the two ministries, not just the Government. Membership in NATO is a national project. It needs a solid parliamentary support (and not just from the current Government coalition) and a solid public support. Comprehensive and correct informing of the public is extremely important.

Number 2: You have to decide once and for all that you actually want to enroll/join your country in NATO. You cannot just say it and not mean it. You cannot be formally inside but with your thinking outside. This is it. You either want to be inside and do it or stay outside and do your own thing, whatever that may be.

Number 3: This one is difficult. You have to be ready at the time of accession talks (I said talks, not negotiations, it is a take it or leave it situation) that you will not only accede to a number of NATO-related agreements but also NATO acquis. To simplify the explanation, let me just say that the acquis means all NATO decisions taken up until that moment. NATO history will become your history. Sounds baffling, buy you have to get used to the idea that you will accept everything as your own. Okay, you don't have to sign this in blood, but you have to mean it if you really want to be a member. Refer to Rule 2. I understand this can be difficult for some nations; it must have been for some former Warsaw Pact countries.

Number 4: It is going to be a long trip. Nothing is going to happen overnight. There are no shortcuts. Take an easy example like Slovenia. We spent 10 years in PfP before acceding to NATO in spite of being a relatively developed nation. It is true that an invitation to join NATO is a political decision. But still, as we say nowadays, NATO is a performance based organisation and performing well will be an incentive for the members to consider an invitation.

Number 5: It is going to be difficult. It is going to take serious reforms in the political-economic, defence-military, resources, security and legislative areas.

Number 6: Co-ordination. Let me say it again: co-ordination. There is no more important word. You cannot leave it to the Foreign Ministry to do their bit and to the Defense Ministry to do the rest. There is a school of thought that the Defense Ministry should have the final say on defense things, the Ministry of Economy on economic things and so on. I do not subscribe to this. Most of the matters discussed at NATO need a co-ordinated response of the Government. This involves the whole Government, and often the Parliament.

On the Government side you should set up a co-ordinating body that meets regularly, reviews progress and pushes the reforms forward. Based upon my own experience, you should actually have two bodies: one at the level of the Prime Minister, involving the Ministers of Foreign Affairs,

Defense and Finance, as well as your Ambassador to NATO. The ministers should hear straight from the horse's mouth what NATO thinks. Being very humble, I know the importance of your Ambassador to NATO. He should also have direct access to these people. They should know ASAP when he feels he has to tell them something. Then there should be a co-ordination body at the level of Ministries and other State bodies, involving a dozen or so of them. It should perhaps be led by a deputy minister level person, a so-called Mr. NATO, if possible someone with a long-term involvement in the project. Also, it should be someone with influence and access to his bosses.

I am stressing this because national co-ordination is important.

E.g., sending troops abroad is not up to the General Staff or the Ministry of Defense. It is up to the Government or even Parliament.

Number 7: There are no sacred cows. You cannot beat around the bush and do reforms only in the easy areas. You should especially tackle the difficult ones. Why not do it first. Let me list a few:

a) Defense planning: outside and without NATO's help you have no idea what the heck this is. It is an enormous undertaking but it will help you save money (and Slovenians fully understand that) and create forces that are actually needed, not something that just happened. NATO has a great tool to help you with the defense reforms: the Planning and Review Process (PARP). It is a means for promoting interoperability with the Alliance, it is open to all partners on a voluntary basis and allows for their self-differentiation. It closely mirrors NATO's defense and force planning system. Defense planning is either done the NATO way or the wrong way.

b) The position of the military. Forget history. The military is definitely no sacred cow. It performs basically two jobs: one is to give the civilians who are in charge military advice, hopefully sound military advice, and the other one is to do the job we give them. That's it.

c) The Security Services. These are the guys that have to be tackled seriously. As I am coming from circles that were in the Eighties checked on and followed by these guys and I did not find them very impressive, I have every reason to say that the services should be streamlined and made finally useful. We live in a world of asymmetric threats, terrorism, spread of Weapons of Mass Destruction, so there is a need for Intelligence. Let us make sure that in this case Intelligence is not an oxymoron. And, lastly, if you want to be an Ally, such services should cease immediately to act against NATO.

Number 8: You cannot hide anything. In NATO transparency is not just a slogan. Quite the opposite, it pervades all our work. So in the process, especially the Planning and Review Process in the Partnership for Peace and later in NATO's Force Planning process you will have to honestly present everything you are doing in the before mentioned 5 areas and be ready constructively to face comments, criticisms, and proposals both of our International Staff and especially the Allies. And that is what each Ally does regularly every two years with the rest of the Allies in the area of defense. Years ago it would have been hard to imagine a Slovenian member of International Staff assessing the U.S. Army or Slovenian diplomats commenting on the British defense planning. But that is how we do things in NATO. And it works! So, again: you cannot hide anything. With your future Allies there should be no secrecy.

Number 9: Although we say (and before our accession we were being told for years by the 19 Allies) that on its way to NATO membership each nation will be judged on its own merits, life is never that simple. Formally this is, of course, true and you have to invest all this energy into carrying out your reforms and presenting them to us and expecting our assessments, comments, critiques etc. But if you are realistic you will know that out there, there is a wider world and that what is happening there will affect your chances. But, let me be perfectly clear, or should I say: read my lips: this is no excuse for non-performing or under-performing. But there is an element in the wider world, where you can be more of an architect of your future: the Western Balkans region. Its success will be the success of each and the success of each will be the success of all. So my advice is to do as much as you can for wider security and co-operation in the region. Three countries of the Region are already involved in the Membership Action Plan, a NATO tool, as well in a regional initiative, the so-called Adriatic Charter. I have used every opportunity to urge Macedonia, Albania and Croatia to invite Serbia and Montenegro and Bosnia-Herzegovina into this interest grouping. Together you could do more and Slovenia knows that very well. We instigated, together with Lithuania, the founding of the Vilnius Group, which proved very useful for our common endeavour. And we learned NATO preferred dealing with groups of countries. So I believe that if you all pull together, - Serbia, with Kosovo, and Montenegro, and Bosnia-Herzegovina and Macedonia, and Albania and Croatia, the success of each will be the success of all. Regional co-operation, regional confidence and security building measures, protection of minorities, and border management are all measures that go hand in hand with your aspirations for Euro-Atlantic integration. Good luck.

Number 10. You are not alone. Finally some good news you will say. The moment you enter PfP, especially if your interest lies in full-fledged membership, you are not out in the cold any longer. You will be a part of the family that has grown together on the basis of common values. And, just for the sake of it, let me quote from the Washington Treaty: "The Parties of this Treaty are determined to safeguard the freedom, common heritage, and civilization of their peoples, founded on the principles of democracy, individual liberty and the rule of law." We take our common security very seriously and we will go to all lengths to assure it. The decision to opt for NATO membership is a smart decision. It means you are re-joining the mainstream of our civilization. And I would like to congratulate you all.

Thank you.

MACEDONIA, NOT FYROM!

On 6 May 2005 I had this speech at the University of Skopje. The visit was organized by my friend, Macedonian Ambassador Nano Ružin and the Atlantic Council of Macedonia. I have been a rare person who never used the cobbled together Greek-inspired name "the Former Yugoslav Republic of Macedonia" or the terrible acronym FYROM, in spite of it peppering every single instruction on the country I ever received. One of the reasons was that I was vitally involved in the recognition of Macedonia by the Slovenian Parliament. Another one was that my father published a Macedonia travelogue in the late 1940's. My wife and I had a good time both in Skopje where we were welcomed by Prime Minister Vlado Bučkovski, and treated to a nice lunch/dinner that spanned at least three hours. Later in life Bučkovski was sentenced for abuse of power when he had served, previous to his premiership, as Minister of Defense. The following day I took my wife to Lake Ohrid for some rest – paying our own way mind you – that included a quick hop into still mysterious Albania. I was also supposed to speak at the University of Tetovo but for some reason the visit there did not materialize

Good morning,

It is a true honor and pleasure for me to be able to address you as a NATO Ambassador, the Permanent Representative on the North Atlantic Council of a country, which has recently become a NATO and European Union member and which shares 7 decades of common history with you.

I'm so happy to see among you Nano Ružin, my friend and colleague, the excellent Macedonian Ambassador to NATO.

Talking of history, this is my first time in Macedonia. The only claim to fame I might have here is that as Chairman of the Foreign Affairs Committee in the Slovenian parliament I formally proposed almost a decade and half ago for Slovenia to recognize the Republic of Macedonia. And the rest is history.

Going farther into history, my father, a Slovenian journalist travelled here almost 60 years ago and then published a serial of articles on the new emancipated Macedonia. Just recently, I reread the serial. And there was so much passion. Being here, I understand it now.

And the emancipation and the history of your joining the Euro-Atlantic structures is not over. There is still plenty of work. It gives me great pleasure to be able to address young people, students, future presidents and prime ministers and ministers and ambassadors members of the Atlantic Council.

I am a fan of Atlantic Councils. Looking around I know why I am a fan of Atlantic Councils. I was actually a member of the British Atlantic Council back in the last century.

I was also a member of the Slovenian one. I tried to get the job of the President. I tried to persuade the first President to get me the position, when he was about to leave.

I was unlucky. So I had to take the next best job – of the Ambassador to NATO. And the former President ended up by being a member of my staff. So it goes.

I am definitely a fan of grassroots movements. I did my share in the Sixties and Seventies, marching against the War, believing in slogans such as Make Love Not War.

But there is nothing un-natural that a former California hippie becomes Ambassador to NATO.

To achieve peace you need a strong defense Alliance. And to make our Alliance strong in the changing security environment you have to adapt it. NATO has demonstrated time and time again that it is capable of re-inventing itself to suit the current security needs.

II. In my address to you today I would like to start with more general topics and then follow with more practical, nitty-gritty ones, everything that comprises the why and how of joining the North Atlantic Treaty Organization.

Let us first check out today's security environment, and NATO's role within it. Let me briefly tackle how NATO has transformed itself in three key areas – the way we in NATO think about security, about our capabilities, and about our relationships, including Macedonia.

Back in my happy hippie student days, the Cold War was at its height and people viewed NATO's purpose at that time as keeping the Soviet Union at bay. We, who lived together in the former federation, know that the relatively liberal Communism we enjoyed was on account of NATO's existence.

On the other hand today's threat to our values no longer comes from the Warsaw Pact with its aggressive ideology supported by a massive nuclear and conventional military machine. Today's threat comes from failed states, from terrorism, and from the proliferation of weapons of mass destruction.

These new threats are global in nature – they could arise anywhere - but their implications affect us all. Some Slovenians at a time in the past believed that there existed a "Valley of Peace." Unfortunately it does not, especially when we are threatened by assymmetric threats.

An Alliance sitting pretty, waiting to be attacked, with huge numbers of obsolete forces with thousands of tanks, dedicated to territorial defence, and working in total isolation from other international organizations and institutions, would rapidly lose relevance in this new threat environment. This is the reason why transformation is needed.

III. First of all: transformation of how we think about our security, and how we use the Alliance. A clear geographic delineation of new threats is simply no longer possible. If we wish to continue safeguarding our values, which was one of the main reasons for forming the Alliance, then we cannot continue to view the North-Atlantic area in isolation from the rest of the world.

So, at NATO, we have agreed that we must tackle these threats when and where they arise, otherwise they will end up on our doorstep, and it will be too late to deal with them effectively.

Former NATO Secretary General Lord Robertson used to say: "If we don't go to Afghanistan, Afghanistan will come to us." I keep quoting him in Slovenia, promoting even larger contributions to Alliance operations abroad.

So we have changed the way in which we were thinking.

This is reflected in how we use the Alliance. And that is why NATO decided to deploy naval forces into the Mediterranean where they monitor shipping and provide a potent deterrent to terrorism at sea, as well as to those who seek to move illegal cargoes.

In Afghanistan we are taking a leading role, under a United Nations Security Council mandate, in assisting the Afghan authorities to bring security and stability back to their country so that democracy can take root. The presence of each country is important. Macedonia is doing a lot for our common security and at the same time your participation in operations helps transform your own military.

We retain a strong presence in Kosovo, where we continue to provide the essential security to permit discussions about the province's future status. There is no one who knows more about the importance of NATO's presence in Kosovo than you Macedonians and we appreciate your Host Nation Support very much.

Although NATO no longer has responsibility for peacekeeping in Bosnia and Herzegovina, that country's new found security, stability and reconstruction were made possible by NATO's implementation of the Dayton Peace Agreement.

And in Iraq, again under a United Nations' mandate, we are assisting the Iraqi forces with their training in preparation for them to take full responsibility for their own security following the successful elections earlier this week.

These commitments are a clear demonstration of the transformed way NATO is thinking about security and the way it is being employed.

IV The second area of transformation concerns our military capabilities. At this point, it is worth remembering that NATO does not own any combat forces itself. It is not a trans-national army. It has to rely on the sovereign nations that make up the Alliance voluntarily, placing their forces under NATO command.

But I am sure you already know that, striving for the membership in the Alliance. I can tell you, the countries striving for membership and those who just entered the Alliance have the greatest knowledge about it.

NATO needed to encourage Allies to realise that static forces dedicated to national territorial defence are obsolete against the threats we face today.

Allies now need forces that can react quickly, that can operate in a wide variety of environments, that can be deployed over strategic distances, and that can be sustained a long way from their homeland for considerable periods.

We talk about the 40/8 formula. It is not very difficult to explain what it is all about and it does not require any statistics (that I hated during my student years). But it is quite difficult to implement. It means having 40 % of your military ready to act and at least 8% of your troops present in the operations.

In addition, we need to have a better mix of capabilities across the full range of possible military tasks. At the same time as we are fighting to keep peace, we will be busy rebuilding the infrastructure and encouraging the development of a society that will also share our values. It is absolutely pointless providing enhanced security if the people do not see any improvement in other aspects of their lives.

V Next, I wish to highlight the transformation in our relationships with others – both other institutions and other states. When the threats are global, we have to ensure that the responses are coordinated globally. We already enjoy a good relationship with the United Nations, and this relationship will have to grow even closer.

But arguably the most significant relationship for NATO is the one with the European Union. You know this very well as you are striving to join both.

As the European Union further develops its own security and defence policy, it will be necessary to increase the cooperation between NATO and the EU. Our current relationship is poor and focused primarily on crisis management in the Balkans, and on planning modernisation of our forces. But now is the time to broaden this agenda.

We ought to work closely together, while at the same time acknowledging that the two organizations have different strengths and responsibilities.

Especially this year, we Slovenians cherish the relationship between NATO and the OSCE very much, since we are chairing the OSCE. The OSCE has nearly the same membership as EAPC/PfP, but different areas of cooperation between countries.

But to be blunt: the major international organizations still have not found a useful way how to optimise their resources and consequently results. Too often they do not even talk to each other, they duplicate work etc.

I believe, when facing crisis areas, the major international organizations such as the UN, the OSCE, the European Union and NATO should make common assessments of situation, formulate common strategies, have a clear division of labor, and then consult and coordinate their work. But it is going to be an uphill struggle.

VI. I have already touched upon the links with states that are not Allies. NATO has formal partnership arrangements with 20 countries stretching from the tip of North Europe down to the Balkans, out to the strategically important regions of the Caucasus and Central Asia within the Euro-Atlantic Partnership Council and the Partnership for Peace. Of course, Macedonia is also a part of it.

These partner countries include Russia and Ukraine, with whom we simultaneously have special relationships.

But perhaps there is no region that will have a greater impact on our security than the region of the Middle East. It is therefore vital for NATO to be engaged in this region. We already have our "Mediterranean Dialogue". This provides established links with seven countries, stretching from western North Africa around the southern Mediterranean rim to the Middle East.

And we recently launched our Istanbul Cooperation Initiative. Through this initiative, we are discussing possibilities for cooperation with interested countries in the Gulf region and perhaps wider. And we are present, of course, in Iraq, where we have a training mission.

Let me also mention the countries with which we have informal contacts, such as China and Japan, Australia and New Zealand, India and Pakistan, South Korea and countries in South America.

These transformed relationships permit NATO and its Allies to play a vital role in shaping the security environment in line with our strategic interests and shared values, and they promote NATO as a forum for political consultation and discussion.

Let me conclude this point with one message: NATO has transformed! But NATO's fundamental purpose endures – and that is as the unique transatlantic political-military framework through which North America and Europe can pursue their shared security interests, shape the environment in line with their common values, and provide mutual protection.

VII. Let me say something about further enlargement that Slovenia supports strongly.

Since NATO is a performance based organization, pretty high standards need to be met to be able to become its member. And to help countries meet those expectations, Membership Action Plan, MAP in short, was launched in 1999.

At first we, Slovenians, were suspicious of MAP. We were not sure if it was not just a delaying tactic of the Alliance. A toy that we could play with…for ages…

But in the following few years we learned MAP was very useful. It was not a toy but a tool. It on the one hand helped us structure better our reforms and on the other it helped NATO understand us better.

It is quite useful to get to know the partner you are going to spend the rest of your life with, before you say the final "I do." In NATO there are no arranged marriages, as we had in our former Federation.

I am not sure you know how the whole MAP process goes.

Let me try to explain it in a few words. Every year a Candidate, or Aspirant Country, has to prepare an Annual National Program where it briefs NATO (the International Staff and the twenty-six members) on certain issues related to fulfilling the requirements of membership. Within each segment it provides an update on reforms and explains what it intends to do in the coming year.

There are five chapters in MAP:

- Political economic issues: where the candidate country has to demonstrate that it fulfills Political and Economic criteria.
- Defense and military issues: where the candidate country has to present the reforms leading to a usable force that can contribute to Allied operations.
- Resources: where the country has to demonstrate it will be able to afford the obligations and have the people to carry them out.
- Security: where the candidate country has to show that the NATO's document will be safe.
- And Legal issues: demonstrating that the candidate country will sort out all the legal paperwork.

With MAP the aspirant country's Government formally confirms its willingness and ability to respect the obligations and commitments under the North Atlantic Treaty and the Study on NATO Enlargement, and provides a timetable for the completion of reforms.

And the Alliance, on the other hand, checks each year, if required reforms have been completed as promised.

VIII. Let me conclude, before I give you the floor for any possible questions, hopefully not too difficult, by touching upon a few "nitty-gritty truths" I learned as Slovenia went down the difficult bumpy road to membership in NATO and that I think could apply to any other applicant country. Sometimes we have heads full of grandiose thoughts and values and stuff but forget the basics. Here they are:

Truth #1: You are *enrolling the whole country in NATO*, not just the Ambassador and his Mission in Brussels, not just the NATO departments in the MFA and the MOD, not just the two ministries, not just the Government.

Truth #2: To this end (reference to the Truth no 1) it is very important to *explain to the people*, like I am doing it now, what NATO is, what its relevance today is, what NATO does and how it has and will contribute to the better wellbeing of Macedonia.

I know you have today strong public support to join NATO, however, you have been striving to join NATO for quite some time and it is not over yet. Some people may change their minds. But will not, if somebody explains to them regularly what it is all about. You know very well this is called Public Diplomacy. Because in case of a referendum, it will only be the choice between a Yes and a No.

Truth #3: *It is a long trip.* Nothing is going to happen overnight. Take an easy example like Slovenia. We spent 10 years in PfP before acceding to membership in spite of being a relatively developed nation. It is true: an invitation to join NATO is a political decision. But still, as we like to repeat nowadays, NATO is a performance based organization and performing well will be an incentive for the members to consider an invitation.

Truth #4: It is going to be difficult. It is going to take *implementation of serious reforms* in the political-economic, defense-military, resources, security and legislative areas.

Truth #5: *Coordination.* Let me say it again: coordination. There is no more important word. You cannot leave it to the Foreign Ministry to do their bit and to the Defense Ministry to do the rest. It involves the whole Government, as well as the Parliament.

Truth #6: There are no sacred cows. You cannot beat around the bush and do *reforms only in the easy areas. You should especially tackle the difficult ones.* Why not do them first?

Truth #7: You cannot hide anything. In *NATO transparency* is not just a slogan. Quite the opposite, it pervades all our work. Years ago it would have been hard to imagine a Slovenian member of NATO's International Staff assessing the U.S. Army or Slovenian diplomats commenting British defense planning. But that is how we do things in NATO. And it works! So, again: you cannot hide anything. With your future Allies there should be no secrecy.

Truth #8: Although we say (and before our accession we were being told the same thing for years by the 19 Allies) that on its way to NATO membership *each nation will be judged on its own merits*, life is never that simple. Formally this is, of course true, and you have to invest all this energy into carrying out your reforms and presenting them to us and expecting our assessments, comments, critiques etc.

But if you are realistic, you will know that out there, there is a *wider world* and that what is happening there will affect your chances. But, let me be perfectly clear: this is no excuse for non-performing or under-performing.

But there is an element in the wider world, where you can be more of an architect of your future: the *Western Balkans region*. Its success will be the success of each and the success of each will be the success of all. So my advice is to do as much as you can for *wider security and cooperation in the region*.

Three countries of the Region are already involved in the Membership Action Plan, a NATO tool, as well in a regional initiative, the so-called Adriatic Charter. I will use this opportunity again to urge you, Macedonia, to promote invitation of Serbia and Montenegro and Bosnia-Herzegovina into the interest grouping, namely the Adriatic Charter.

Together you could do more and Slovenia knows that very well. We instigated, together with Lithuania, the founding of the Vilnius Group which proved very useful for our common endeavor. And we learned NATO preferred dealing with groups of countries.

So I believe that if you all pull together, Macedonia, and Albania and Croatia, Serbia, with Kosovo, and Montenegro, and Bosnia-Herzegovina, the success of each will be the success of all.

Regional cooperation, regional confidence and security building measures, protection of minorities, border management are all measures that go hand in hand with your aspirations for Euro-Atlantic integration.

Truth #9. *You are not alone.* Finally some good news, you will say. You are a part of the family that has grown together on the basis of common values. And, just for the sake of it, let me quote from the Washington Treaty: "The Parties of this Treaty are determined to safeguard the freedom, common heritage, and civilisation of their peoples, founded on the principles of democracy, individual liberty and the rule of law." We take our common security very seriously and we will go to all lengths to assure it.

Let me end by saying: the decision to opt for NATO membership is a smart decision. It is also a difficult decision because it forces you to do serious reforms. But that is the only way to create a strong Alliance. I am sure you would not want to join a weak Alliance.

Now I will happily take any questions.

Thank you.

OFFERING ASSISTANCE TO SERBIA

On 4 May 2005, NAC met with Serbia and Montenegro in the person of Minister of Defense Prvoslav Davinić, accompanied by Ambassador Branko Milinković. The following year even that remnant of Yugoslavia disbanded and both Serbia and Montenegro went their own ways.

Thank you Secretary General,

May I extend a warm welcome to you, Minister Davinić, and the members of your delegation, especially our colleague Ambassador Milinković.

Slovenia strongly supports Serbia and Montenegro's aspirations to join the PFP, as soon as the conditions are met.

We believe that the Defence Strategy document, adopted at the end of 2004, which for the first time stated that SAM's strategic goal is NATO membership, was a major step forward for the Serbia and Montenegro State Union.

Knowing the importance of public support, I was personally very much encouraged by the recent Faktor Plus opinion poll, which showed that 43.8 percent of Serbs supported NATO accession (and 68.4 PfP accession).

It is especially encouraging that in the past few months, considerable progress has been made regarding the ICTY co-operation.

Slovenia has offered its assistance in the past and has carried out several activities within the Tailored Co-operation Program. Particularly in the field of public diplomacy we can do a lot more. In our experience, public diplomacy, and a centered public information campaign were extremely important elements on the road to NATO. We are planning to organise in the Fall (we hope with another Ally) a seminar on this issue. I am looking forward to taking part in a SEEGROUP seminar next week in Belgrade.

May I urge you, Minister that SAM continues to move ahead on reforms. As we like to say nowadays, NATO is a performance based organisation.

I would like to ask you, Minister two questions: First, when do you think SAM could sign the security agreement with NATO, and secondly, how are the talks on the agreement on the Land Lines of Communications proceeding?

Thank you.

PLAYING WITH THE
NUCLEAR BUTTON

The following is what NATO publicly tells about this body: "The Nuclear Planning Group (NPG) acts as the senior body on nuclear matters in the Alliance and discusses specific policy issues associated with nuclear forces. The Alliance's nuclear policy is kept under constant review and is modified and adapted in the light of new developments. The NPG reviews the Alliance's nuclear policy in light of the ever-changing security environment. While the North Atlantic Council is the ultimate authority within NATO, the NPG acts as the senior body on nuclear matters in the Alliance. The NPG discusses specific policy issues associated with nuclear forces and wider issues such as nuclear arms control and nuclear proliferation. All members, with the exception of France which has decided not to participate, are part of the NPG irrespective of whether or not they themselves maintain nuclear weapons." This little intervention was delivered at the 2005 Nuclear Consultation Seminar od 26 April where the Ambassadors, members of the Nuclear Planning Group, played the game of an international conflict, involving three imaginary states. I have been and remain a firm believer in nuclear deterrence. I was going to start my intervention with "I was very careful not to push the wrong button as we are talking about nuclear weapons…" but perhaps I managed to restrain myself. My record is not clear on this.

Secretary General,

Nuclear weapons can be an important deterrent only if the opponent is convinced that the Alliance is actually capable, prepared and determined to use them in a timely manner. For that, unity of the Alliance members is extremely important. In all the public messages, members have to act as a unified bloc, determined to answer all possible threats to the territory of the Alliance Members.

In case we can actually trust – and that is a crucial question – the intelligence reports and there is a real chance of an incoming invasion of the part of the Alliance territory and a threat to use WMD against its members, the Alliance has to act swiftly and decisively. The SACEUR should be tasked to prepare the Alliance Sub-Strategic Nuclear Forces to the highest level of preparedness. I believe that should be done in an overt fashion.

At the same time it is extremely important that the international actors and world public is informed about the events and efforts Nato has put in to find a peaceful solution of the current crisis. The politico-military actions should be closely aligned with appropriate declaratory measures.

Thank you.

REAFFIRMING SUPPORT
FOR UKRAINE

On 18 April 2005, the NUC at Ambassadorial level met. Therefore, it was the 26 NATO Ambassadors and Ambassador Volodymir Khandogyi on the Ukrainian side. He has had a very important diplomatic career, last time I looked as Ambassador to London. We were friends, perhaps also because we both had cats; his was named Bush and ours Sox for short. When Slovenia was upgraded to NATO membership, we left our previous Mission offices, mostly designed by myself, to Ukraine.

Thank you, Secretary General,

You will recall that the Slovenian Prime Minister Janša made it clear during the NUC Summit two months ago that Slovenia supports Ukraine's aspiration towards joining the Membership Action Plan. We are convinced, based on our own experience, having gone first through cooperation with NATO via Partnership for Peace, followed by several years of Individual Dialogue, which continued in the Membership Action Plan, that the MAP is the best mechanism in existence for an aspirant country to implement relevant reforms and for the Allies to guide implementation of the reforms.

As a pre-step to the membership action Plan, and following the usual routine with aspirants, we are happy that NATO can offer Ukraine at this point an "Intensified Dialogue on Ukraine's aspirations to membership and relevant reforms…" which will cover the full range of political, military, financial and security issues related to possible NATO membership.

From our own experience we know that the path of reforms will not be easy, which is also obvious from the list of short term actions. Slovenia is willing to help you, Ambassador Khandogy, on your way with our advice. Let me just mention one area, where Slovenia had a lot of experience during our path to the Alliance – public diplomacy.

We also look forward in Vilnius to the exchange of letters on Ukrainian Contribution to Operation Active Endeavor.

Let me conclude with a question to Ambassador Khandogyi: I remember from the speech of your President last February that one of his and your Government's priorities is to get "rapid and convincing economic results." To this end, he was willing to hold in Kiev a so-called "Ukrainian Davos." I would like to know what the present stay of play on this issue is.

At the end, I would also like to support the idea of one NUC being held in Ukraine this year. It would be useful to see the progress being made in implementing different kinds of reforms.

Thank you.

SHORT INTERVENTION/ MAJOR DECISION

On 6 April 2005, NAC discussed, under Agenda Item 2, Afghanistan, for the umpteenth time. I visited the country a few times and was crucially involved, in both Ljubljana and Brussels, in the decision-making on Slovenia's participation in the ISAF, especially troop deployment to Herat. Also, after my talks with President Hamid Karzai, Minister of Foreign Affairs Abdullah Abdullah and Governor of Herat Sayed Mohammad Khairkhah I presented proposals to the Slovenian Government for reconstruction and development projects in Herat, unfortunately without success. Here's my brief intervention on our plans to move west from our initial positions in and around Kabul.

Thank you, Secretary General,

I would just like to inform that decision has just been reached in Slovenia that we are going to contribute to PRT and FSB Herat both militarily as well as with civilian projects, related to reconstruction and development.

To study and then recommend this option I went to Kabul and Herat two weeks ago, and I would like to express my appreciation for all the support and help given by SACEUR General Jones and his staff.

Our contribution will be based on the capabilities we currently have in Kabul and we are thinking of developing civilian projects in the area of infrastructure and agriculture.

Thank you.

UKRAINE OVER LUNCH

Ambassador Bogdan Mazuru, my Romanian colleague on the NAC organized a working lunch on Tuesday, 5 April 2005, to discuss Ukraine, with NATO's Deputy Secretary General Ambassador Alessandro Minuto-Rizzo as the Guest of Honor. My friend Bogdan, who later served in Germany, France and Austria, had a nice Residence on the border between Brussels and Flanders, a 10-minute car ride from the NATO HQ. I have kept the menu: *asperges aux morilles et dentelles de parmesan, gigot d'agneau, salade aux radis roses, carpaccio d'ananas, white wine: Castle Rock, Feteasca Regala – 2002, red wine: Prahova Valley Feteasca Neagra – 2000.* The guest of Honor had a little introduction to the theme.

Thank you very much, Bogdan, and thank you Alessandro,

I remember the enthusiasm, goodwill and major support from all of us in the times of Orange revolution and especially after Yushchenko was elected and officially declared President of Ukraine.

I also remember NUC and NAC at the level of Heads of State or Government last February, wholeheartedly welcoming and supporting Ukraine's ambitions/aspirations to full Euro-Atlantic integration, based on the commitment to the implementation of the reform objectives.

My Prime Minister vocally supported Ukraine's aspirations towards joining the Membership Plan. This remains our view also after the discussions in the Political Committee and our level.

We cannot offer Yushchenko even less than we offered Kuchma, and I refer to the Reykyavik 2002 communique, where we already offered intensified consultation on political economic and defense issues!

However, as consensus builders, we can agree on offering Ukraine a bit less: "Individual Dialogue on Membership Questions," but this is as far as we can go. We would also like to offer Ukrainians a vision of being able to join the Membership Action Plan as soon as they demonstrate that implementation of their reforms is under way.

Thank you.

MEETING THE KING OF BOSNIA

NAC met on 5 April 2005 with Paddy Ashdown, International Community's High Representative for Bosnia and Herzegovina, with powers equaling a dictator. He was called by some the King or Tyrant of Bosnia. I had known him since the late 1980's when he was the leader of the U.K. Liberal Democrats; both during the time when I was involved in political life in Slovenia, as well as later when I served in London. He almost made it to be a NATO Secretary General after Javier Solana, but ultimately the job went to the more government-experienced George Robertson. He was a fun person, almost as much as George was. On this occasion, he was in Brussels to report on the progress of Bosnia and Herzegovina.

Thank You, Chairman.

Let me also extend a warm welcome to you, Lord Ashdown.

Slovenia is deeply interested in BiH security and development – like all of us – but also being almost a neighbor, at the closest point lying just 25 miles away – the nearest NATO Ally.

Thank you very much for today's captivating briefing. We believe that you've been doing an outstanding job and that Bosnia and Herzegovina, under your guidance, has achieved considerable progress.

Particularly in regard to the co-operation with ICTY, the past few months have started to show results. We hope that this momentum will keep up and that the Foreign Ministers at their upcoming meeting in Vilnius can take stock and welcome progress made since last December.

However, we agree with you that full membership in PfP requires full cooperation with ICTY. And we cannot evade linkage with SAM.

I would like to ask you to comment on the reports that Bosnia and Herzegovina signed an agreement on defense co-operation with Iran. Is this in line with the defense reforms that we want to see on Bosnia's way to PfP and eventually NATO?

Thank you, Chairman.

LECTURING ALBANIAN
PRIME MINISTER

On 24 March 2005, the North Atlantic Council met with Albanian Prime Minister Fatos Nano, who was in town, lobbying for NATO's and EU's support in their quest for membership in the two organizations. As usual, he presented his county's achievements and plans for the future, a bit embellished, as it was the usual for visiting Prime Ministers and Presidents... And a few of us reacted, mostly with kind words...

Thank you, Secretary General,

Let me also warmly welcome you, Prime Minister, and your delegation, especially our friend and colleague Ambassador Ilir Boçka.

Slovenia welcomes and supports Albania's determination to join NATO. We are always happy to offer our assistance in the implementation of reforms in all the five chapters of MAP that we know so well!

We are pleased that the recent PARP assessment of Albania was positive and that the necessary legal framework has been established. I am confident that the imbalance between the defense plans and the resources needed can be resolved for the benefit of a transformed, modernized and capable Force. Your progress in the area of economic development sounds very promising, in order to achieve that.

Although on the way to membership each nation should be judged on its own merits, the security problems of the nations and entities in the

Western Balkans being intermingled to such an extent that the security of each depends on the security of all.

In this vein we would especially like to commend Albania's role as a moderating factor in the region and its active involvement in regional security initiatives.

We look forward to seeing Albania in our midst, Prime Minister!

Thank you, Secretary General.

LOOKING AT NATO IN 2015

The North Atlantic Council decided to discuss at an "Away Day" what NATO will or should look like in ten years' time, namely in 2015. I think we went to some castle or other that abound in Belgium on 15 March 2005. Perhaps I took the event too seriously and prepared a think piece that was quite out of line with my colleagues' contributions that like the "food for thought paper," prepared for us by the International Staff, did not project their thinking much beyond the current state of affairs on NATO's plate. Just a short note: in my intervention I referred to Karel, where I meant the long serving Czech Ambassador Karel Kovanda, and Lubomir, where I meant Lubomir Ivanov, the Bulgarian Ambasasador. Secretary General Jaap de Hoop Scheffer did not agree with my first wise advice that the next time we should meet in a Jacuzzi.

Thank you Secretary General,

For bringing us here, a great place to relax. Perhaps next time we could meet in a pool, a sauna or a Jacuzzi...

Speaking today on my own behalf – not Slovenia's, I was going to say that we should tape our discussion here today, thinking that it would be fun to watch the tapes of the Away Day back in 1985 when our predecessors were discussing NATO in 1995, as well as Away Day in 1995 when they were discussing what NATO would look like in 2005.

Today, of course, we would digitally record it, not tape it, and hopefully the players in 2015 would still be able to play our DVD's. I cannot assure the technological part but I am sure our Permreps in 2015 would have a lot of fun listening to us.

Okay, if there are no tapes from '85 and '95, perhaps we could just ask Karel about it. I just hope nothing too dramatic will happen here today so that we would then have to talk of a pre- and post-3/15 period.

I appreciate the paper prepared by the Policy Planning Unit. It is a useful backdrop and very stimulating. Thank you, Jaap, for providing it. I enjoyed it having been a Science Fiction fan since the age of 6, as well as a minor SF author later on. Science Fiction combines both futurology and escapism, and I am glad we have escaped Brussels to look at NATO's future.

Before I come to a few comments which are hard to divide into the three proposed discussions, may I, tongue in cheek, paraphrase a quote from my book of 1001 Laws of Survival: "Things have been getting from bad to worse for the past 7 billion years, ever since the Big Bang. So why should the next 10 years be any different?" I hope my comments will be taken with a pinch of salt. Anyway, as we know, "Forecasters study every other possibility, except for what actually happens."

I. The General Security Environment

1. I feel the Food for Thought Paper is good at identifying different existing and some potential threats.

2. My general observation however is, that it presents us with the current international security environment, rather than with a future one. I sort-of missed the name of Ukraine, if not already seen as part of NATO, and the name of the OSCE (if we do not see OSCE as existing in 2015 then we should warn Lubomir that he might chair over the last year of its existence, as I understand Bulgaria is a candidate for 2014 Chairmanship).

3. Predicting the future can be, as stated in the paper itself, very ungrateful. Not for the chance of failing to predict the future, but for the fact that the tensions, quarrels, conflicts and wars that we predict for 2015 are those whose beginning we, as the international Community, are detecting to feel and address at this moment and in the years to follow.

4. As I see it, in spite of or thanks to the globalists the world will be more globalized in the good and, I am afraid, in the bad,

threatening, violent way. Let me mentions just a few; and I have more questions than answers.

5. The rise of more violent, fundamental Islamic extremism. Can we expect that democracy in any recognizable form will take root in Islamic societies or will they go the opposite way? Can this be reversed by an eventual success of the International Community's efforts in the Israeli/Palestinian conflict? Or should we expect a clash of Islamism and our civilization?

6. Africa and other poorer regions of the world. The rise of desperation and resentment of the poor parts of the world, as they keep getting poorer, while we get richer. Can this be checked by more generous humanitarian aid? Or will they come after us? Will AIDS still reign or will a miracle cure result in a population explosion? Are there going to be unprecedented mass migrations?

7. The Balkans: is the region on the way to Euro-Atlantic integration or can it still be a powder keg in 2015? Should we act in the region on a case-by-case basis as we have been doing so far or should we tackle the whole group of, say, seven entities (Albania, Bosnia-Herzegovina, Croatia, Kosovo, Macedonia, Montenegro, Serbia) together? All their problems, and therefore solutions, are intermingled. Even in 2015 they will be reflecting what happened in 1389. I believe that without tackling the region in a regional way, we will not succeed in bringing them all into Euro-Atlantic structures. E.g., if we take Croatia in individually, can it ever agree to Serbia being a member? If we take in Serbia on its own, can Kosovo ever hope to receive an invitation? Even Macedonia, that has been behaving admirably, is a hostage to the situation on its Serbia and Kosovo borders.

8. China. Is China on the way to become a global military power? Why is it spending so much on defense out of proportion with the threats of today, as we see them? Are we witnessing the beginning of the end of democratic and de facto independent Taiwan? Does China need more *Lebensraum*? If yes, is that Siberia or Indochina? Do they see NATO as a future adversary and are getting ready for it or are they getting ready for a common global threat that we have not identified yet?

9. Russia: are the democratic processes irreversible or will an authoritarian if not totalitarian Russia rise once again?

10. Global warming, natural or man-made disasters. Can a series of such events threaten our civilization?

11. Can we envisage a combination of the before-mentioned events that would demand a much more demanding role of NATO than we know today?

12. I was hoping I would not mention a comet... But here I go: Armageddon?

II. NATO's role, capabilities, programs, relationships

1. Firstly, I believe there will be a NATO in 2015.

2. Why? Because Safeguarding the freedom, common heritage and civilization of our peoples, founded on the principles of democracy, individual liberty, and the rule of law will still be necessary in 2015 and beyond – and perhaps more than now.

3. However, NATO should not only be a paper tiger. Until my arrival in Brussels when I only knew NATO from the outside, I believed in its omnipotence. Now, from the inside, seeing difficult search for consensus, painful force generation, obsolete armed forces, low percentage of GDP spent on defense... it sometimes feels NATO's harshest critics have got it almost right. So we have to get our act together. Unfortunately, our discussion here will not be a catalyst for a stronger NATO. Unfortunately, only another 9/11 or Pearl Harbor or a nuclear attack or dirty bomb upon a major city in a NATO country will result in our public and politicians demanding a change.

4. If NATO is a transatlantic organization, bringing together North America and Europe, should we not strive to bring in the rest of North America, namely Mexico, as well as Europe, especially the Western European partners that are capable of contributing so much? The threats that we and they are and will be facing in the future should make neutrality and non-alignment obsolete.

5. What should our relationship with the European Union be? I believe in 2015 our memberships will be even more alike. A few years ago

one of the fathers of the Atom bomb asked me if NATO and the European Union would ever merge. Maybe not merge, but either there will be more synergy, or there will be more problems. With the European Union, more than with any other organization, we should form common assessments, common strategies, have a division of labor and consultations. We should get as soon as possible over the present problems of not being able to talk to each other.

6. But if threats are global, so perhaps NATO has to be a global organization. If now NATO is a Euro-Atlantic Alliance and hardly coping with all the challenges it is facing, it would fail if faced with larger global risks. To face successfully global threats it would need to:

   a. Expand its membership globally to natural allies in Western Europe, Australia, New Zealand, Japan and elsewhere.

   b. Nations would need to raise defense expenditures to well over 2% of GDP and achieve real usability of forces.

   c. NATO would need to set up a large range of its own assets.

   d. We should opt for common funding of operations.

   e. In short, a deep reform of the Alliance, by making it mean but not necessarily lean.

   f. NATO would need to be the engine of public diplomacy in Member States and elsewhere.

   g. If threatened by rising new powers should we only be ready to counteract asymmetric threats, or should we also be ready to face a more conventional situation? Should therefore the territorial capabilities really be scrapped?

   h. Preemption, not just prevention would be the name of the game.

III. Internal organization

We need a think cell – an intelligent intelligence unit – if that is not an oxymoron – to detect events that could lead to new potential threats to our nations and the Alliance and follow the development of already present and detected threats that we are not currently dealing with.

Thank you.

SLOVENIA'S SECOND NATO SUMMIT

This was my proposed text of Slovenia's new Prime Minister Janez Janša's intervention for NATO's Summit in Brussels on 22 February 2005. I do not have any recollection of what was actually used. It was one of those laid back Summits that were usually organized at the HQ in Brussels at the start of a U.S. President's term, in this case obviously George W. Bush's 2nd term. "Mr. President" in the text refers to him.

Secretary General, President d'Honeur, Mr President, Colleagues,

The opening addresses this morning were most inspiring, both setting the tone as well as laying the cornerstones for our discussions today. I was especially moved listening to President Bush. We have always appreciated the historic U.S. leadership in bringing North America and Europe closer together on the basis of shared values, one expression of that being the creation of the Atlantic Alliance. We have appreciated the U.S. leadership in winning the Cold War and we appreciate their leadership in making this Alliance stronger today.

Preoccupied with the everyday business of planning and carrying out operations, we sometimes forget what the Alliance is all about. After all, our Alliance was founded to safeguard the freedom, common heritage and civilization of our peoples, founded on the principles of democracy, individual liberty and the rule of law, as well as promoting stability and prosperity.

Slovenia deeply shares the feelings of peoples struggling against tyranny. Not long ago we had to rise as people and as a nation to defend our basic human rights, so long denied. Subscribing to these ideals, and not merely thinking in terms of our own security, we sent our troops to participate in NATO's operations abroad, fully realizing that we have an obligation to share freedom's blessings.

We have witnessed NATO react and adapt to current challenges time and time again since its inception over 55 years ago. The Alliance has not only grown into the single global military Alliance it is today but also into an effective framework for transatlantic security consultations and decisions. However, with all the security challenges facing us today we should make NATO even more active and relevant in the political transatlantic dialogue. The link between Europe and North America is the bedrock of our common security. If there was no NATO we would have to invent it.

It is true; NATO cannot act just on its own. The Alliance should, whenever possible, strive for synergy, establish common strategies, a clear division of labor and coordinate its activities with other international organizations, especially with the European Union, where our strategic partnership is of utmost importance, the United Nations, as well as with the OSCE. At the same time, the Alliance cannot only be an executor of the tasks given by other organizations. Its political role, when dealing with international crises, should be strengthened.

Let me just add that whenever possible NATO should seek partners' involvement. In this framework I wholeheartedly support closer attention to our relations with Russia and am reassured by our overwhelming support for the Ukraine demonstrated earlier today.

The challenges in Afghanistan, our first priority, in the Balkans and in Iraq will still require a lot of our energy and resources over a number of years. But we may face other challenges soon. While we all feel encouraged about the prospects for peace after the recent events in the Middle East we cannot turn a blind eye to what we as NATO could contribute to the process, if asked by the two parties and on the basis of an eventual UN mandate. The Alliance should not shy away from discussing the Middle East Peace Process. There is no doubt that the easing of the situation between Israel and the Palestinian Authority would have a positive effect on the situation in the broader region where NATO is so heavily involved.

Colleagues, let me close by saying a few words of how we see our recent Alliance membership from the two sides of the same coin. Firstly, the transformation of the Slovenian Armed Forces is running hand in hand with the Alliance's transformation and we intend to achieve the 40/8 formula in a few years so that Slovenian troops will be fully trained, well equipped, deployable and sustainable for Allied operations wherever we might decide together it is necessary for collective defense or other purposes.

And, secondly, our participation in operations is steadily growing; we will remain in Bosnia-Herzegovina, increase our troop numbers in Kosovo by 200 percent this year, we are present with our reconnaissance platoon and firefighters in Afghanistan and intend to support ISAF expansion by contributing to a Provincial Reconstruction Team in the next months. To the post-election Iraq we are donating a corps size quantity of weapons and military equipment, worth over 5 million Euros, we are contributing 100.000 Euros to the Trust Fund and will help train Iraqi forces outside of Iraq. Also, we will not apply caveats to Slovenian officers in NATO integrated structures that would exclude them from serving in NATO's Iraq training mission. We are also considering participation in operation Active Endeavor.

We take our NATO membership seriously. We do not want to be a bystander or a free rider. As a stakeholder in this organization we will keep taking our share of responsibility.

Thank you.

PRIME MINISTER TRUSTING
MY ADVICE

The meeting took place on 22 February 2005 in Brussels. It was customary to use the opportunity of the NATO Summit to have also other NATO-related Summits, such as the Euro-Atlantic Partnership Council (EAPC), NATO-Russia Council (NRC) and NATO-Ukraine Commission. When the new form of relationship was being debated, Allies wanted to put their relationship with the large countries such as Russia and Ukraine, on a sort of pedestal, separate from the EAPC bunch, but grading Russia higher than Ukraine, thus the "Commission," not "Council." It was just playing with words... The published text is as delivered by Prime Minister Janša at the NUC Summit. Although I sent my proposal via the Slovenian Ministry of Foreign Affairs, what Prime Minister brought with him from Ljubljana was much rehashed and, as I felt, weak. So I, in a way, pushed my text into P.M.'s hands and asked him that he should use it. What you see in the triple parentheses started in the original text as my personal instruction to him, in Slovenian: "In case Yuschenko asks for the Membership Action Plan, I propose the following: ..." When in his speech President Yushchenko did ask for Ukraine to be given its own Membership Action Plan, I, just in case, stepped to the front NAC table and peered over my P.M.'s shoulder. I saw that he had crossed out with a pencil the proposed addition. I told him that now that Yushchenko had actually asked for MAP, he should support him, and that he would probably be the first Head of State or Government

to do so. And he did utter it and, as far as I remember, was the first one to do so.

Secretary General,

I would also like to add a warm welcome to President Yuschenko. The popular movement in Ukraine to defend democratic values, an important one being free and fair elections, was an inspiration to all of us. I personally know very well what the support of freedom loving people in the streets means. A decade and a half ago many Slovenians were freedom fighters themselves. We freely chose sovereignty, independence, but not isolation. We opted for full Euro-Atlantic integration and our endeavors brought us into membership of this Alliance, as well as the European Union, less than a year ago.

I salute your vision, Mr. President, of a Ukraine that will stand shoulder to shoulder with other democratic nations in the Euro-Atlantic area. The road to integration is open but not short; from our own experience we know that political, economic and military reforms are difficult but not insurmountable.

We welcome Ukraine's willingness to support NATO's anti-terrorist naval operations in the Mediterranean. We also look forward to working with you on the basis of the existing Charter on Distinctive Partnership, the annual Action Plans and other possible forms of enhanced cooperation. ((((Slovenia is a staunch believer in NATO's Open Door Policy and supports your aspirations towards joining the Membership Action Plan.)))

I wish you all the best on this road. Slovenia stands ready to support you the best it can.

Thank you.

COMPARING SLOVENIA AND UKRAINE

The **NATO-Ukraine Commission (NUC) is the decision-making body responsible for developing the NATO-Ukraine relationship and for directing cooperative activities. It also provides a forum for consultation between the Allies and Ukraine on security issues of common concern. It was established, on 9 July 1997 at the Madrid NATO Summit, well remembered in Slovenia for not issuing an invitation to my country to join NATO. Personally – in spite of being a supporter of Ukraine's move forward – I had some concern over the diminishing role of the EAPC and, as far Ukraine was concerned, giving it too much advantage in comparison with the so-called Aspirant Countries, struggling through their ornery Membership Action Plans. This little intervention of mine was delivered at a NUC Ambassadorial on 3 December 2004; agenda item: "Preparation of the NUC meeting at the level of Foreign Ministers on 9 December 2004."**

Thank you, Chairman,

I would also like to thank you, ambassador Khandogyi, for your statement. Democratic Slovenia was born from a popular uprising against undemocratic practices, and later on the basis of the result of free and fair elections.
Actually, the man whose basic human rights we were supporting 16 years ago in the streets of Ljubljana, will be leading from today on the new Slovenian Government.

It is clear then that we pay a lot of attention when the basic values and democratic standards are in peril in a friendly partner nation.

We urge rapid, non-violent solution of the present political crisis. At the same time we strongly believe that the will of the people and democratic procedures must be reflected in the outcome of the presidential elections. We support all democratic measures to secure unity and territorial integrity of Ukraine and firmly stand behind a stable and democratic Ukraine, moving closer to Euro-Atlantic institutions.

Both NATO and Ukraine have a long-term interest to work together. These are difficult times for Ukraine and the Ukrainian people and at least what we – as NATO – can do for Ukraine today, is to show support in every possible way.

Thank you.

CROATIA MISBEHAVING – AS ALWAYS

On 29 September 2004 I addressed the North Atlantic Council about the proclaimed intentions of the partner country Croatia to create unilaterally a new regime in the North Adriatic that would not only affect Slovenia but would severly affect especially ships registered in non-EU NATO member states. It was another case of Croatia's long series of actions that ran contrary to good neighborly relations. I used the opportunity to flag also Croatia's unilateral withdrawal from the Treaty on the State Border between Slovenia and Croatia, as well as the daily tresspassing of Croatian fishing boats, often accompanied by the Croatian police, in the sea under the sovereignty of Slovenia. Unfortunately, Slovenia never acted with enough resolve facing the neighboring country and little by little allowed it to enter both NATO and the EU without having the open issues with the neighbor first resolved. In both cases I was (on record) for the opposite course of actions, namely: 1. Croatia needs to resolve the open issues with neighboring countries first, 2. following that Slovenia will agree on Croatia's entry into NATO and the EU. In both cases we held a trump card in our hands but unwisely did not use it.

Secretary General,

I would like to inform the Council about Croatia's unilateral proclamation of an Exclusive Economic Zone which will take effect in 4 days' time on October 3, in the context of Croatia's relations with the Alliance.

I believe you are all aware that Slovenia has invested a lot of energy and goodwill in fostering good neighborly relations in the Western Balkans, its South East neighborhood. I will not dwell closely on the relations with the other States of the region but would like to highlight a few points on our neighboring partner nation Croatia.

To mention just the most recent years, back at the 1999 Washington Summit Slovenia supported Croatia in its efforts to join the Partnership for Peace. In 2001 Slovenia became a proponent of Croatia becoming a member of the Vilnius Group. We welcomed very much the invitation to Croatia to join the Membership Action Plan process.

Slovenia has for the past 3 years been expecting that Croatia would agree to ratify the Treaty on the State Border between Slovenia and Croatia, agreed by the Prime Ministers and endorsed by the Governments, unfortunately to no avail. Quite the opposite, Croatia has unilaterally withdrawn from the reached consensual solution.

Slovenia has been consistently promoting good neighborly relations, even in spite of continuing, sometimes daily incidents, especially involving the trespassing of Croatian fishing boats, in most cases accompanied by Croatian police boats, in the sea under the sovereignty of the Republic of Slovenia.

Also, Slovenian troops have been prevented from taking part in an exercise in Croatia, Slovenian companies and homeowners are on a regular basis treated in a discriminatory way.

The most recent incident, which happened exactly a week ago, involved the Croatian Border Police which detained 12 Slovenian citizens, including 2 MP's …. **on the Slovenian territory**! They were taken to Croatia and held under humiliating conditions for an extended period of time

These acts of Croatia contravene the principle of good neighborly relations and are contrary, we believe, to Euro-Atlantic principles and standards. By its involvement in the Membership Action Plan Croatia has committed itself to pursue and constructively promote cooperation and good neighborly relations and to demonstrate its ability to take on Allied responsibilities.

Let me now come to my point.

We first formally informed the Alliance about Croatia's plans to unilaterally proclaim a "Protected Ecological Fishing Zone" in the Adriatic

Sea just over a year ago. Slovenia has raised this question bilaterally, in the framework of the EU and other international organizations.

Last May I raised the question of this unilateral move in the Council's meeting with Foreign Minister of Croatia Žužul. I never received any answer whatsoever.

In spite of concerns about such unilateral moves in different fora Croatia still plans to establish the above mentioned Zone come this Sunday.

As a result of talks with the European Union last summer, Croatia has now excluded ships registered in the EU member states from the new regime.

However, ships of other countries (including non-EU member NATO nations) in the high seas, on the way, say to the Slovenian Port of Koper – or just about anywhere in the Adriatic – could be stopped and boarded, if suspected of not complying with Croatian regulations. Most probably also military ships.

Slovenia cannot accept unilateral acts that could hinder its access to the high seas and the access of ships of other countries to the Slovenian ports.

We are concerned that a nation that we have been supporting to join the Alliance is not behaving in conformance with the principles it has proclaimed. We are also very much concerned that Croatia never discussed this move with the Alliance.

Thank you.

SLOVENIA'S FIRST NATO SUMMIT

I always prepared a draft speech for the Prime Minister, Minister of Foreign Affairs or Minister of Defense when they attended Summits or Ministerials. Usually they showed up with texts prepared in the capital and most of the time I managed to persuade them to use my version. In this case, you can see first my draft and then the version, delivered by our Prime Minister in Istanbul at the Meeting of the North Atlantic Council at the level of Heads of State or Government on June 28, 2004. I was impressed by how much of my original text was kept intact. PM Anton Rop, politically not from my neck of the woods, who arrived one day late on account of some Euro-related business in Ljubljana, delegated me in his absence as Head of Delegation. This did not go down well with the then Defense Minister, who was already there and was expecting to have that honor. That appointment opened the door to my wife Magdalena and I attending the 37-person Gala Black Tie Dinner on the eve of the Summit with Presidents, Prime Ministers and a couple of mere Ministers of Foreign Affairs of the other 25 NATO member states, accompanied by a half dozen wives. This may not be the right opportunity to relate the stories about our meetings with George and Laura Bush or Recep Tayyip Erdoğan and others.

Secretary General, Colleagues,

It is indeed a great pleasure for me to be at this historic Summit here in Istanbul which for the first time gathers the Heads of State or

Government of Twenty Six members of the Alliance. I would like to extend my congratulations and warm thanks to our host President Sezer for the wonderful hospitality and for the Herculean task of organizing this event.

While half a decade ago there were concerns that the enlargement of the Alliance would weaken it and transform it into a paper tiger or a debating club, it is clear today that the Transatlantic Alliance is stronger and more vibrant than ever.

And we all have no choice if we want to be able to face the security challenges and threats of today and tomorrow. While Slovenia from the outset of its relationship with NATO first only followed the Alliance from the sidelines, then through its initial involvement as a partner nation, it now holds NATO's destiny in its hands with the rest of its members. We treasure the confidence we have been entrusted with with membership and are fully aware of its responsibility.

Working together with the Alliance is not new to us. Formerly a virtual, or better, a de-facto Ally, we contributed a substantial part of our resources to NATO's operations in the Western Balkans. We knew that the Alliance's success was also our success. We knew where the threat to our security and stability was coming from and we dealt with it. And our involvement had and has wide public support in Slovenia. The profound understanding of the public that the Alliance, with Slovenia's involvement, was successfully involved in making Slovenia safe played a major part in the overwhelming popular support for NATO membership in our referendum last year.

We have learned from this the importance of public diplomacy. While it was easier to convince the public of the necessity of contributing troops in our neighborhood, [almost our backyard,] we have to work harder the farther our troops will have to travel. This is far from an academic question, as the credibility of the Alliance will be on the line wherever it gets involved.

However, public diplomacy is not the primary question. The question not only Slovenia has to answer is, how much are we ready to invest to fulfill our political ambitions? And I believe that we have to ask ourselves this question time and time again when we discuss whether or not to get involved in another operation.

For Slovenia it was not always easy to provide the necessary capabilities as we are still just building up our armed forces. However, our fully professional force has been developing fully along the line of NATO's thinking, away from the territorial defense principle towards a well trained, well equipped, movable, in one word: fully usable force that can be deployed wherever deemed necessary. Slovenia cannot provide vast capabilities, but whatever we do and will provide is going to be of high quality, as demonstrated for instance by our contribution to the NATO Response Force.

Let me touch upon our common major responsibility right now. The ISAF operation in Afghanistan is not only crucial for the future of Afghanistan and its people, but also of vital importance for the credibility of the Alliance as a global force for peace and stability.

Slovenia is committed to supporting the Government of Afghanistan in providing security and reconstruction assistance. Over the past two years we have donated military equipment for three battalions of the Afghan National Army and provided specialist training for the Kabul police force. At the present time we are participating in ISAF with a Reconnaissance Team, a National Support Element and a Staff Component in the HQ.

Fully aware of the importance of the upcoming Presidential elections and to fulfill our commitment to the people of Afghanistan through progressive expansion of the NATO mission throughout the country, Slovenia will substantially increase its contribution in the ISAF operation. We will double our troop contribution during the election period. We have already announced the contribution of a fire fighting squad to the Kabul International Airport and we will contribute to one of NATO's new Provincial Reconstruction teams before the end of the year to help extend the area of security and development beyond Kabul.

Let me also tackle the question of Iraq. Slovenia has provided reconstruction and humanitarian aid to Iraq, as well as training for Iraqi police officers and businessmen. Our approach to Iraq has not wavered and that is why we have welcomed the unanimous adoption of UNSCR 1546. We believe it opens the way for our more substantial involvement as we are committed to helping the people of Iraq create the conditions for long-term development of their country.

We welcomed the discussion to determine the best way for NATO to contribute to that process, specifically in the area of increasing the capacity of Iraqi security forces to take full responsibility for the security of Iraq.

We are convinced that NATO can help in creating the necessary conditions for a stable Iraq that will no longer need international forces. We should be receptive to any potential requests for assistance from the Iraqi interim government, coordinate our contribution with other international organizations, and make sure that our new commitments in Iraq in no way jeopardize our other on-going operations in Afghanistan and the Balkans.

Let me close by getting back where I started. The Balkans. Although our thoughts go as far as Afghanistan and Iraq we are not forgetting the Balkans. Slovenia is going to remain involved in Bosnia-Herzegovina, both in the newly created EUFOR as well as in the NATO HQ with our capabilities that have already proved their worth there.

Concerned about the fragile situation in Kosovo we are going to substantially increase and upgrade our presence by contributing a military police platoon and certain intelligence capabilities.

All in all, Slovenia wants to put money where its mouth is. We are committed to the Alliance and its missions and, although small, we intend to punch above our weight.

Thank you.

*

Secretary General, Colleagues,

It is a great pleasure for me to be at this historic Summit here in Istanbul which for the first time gathers the Heads of State or Government of Twenty Six members of the Alliance.

While half a decade ago there were concerns that the enlargement of the Alliance would weaken it and transform it into a debating club, it is clear today that the Transatlantic Alliance is strong and vibrant facing together 21st century threats.

There is no doubt; we have to work together if we want to be able to face the security challenges and threats of today and tomorrow.

Let me touch upon our common major responsibility right now. The ISAF operation in Afghanistan is not only crucial for the future of

Afghanistan and its people, but also of vital importance for the credibility of the Alliance as a global force for peace and stability.

Slovenia is committed to supporting the Government of Afghanistan in providing security and reconstruction assistance. At the present time we are participating in ISAF with our forces.

Fully aware of the importance of the upcoming Presidential elections and to fulfil our commitment to the people of Afghanistan through progressive expansion of the NATO mission all over the country, Slovenia will increase its contribution in the ISAF operation.

Let me also tackle the question of Iraq. Slovenia has provided reconstruction and humanitarian aid to Iraq, as well as training for Iraqi police officers.

We have welcomed the unanimous adoption of UNSCR 1546 also because it opens the way for increased assistance of the international community as we are all committed to helping the people of Iraq create the conditions for long-term stability and development of their country.

We welcome the determination to contribute to that process, specifically in the area of increasing the capacity of Iraqi security forces to take full responsibility for the security of Iraq.

We are convinced that we (NATO) can help in creating the necessary conditions for a stable Iraq that will no longer need international forces.

Let me close by the Balkans. Although our thoughts go as far as Afghanistan and Iraq we are not forgetting the Balkans. We welcome the developing cooperation between NATO and the EU on the basis of Berlin Plus. Slovenia is going to remain involved in Bosnia-Herzegovina, both in the newly created EUFOR as well as in the NATO Headquarters with our capabilities that have already proved their worth there.

Concerned about the fragile situation in Kosovo we are going to increase and upgrade our presence by contributing a military police platoon and personnel in KFOR Headquarters.

Secretary General, Colleagues,

We go further and Slovenia remains committed to the Alliance and its missions.

Thank you.

OPENING THE PERMANENT MISSION

As the status of NATO candidate countries kept changing, so did the location of their diplomatic representations. When I first arrived in Brussels in January 1999, our Mission to NATO was stationed in a rented Hewlett-Packard building situated right next to the NATO HQ. Then we progressed to a newly built structure within the compound and, finally, after having received at the Prague Summit the formal invitation to start accession negotiations, NATO built for the newcomers a new four-story building, physically connected to the rest of the HQ. I opted for the top floor, saying: "No one is going to .... on us." Then after having moved in it was time to officially open the Mission. I had my Foreign and Defense Ministers together with Secretary General of NATO attending, as well as some NAC colleagues; while my staff gathered there in awe. I delivered this speech in the great new meeting hall on 17 May 2004, finally as the Permanent Representative of Slovenia on the North Atlantic Council. Almost a decade and a half would then have to pass for the completely new 1 billion plus Euro NATO HQ to be built across the street from the old one. In 1999, I had been told it would take 5 years...

Secretary General Jaap de Hoop Scheffer, Ministers Dr. Dimitrij Rupel and Dr. Anton Grizold, Ambassadors, Ladies and Gentlemen, Colleagues,

There has been talk about the importance of Slovenia's NATO accession on many occasions. As I am speaking not only to the convinced but also to those who have been seized with this project, I am not going to repeat everything that we have been repeating for years to the unconvinced.

To me personally a vision from a decade and a half ago when we were setting up the foundations of our state has come true.

Today I have the opportunity to thank all the colleagues, especially those who were either at home or here at the NATO HQ in Brussels or at SHAPE in Mons breaking the ground; and not only from 9 to 5 but often late into the night, day in day out. We should also remember those who have since moved on to other duties but who had contributed unselfishly.

You were the source of a flood of proposals, ideas, how to speed up the adaptation of our country to Alliance criteria in the political and economic area, in defense-military issues, resource issues, security issues and legal issues. Our nagging sometimes did not result in an enthusiastic response, however the progress achieved and the membership earned clearly demonstrate that we were on the right track.

Today both ministers who had the key roles in our accession to NATO officially opened the new premises of the Slovenian Permanent Mission, actually the fourth abode of our diplomats who cover the North Atlantic Alliance, from the initial times under the baton of Ambassador Dr Boris Cizelj. As all things must pass, our stay in this building will last only about a decade until the completion of the new NATO building on a new location.

However, Slovenia is in NATO for the long haul. We have committed seriously to link our destiny with the destiny of the Allies. While for many Slovenians this Alliance will hardly be visible in everyday life, you are going to be the ones not only observing it but living and developing it on a daily basis. If the Mission fulfills conscientiously its mission, there should be no doubt that Slovenia will be a useful member of the most successful defense alliance of all times.

Perhaps some of you were surprised, when faced with the statue of Dr. France Prešeren (SecGen: Prešeren is the greatest Slovenian poet and two stanzas of his poem A Toast are used for the Slovenian National Anthem). However, was it not him who foretold the Slovenians two things: Firstly, that they are able to form a nation from out of disparate and disparaged parts, and, Secondly, that we »*Will live to see that bright day's birth/When 'neath the sun's rotation/Dissent is banished from the earth/All will be/Kinfolk free/With neighbours none in enmity.*« (SecGen: the translation is only a very poor rendering of the original.)

I see his rhymes as the motto of our active engagement in NATO. In the organization which is based on ensuring international peace, security, liberty, justice, democracy, common heritage and the rule of law. The 7 lines Prešeren penned 160 years ago are actually the gist of the 14 articles of the North Atlantic Treaty.

The Slovenian nation has therefore 160 years after the resonant words of a visionary become with membership in two of the most important international organizations a global player in ensuring those basic values that are the prerequisite for our survival and development and that of the future generations.

The Slovenian Permanent Mission, which will continue to have an integrated structure, has in its political, defense and military sections dedicated experts who, on the basis of clear and coordinated national positions, will be able to represent well the Slovenian interests in the framework of shaping NATO's decisions, both on further transformation as well as its operations which are becoming more and more demanding.

At the close, before I pass the floor to the Ministers, I propose that we remember the Slovenian troops that in NATO's operations, led from this HQ, day after day, hour after hour, stand on the bastions of our liberty, security and international peace.

Thank you.

FACING CROATIA IN THE
NAC FOR THE FIRST TIME

A high-level delegation from Croatia, headed by Minister of Foreign Affairs Miomir Žužul and Minister of Defense Berislav Rončević, presented to the North Atlantic Council on 30 April 2004 the Croatian progress report towards its eventual membership in NATO. This was the first time Slovenia could, as a full-fledged member of NATO, address a NATO membership aspirant that we neighbor on and had (and still have) rather difficult relationship with. I was especially happy to see their first representative to NATO, Ambassador Tus, who performed his duties with rare grace. I was the second NAC member to intervene, out of 16 Alliance members that reacted to the Croatian opening presentation. Comparing the Croatian reactions to interventions and question with later meetings with their high-level representatives, I can conclude that they were the most civilized ever. While evading directly answering my more or less obvious displeasure with Croatia's handling especially the banning of some Slovenian investments and unilaterally proclaiming a zone on our sea border the whereabouts of it had not been agreed, in their replies, they paid a lot of tribute to working with Slovenia.

Thank you, Chair

I would like to extend a warm welcome on behalf of the Slovenian delegation to Ministers Žužul and Rončević, as well as my colleague and friend Ambassador Anton Tus, and the other members of the Croatian delegation

It is probably just a coincidence that this meeting is happening today, after Slovenia's accession to NATO and on the eve of its accession to the European Union.

Let me be a little bit personal. I remember well that we started out on this path together on June 25 1991, when both Slovenia and Croatia declared independence. I remember well the heady moment when I raised my hand in the Parliament for this bold move, and then hearing that Croatia had beat us to it by an hour.

Both countries had the vision of their European and Euro Atlantic integration and have spent the past 13 years on this, often very difficult, path.

Slovenia has profited a lot from the support and advice of the Allies and especially from the neighboring countries that had to go through a similar process. As a neighboring country we are especially interested in seeing Croatia proceed further towards Euro Atlantic integration. We will do our utmost to assist you if you wish so.

Our relations with Croatia are based on mutual friendship and understanding and good bilateral economic and political ties. These relations have resulted in the signature of a number of bilateral agreements, and many of them have already entered into force.

I would firstly like to commend the viable progress made in many areas of reform. Especially impressive is the growth of the Croatian economy and the improvement of its macroeconomic situation.

A good indicator of the overall political and economic improvement is the steady growth of foreign investments. We are pleased that among the foreign investors Slovenian companies represent and important share.

Unfortunately, there have also been cases when foreign investors have not been successful in bids because of powerful lobbies and popular discontent, as referred to in Para 34 of the Progress Report.

We hope that the Croatian government takes the necessary measures to further improve the conditions for foreign companies in Croatia to do business on equal footing with Croatian companies.

We know from our own experience that privatization is an arduous and difficult process. Private property is a *sine qua non* of a working market economy and is the basis of individual and political freedoms. We therefore encourage Croatia to proceed on with the privatization issue.

We would like to commend Croatia on its political involvement in the regional initiatives of the Western Balkans and its concern to improve relations with the neighboring countries, consequently playing an important role in the stabilization process of the region.

I would like to express concern with the unilateral proclamation by Croatia of an ecological and fishery zone in the Adriatic Sea, referring to Para 16 of the Progress Report.

We believe the protection of the Adriatic Sea within a multilateral framework is the most effective way to undertake such issues.

The first question I would therefore like to ask is why Croatia has not addressed the issue of such a zone in the Adriatic Sea within a multilateral framework, for instance within the Adriatic-Ionian Initiative?

My second question concerns the membership of Bosnia-Herzegovina and Serbia and Montenegro in the Adriatic Charter, PfP and the MAP. What are Croatia's views on this?

Regarding the defense/military issues we belio3eve that Croatia has already taken some important steps in the right direction in her reform process. We highly commend Croatia for this effort. On the other hand, significant further work still remains to be done.

We believe that a Strategic Defense Review, which according to our understanding is to be finalized by the end of 2004, lies at the heart of a successful reform of the Croatian Armed Forces. In this regard we would like to underline that a comprehensive and methodologically correct process of the SDR, without any shortcuts, is precondition for final success.

I would like to emphasize that timely and close consultation with the Alliance throughout the ongoing SDR is in our view an essential part of this process. Specifically, we would expect that Croatia informs the Alliance and indeed consults with the Allies collectively before any final decisions on the outcome of the SDT or the Long-term Development Plan to 2015 are being made.

It is in our interest that Croatia successfully concludes her SDR and creates a sound basis for her reform process. We are standing ready to support Zagreb in this endeavor.

At the end I would like to extend ouir full support on your way in joining the Alliance.

Thank you, Chair.

AFGHANISTAN WILL COME TO US

This is the interview Slovenia News, a Government rag, published on March 16, 2004, ISSN-1581-4602, under the title IF WE DON'T GO TO AFGHANISTAN, AFGHANISTAN WILL COME TO US. I think I used George Robertson's quote. I may have mentioned the author to the interviewer Vesna Žarković from the Gov't s PR and Media Office. The interview was in the Slovenian language and then translated into English. In spite of inaccuracies in the text, I will not correct anything, except turn British spelling into American, which I prefer. I did not appreciate her addressing me "mister" or being an ambassador of the Slovenian mission, I was Ambassador to NATO ... The interview was improved by her including a photo, taken by my spouse, the Ambassadress Magdalena Šinkovec a.k.a. Majda, on the terrace of my Residence, of yours truly presenting a V7 plaque of thanks to Lord Robertson. The text started with her brief introduction: "the enlargement of NATO to seven countries, among them Slovenia, will most likely take place before 2 April. The United States is planning to have the seven newcomers deposit the North Atlantic Treaty ratification documents the last week of March at a special ceremony that is expected to take place in Chicago."

The day of deposit officially counts as the day of accession to the Alliance. The United States, the depositary of the North Atlantic Treaty, NATO's founding document, has not taken a final decision on the exact date, since it depends on when ratification will be completed in the seven invited states. Mister Matjaž Šinkovec, Ambassador of the Slovenian Permanent Mission to NATO, can you explain what is happening with the ratification process in Slovenia?

As we speak, the U.S., in its capacity of depositary, has not yet decided when the ratification documents will be deposited. We expect that this event will be held by 2 April at the latest, when the raising of the flags of the seven new NATO members is to take place at NATO headquarters in Brussels. In Slovenia, the ratification process began when the government put forward the North Atlantic Treaty ratification bill on January 22. On February 17 the foreign policy committee debated the bill and a week later the document was adopted in parliament. It stepped into force on March 6. Slovenia is therefore ready to deposit its ratification instruments. However, the invitees will deposit their accession documents on the same day. So far, six of the seven countries have carried out the necessary internal legal steps for this, so only one country remains. Slovenia will become a member of NATO on the day it deposits its accession documents. Having joined NATO, Slovenia will also have to accede to nine other agreements and protocols that deal with cooperation with and within NATO.

The Alliance is planning to hold a ceremony at NATO headquarters in Brussels on 2 April, when the foreign ministers of the member states will hold an informal meeting. What will be going on then?

We are still debating the level that this meeting will be held at as well as the program. As is the case with all other matters, we have to reach a consensual agreement on this. A special celebration should be held during the course of this occasion, at which the flags of the seven newcomers to NATO will be raised and their national anthems played. Moreover, the representatives of these countries are due to issue statements in a separate ceremony. This event is expected to be followed by an informal meeting of foreign ministers from the 26 member states that will be dedicated to preparations for June's NATO summit in Istanbul.

A new wing of the main building at NATO headquarters is set to open on March 17. What will this bring for the Slovenian mission to NATO?

Actually, it will be "business as usual." A move from one to the other building represents the provisions of the right conditions, especially from a security point of view, in which the mission will be able to fulfill all the tasks assigned to it as a full member. We have been functioning as a de facto member since last June, but on the day of membership we will be assuming full responsibility for the operations of the Alliance. The move will also represent a significant improvement in the working conditions for the members of the mission, while it will also give us the necessary facilities to accept larger groups from Slovenia that wish to get acquainted with NATO and our role and activities within it.

Retired British General Jeremy Mackenzie assessed during a recent visit to Slovenia that the Slovenian Armed Forces are very well prepared for NATO membership. However, the real work is only just beginning, given the membership is different from preparations. What does "real work" encompass?

Because of the principle of consensus used by NATO, Slovenia will shoulder a part of the responsibility, together with other members, for each decision. A political decision to support a NATO military intervention will have to be backed up with a contribution of military units. One must understand that, as a member of NATO, Slovenia will no longer participate only in peacekeeping operations, but also in the most intensive military tasks, if the need arises. For example, this could happen if Article 5 of the Washington Treaty (collective defense) is invoked.

What will NATO do to safeguard Slovenian airspace, given that Slovenia cannot do that on its own?

By entering NATO, Slovenia will become a part of its integrated air defense system. Since Slovenia alone does not have the capabilities to police its airspace in times of peace, it will be left up to the Alliance to take care of this. NATO's solution to protecting the alliance's airspace will therefore be activated on the day of membership. This means that certain members that have fighter aircraft will help to safeguard Slovenian airspace. A final decision has not been taken yet on this, although it is expected to happen in the near future.

Does Slovenia agree to all of NATO's demands?

The Alliance is founded on the principle of cooperation, where things don't happen on the basis of demands. The decision to join this organization, in which our responsibilities are clear, was made of our own accord. Extensive talks were held about this. We know what capabilities the member states have to provide so that the Alliance can perform the tasks that get decided on consensually by its member states. But in the end, the contribution of each nation depends only on that country itself.

Can we expect that the Slovenian mission to NATO will be bolstered staff-wise as a result of the country's entrance?

When I arrived at the mission it was adapted to the work of a partner nation that had a clearly defined ambition to become a member state. Along with the head of the mission, three political diplomats and three officers worked here back then, with another officer working at the Supreme Headquarters Allied Powers Europe near Mons. Together with the administration, 12 people worked at the permanent mission. Since then, the number of staff members has grown as the number of tasks increased (adoption of the Membership Action Plan in 1999, the invitation to accession talks in autumn of 2002, the signing of the accession protocol in spring of 2003, the beginning of participation in the work of the North Atlantic Council and most of the working bodies in the summer of 2003) so that it now has six diplomats in the political sector and six in the defense sector, as well as six officers at the military headquarters and four officer at Mons. So altogether there are 32 employees at the mission, administrative staff included. Whereas the number of staff members has increased three-fold, both on account of participation in some 300 NATO working bodies and the processing of tens of thousands of documents. Although there is – more or less – a sufficient number of diplomats, we are still short of administrative and clerical staff.

Given NATO's role as forum for trans-Atlantic cooperation and its importance in resolving problem in the international community that are the source of threats to global security, such as Iraq and

Afghanistan, one wonders how much sense it makes for Slovenia to take part in this, especially because of the smallness of its armed forces. Wouldn't it be better to send more soldiers to the Balkans' mission and thereby apply the comparative advantage that we have there (such as the knowledge of the language, culture and terrain...)?

The guiding principle of NATO is the division of the responsibility for defense and the protection of all allies in missions irrespective of their capabilities. Notwithstanding the fact that it has a comparative advantage in the Balkans and that it has sent most of its forces there so far, Slovenia is ready to contribute to international security also by participating in other NATO operations. Let me put it this way: "If we don't go to Afghanistan, Afghanistan will come to us." What I want to say is that the situation in Afghanistan affects Slovenia's security, not only through international terrorism, but other means as well. For example, 80 percent of the poppy seeds that are used for drugs which are destined for Western Europe and in some cases pass through Slovenia are produced in Afghanistan. What is more, a deterioration of security conditions in Afghanistan could well lead to larger waves of refugees heading towards the EU, which would also affect Slovenia. This is why we have decided to make a contribution that reflects our capabilities. The first Slovenian unit, which has been tasked foremost with reconnaissance missions around Kabul, arrived in Afghanistan last week. Shortly, a fire fighting team should be send to the Kabul airport. We have also made contributions to the training and equipping of the Afghan security forces, as well as to demining efforts.

What is your assessment of the relations between NATO and the EU?

Relations between NATO and the EU are good and have been developing in the right direction. Much has been achieved in recent years, especially if you consider that there was no dialogue – no mechanism for dialogue even – between the organizations. NATO and the EU work together in different fields and with the aim of avoiding duplication of work and ensuring coordinated and united response of the international community to security and other challenges. Joint meetings are being staged on the political level and there is permanent dialogue between the international secretariats of both organizations. The most important matter that the two organizations are currently dealing with together is the transfer of the military operation in Bosnia-Herzegovina. Slovenia will soon begin taking part in regular joint meetings of NATO and the EU (NAC-PSC, Political Security Committee), which should give us the opportunity to have an even more direct say on the future development of good relations between the organizations. After all, this is our interest.

BIRDS OF A FEATHER

I was asked by the Youth Atlantic Treaty Association, a.k.a.YATA, to address the participants of their seminar "NATO's New Members: Expectations and Challenges," taking place at the NATO HQ on 16 September 2003. The title of my address was, how original, "The Future of NATO." I believe it was Katerina Culiberg, a young SDS activist, who proposed me as speaker. I liked the audience at the first glance: it was composed mostly of young women. True, very ambitious, but still...

Good morning.

Very happy to meet you all...

When I first found out I had to address a group called YATA I thought you were from a large Slovenian chicken company with the same name. My colleague Barbara, having one of her jobs called Ambassador's Pet, soon corrected me.

Still, I had to find a deeper reason why we had to meet. I found one. YATA means *flock* in Slovenian.

My last name Šinkovec translates as Finch in English. And Birds of a feather flock together.

So I hope we'll have a good time together.

Then another thing happened. I was told NATO's camera would be here. This whole thing would be available on the NATO website.

When I was still in politics, ages ago, I craved attention, I craved publicity. Well, like all... honest... politicians...

But ever since, I prefer to evade limelight. I prefer Chatham House Rules.

So we asked NATO to spare me this time. And they said they were only doing that for internal use – it would only be on the Intranet!!! The Internal Internet. What an understatement of the year.

But, I guess we'd better get to the subject.

I am a fan of Atlantic Councils. Looking around I know why I am a fan of Atlantic Councils.

I was actually a member of the British Atlantic Council back in the the last century.

I was also a member of the Slovenian one. I tried to get the job of the President. I tried to persuade the first President to get me the position, when he was about to leave.

I was unlucky. So I had to take the next best job – of the Ambassador to NATO.

And the former President ended up being a member of my staff. So it goes.

I am definitely a fan of grassroots movements. I did my share in the Sixties and Seventies. Marching against the War.

You've heard of Make Love Not War...

But there is nothing un-natural that a former California hippie becomes Ambassador to NATO.

You need Peace, Stability, Good Defense to be able to make love.

Okay, I've finally just made my first point.

I hope you will not think that NATO is not a very serious organisation.

Well, you met Secretary General Lord Robertson last night. He keeps us Members of the Council well in line. The Ambassadors, after all, are the people in NATO who decide.

Just the other day he asked us if we knew the difference between the New York Mafia and the Glasgow Mafia.

Well, there's only one difference.

The New York Mafia makes you an offer you cannot refuse.

And the Glasgow Mafia makes you an offer you cannot understand.

Seriously folks...

I understand that you presented a "Memorandum on the future of NATO" to Sec Gen yesterday. So I assume that you, the young people of the world, see a future for our organization.

I am reassured.

The de facto new members are definitely on the same bandwagon with you.

Why else would we want to join this organization?

Slovenia formally decided to run for membership back in 1993.

But the roots of this decision go further back.

My friends have convinced me that it was I who proposed NATO membership for Slovenia when Slovenia was still part of another country... I forget its name for the moment...

But in general, when in Slovenia, we, the grassroots organizations were opting for Freedom, Democracy and Independence... We were not opting for Isolation but – quite the opposite – for Euro-Atlantic Integration.

We did not see NATO just a tool to offer us Collective Defense.

We did not seek membership because of our weaknesses but because of our strengths.

Slovenia has been and is an internally stable and inclusive society.

We have not become a consumer of security.

On the other hand we have contributed to international stability and security, especially in the region to the South East of our borders.

We believe we can achieve even more by working together, meaning working inside NATO.

And the new members were and will be able to join NATO because of the changed world, sometimes for the better, and sometimes for the worse.

Slovenia strongly supports further enlargement; both the enlargement of NATO and the enlargement of the EAPC/PfP.

We believe that with new members that share same values and are in the Euro-Atlantic area it could be easier to preserve peace and stability and fight new global threats.

NATO has prepared several tools for membership.

The Membership Action Plan (MAP) is definitely the main tool.

The Planning and Review Process (PARP, Pronounced P-A-R-P by our Ministers that we write speeches for) helps defence reforms. There is the Individual Partnership Program (IPP), and new tools, such as the Individual Partnership Action Plan (IPAP), for Central Asian and Caucus countries and new PfP members) which helps also with all internal reforms.

I would like at this point to say a few words on the experience we've had with MAP.

At first, after the Washington Summit, where MAP was launched, officially "to best prepare candidate countries for accession," we were suspicious. We were not sure if it was not just a delaying tactic of the Alliance. A Toy we could play with…for ages…

But in the next few years, we learned MAP was very useful. It has on the one hand helped us structure our reforms better. And on the other hand it has helped NATO understand us better.

And it is quite useful to get to know the partner you are going to spend the rest of your life with, before you say the final I Do.

By the way, in two weeks we will be handing over our fifth Annual National Programme of the Membership Action Plan.

I am not sure you know how the whole process goes.

Let me try to explain. Every year a Candidate, or Aspirant Country, has to prepare an Annual National Program where it briefs NATO (the IS, meaning the bureaucrats working for NATO, and the Nineteen) on certain issues related to fulfilling the requirements of membership. Within each segment it provides an update on reforms and explains what it intends to do in the coming year.

There are five chapters in Map:

- political and economic issues,
- defense and military issues,
- resources,
- security
- and legal issues.

In short, in the political and economic chapter we are attempting to demonstrate that we fulfil political and economic criteria.

In the defense and military chapter we have been trying to convey two things. Firstly, how we intended to go from the conscript based armed forces to fully professional ones. The conscription in Slovenia which is to be formally abolished by 2004 has just been put into a moratorium. First the obligatory and then the voluntary reserves will be used until a full professional force is formed by 2010. And, secondly, we are trying to demonstrate how we intend to contribute to the Alliance's capabilities.

The resources: in short: can we afford the obligations?

On security the gist of it is: Will NATO's documents be safe with us?

On legal issues in short: Have we sorted out all the legal paperwork?

In March, when we officially expressed our desire to receive an invitation to accede to the North Atlantic Treaty and confirmed our Government's willingness and ability to respect the obligations and commitments under the North Atlantic Treaty and the Study on NATO Enlargement, we also had to attach a timetable for the completion of reforms.

In the near future the Alliance is going to check if required reforms have been completed as promised.

So, as I have stated before, enlargement contributes to peace and stability and to the completion of internal reforms.

Lately lots of discussions on NATO's relevance now and in the future have been held, also in Slovenia, especially just before the referendum on joining NATO that we had last March.

I am sure that NATO has always been a relevant organization for ensuring peace and stability in Europe.

In the debates in Slovenia before the referendum, some very high level proponents of NATO membership claimed that "Now that NATO has changed it is acceptable to Slovenia., because it was not the Cold War NATO any longer."

Of course not; NATO adapts and reinvents itself.

But I also believe that the Cold War NATO was extremely relevant to Slovenia. Not just that it helped bring the Wall down and release the captive nations of Eastern Europe.

But in our neck of the woods NATO's presence just across the border made it possible for Slovenia (as well as the rest of the now defunct federation) to live in relatively liberal communism, with open borders, private property, relatively open media, mixed economy, etc.

Without NATO we would have probably been occupied by the Warsaw Pact.

*

I have mentioned the changing world. And I have mentioned the good changes.

But there also are the bad.

After 9/11 it has become clear that we can fight the scourge of terrorism only if we fight together.

And this is what NATO offered to the US only a few hours after the terrorist attacks. The Nineteen have decided to invoke Article 5 of Washington Treaty, the article on collective self-defence, the article on solidarity. It was invoked the very first time after the signing of the Northatlantic Treaty back in 1949.

This has reassured countries like Slovenia that Article 5 is very much alive.

So after the enlargement and the new threats, what, in my opinion, is the role of NATO in the future?

The following is as true as it was at NATO's birth: "To safeguard the freedom, common heritage and civilisation founded on the principles of democracy, individual liberty and the rule of Law" – but in a changed environment, of course.

NATO is still the only place where North America and Europe sit at the same table and talk and decide consensually on common security issues.

With terrorism and other threats and instability and changes happening in different countries coming from different sides of the world, e.g. the Balkans, the Caucasus, Central Asia, North Africa or Middle East, there will be more violence, drug trafficking, trade in people, arms smuggling, etc. And NATO as a defense organization has a unique role in all of these things.

If there was no NATO, we would have to invent it.

*

There are a few more points I would like to make:

I have already mentioned consensus. To Slovenia this is one of the most important qualities of NATO. The indispensable principle of consensus. It gives important say also to small countries such as Slovenia. At the same time I want to reassure you that reaching consensus with 26 member countries will be no more difficult than with 19.

What happened in last spring's debates on Article 4 should not make us feel disappointed in NATO's ability to reach consensus. It should make us feel good that also small countries have a say. Otherwise, what sort of organization would we have?

Another important thing is also to increase cooperation with other international organizations, to use resources more effectively and not duplicate the work.

For Slovenia, a country that will join both NATO and the EU next spring, the discussion about the co-operation between the two organisations is of particular importance.

Certainly this will be one of the more often debated issues during the next few months, as the EU's Intergovernmental Conference concludes its work on the EU institutional treaty.

The arrangements that were concluded last year under the so-called Berlin Plus agreement already allow the EU to take advantage of NATO's assets and capabilities and to use them in its military operations. In practice, this meant that in March of this year the EU was able to take over the responsibility for the international mission in Macedonia, and I believe that this should be a model that will be followed in other locations in the future.

As for the predictions that the development of the Common Security and Defence Policy could allow the EU to take over the role of NATO and make NATO obsolete, I think we need to be realistic.

Certainly there is a fair amount of enthusiasm about the idea of a strengthened ESDP in Slovenia and in a number of other EU member and accession states. In addition to that, we are all familiar with the very ambitious proposals for European defense that were put forward at the summit of the four NATO and EU members in May of this year.

However, it is a fact that today NATO remains the only organization with the necessary capabilities to provide for collective security in Europe and to act in other areas of the world when this is necessary. NATO proved its efficiency by bringing security and stability to the Balkans; it is now taking over responsibilities in Afghanistan and in Iraq.

It would be in nobody's interest to weaken NATO by taking away its financial and military resources or its political clout.

If it ain't broke, don't fix it.

No country, including the four countries that appear to champion the idea of a separate European defense structures, can afford to waste limited and precious defense resources on duplication.

I hope that eventually the argument of rationality will prevail (or is that too much to expect of politicians?), and that the debate regarding the NATO-EU relationship will focus not on competition between the two, but rather on the ways they can best complement each other in sharing the extensive burden of European and global security.

Another point:

With the adjustment of the Alliance, its members have to adjust. Slovenia is now creating a more realistic force structure, with substantially smaller wartime strength, which will be capable of supporting the Alliance's policy and missions in a substantial and credible manner. Higher defense spending supports the entire process. »The critical issue is how much we are willing to invest in the safety of our children and grandchildren, « as Lord Robertson once said.

Another point:

One major challenge for us was to explain to the Slovenian public what NATO is going to be all about in the future. The difficult thing at that point was, that NATO was and still is changing. But we were persistent and were able to celebrate a fantastic victory in our referendum. 66% of the people voting decided Slovenia should join NATO.

We keep talking to the public. And the support for NATO and its missions is high, around 56% which, I understand, is not very common in some other member nations.

What was hard to grasp in Slovenia was that young people supported our membership less than the oldtimers, such as me. I do not know all the reasons.

Perhaps Katerina Culiberg has the answer.

More knowledge of NATO would definitely be useful. In your memorandum on the issue of discussion on security and defence matters and highlighting achievements and goals in civil areas you propose to create a Model NATO following the Model UN. I remember with fondness participation in the Model UN during my College years. My kids tell me that both of their high schools here in Brussels had Model NATO clubs. So I guess in some, perhaps rudimentary form, this idea is already alive.

*

Ladies and Gentlemen,

Let me try to wind up.

Besides indisputable benefits, membership will bring along also responsibilities for sharing an equal defence burden with other Allies. In short, the biggest challenge ahead of Slovenia will be twofold: to develop real military capabilities suitable for modern security environment and to be ready to use them, together with other Allies, for the benefit and protection of our citizens.

Slovenia, together with other invitees and members of the Alliance, has recently received its draft Force Proposals 2004, a set of planning targets through which we will develop capabilities sought by NATO. They are extremely demanding, challenging but realistically attainable. If implemented, they will help the Slovenian Armed Forces to develop into a small, professional, and modern fighting force, needed by Slovenia and for the benefit of the wider transatlantic community of nations.

I know that this is a tall order but it is also the only way that we could close the gap in capabilities needed to meet Alliances' ambitions or in other words, to meet modern security challenges. And it holds true for practically every NATO member and invitee.

Before Prague, when we were sometimes more waiting to be invited then trying hard to be invited to join NATO, some of its nations called us complacent. Once I had a whole speech on complacency. It was pretty masochistic. But the speech, as well as our further engagement, finished with the most important word and idea among NATO nations, which is commitment.

I'm talking about commitment to defend »the freedom, common heritage and civilisation founded on the principles of democracy, individual liberty and the rule of Law«.

There we go again.

What is the role of NATO?

The role of NATO in the past and the role of NATO today?

It is so very simple.

After all these years it is still the same.

The threats have changed.

And the way of dealing with them has changed.

However NATO is still here to defend the freedom, common heritage and civilisation founded on the principles of democracy, individual liberty and the rule of law.

With this I conclude my presentation and I will be happy to take any question or listen to your views on the future of NATO or anything else thast may come to your mind.

Thank you.

SUCKING UP TO SECRETARY POWELL

The U.S. Mission to NATO organized on 2 April 2003 a pleasant meeting of the NATO Partner countries aspiring towards NATO membership with Secretary of State Colin Powell. I still have the "family photo" of the meeting. I briefly said everything expected of an ambassador of a country that wanted to enter the Alliance. However, there was a slightly uncomfortable backdrop to the meeting. The Slovenian media –vehemently opposing U.S. intervention in Iraq – had found out about the meeting and the Ministry of Foreign Affairs was besieged with questions about my eventual participation. I called Minister Rupel – who was visiting Macedonia at the time – and asked him whether I should attend. He was both clear and evasive at the same time: he told me that I was the Ambassador and it was my decision to attend or not attend. If things got out of hand in the public – I would be recalled in the fall. I attended and remained Ambassador there for further three and a half years...

Secretary of State,

I appreciate very much the chance to meet with you on this ocassion.

I would like to express our sincere thanks for all the US support we have received over the years for a robust enlargement of NATO. The US was vital in actually making it happen. March 26 was also personally for me, who have supported Slovenia's NATO membership for over a dozen years, a day comparable only to the Independence of Slovenia.

In spite of the elation we will not become complacent. We have our Timetable of Reforms and we will keep to it. The Government with the great support it received in the Referendum on NATO, will be able to take on Allied responsibilities at an accelerated pace.

On Iraq, Slovenia has clearly expressed our interest to do as much as we can in the area of humanitarian aid. We are examining the options for our involvement in the post-conflict time, especially on the basis of lessons learned by our participation in the Balkans.

It is important for us to join NATO. It is important for us to join a strong and relevant NATO. We believe that NATO should play an important role in the post-conflict time in Iraq. The US lead in this, as it is in the Coalition, would be of utmost importance.

Thank you.

GETTING READY TO GO TO IRAQ

This is one of my rare EAPC interventions included in this book. It was delivered on 20 March 2003. Although it requires no further explanation I believe I need to explain that when NATO started getting ready to assist the new Iraqi Government with the security issues I pulled all the stops, often feeling quite alone, to have Slovenia participate in the NATO Training Mission with its instructors. I had to go on my own all the way to the top of the hierarchy to have that materialize. It had been similar with the decision to have our troops deploy to the province of Herat in Afghanistan, when I encounterted stiff opposition from the responsible Defense people who wanted our troops to join the Canadians in Kandahar. Well, in both cases I won. And, mind you, we did not lose a single soldier. Check the tragic Kandahar score...

Secretary General,

I would like to join my colleagues in expressing their regret that the diplomatic efforts to resolve the crisis have failed.

May I express my satisfaction that the EAPC has been convened so soon after the start of combat operations in Irak and that the Invitees have also been briefed about this morning's NAC and DPC meetings. This demonstrates that NATO continues to be the essential forum for transatlantic security consultation.

As NATO has already started to discuss humanitarian and post-conflict issues, I would like to add that the Slovenian Government has already started preparations to join in humanitarian efforts, reconstruction and other post-conflict issues.

Thank you.

COMMITMENT IS THE WORD

I chose "Commitment is the Word" for the title of my second address to the Manfred Wörner Circle, delivered at the NATO HQ on 6 May 2002. It reflected the complaints about NATO aspirants' and especially Slovenia's seeming complacency as far as preparations to fulfil NATO entry requirements were being carried out.

Ladies and Gentlemen,

It is indeed a rare honour to be able to address the Manfred Woerner Circle for the second time in 3 years. I appreciate the invitation very much.

Of course, this can be explained in at least two ways. One is that the first time I did at least a half decent job and the other one is that perhaps it is time to bid farewell.

Actually, neither is right. It is only because I have promised my friend Mr Mueller to provide Slovenian wine if I could introduce the latest special issue of NATO's Nations dedicated to Slovenia.

So three years ago I titled my address »Slovenia and NATO: 20/20 Vision«. It was just before the Washington Summit and I was attempting to imply that if NATO had perfect, 20/20 vision, it would invite Slovenia at the Summit to join the Alliance. And Slovenia would be the twentieth member. **How corny.**

And I guess **my** vision was not that perfect after all.

This time Mr Mueller asked me to give him a title for the speech before I even had any idea what I wanted to say. So I gave him a title and then completely forgot about it.

When I later on sat down and tried to write the address I could not remember what its title was supposed to be.

I only remembered it had to do with a word that started with a C.

So, if you think these days of Slovenia and a C-word then everyone in NATO would seem to think of Complacency. That is the buzz word, the C-word that has been haunting us for a while.

It implied that Slovenians, believing they were the first in the queue before NATO's Open… (hmm)… Door were just sitting on their… (hmm)… and doing nothing, while the rest of the aspirants were hard at work.

It implied at the same time that Slovenians were waiting until they would get a clear signal that the Open Door would actually open and only then we would do what had to be done.

Well, we have heard this so many times so it must be true.

Honestly, we have had a hard look and found out that there was more than just a grain of truth in it. We have been behaving probably too European and have missed out on two very important issues that could adversely affect our candidacy for an invitation at Prague.

Firstly, having had a long standing, binding commitment of just about all political forces of any consequence in Slovenia, we have neglected to a great extent the dialogue with the public. We have been too self-assured and have not, for years, tried to explain the benefits of membership to the ordinary voters. We believed that if they voted for pro-NATO membership parties they were automatically on board. Wrong.

That is why we were caught with our pants down when the NATO opposition pounced. The public support for NATO membership was always above 50%, which is a healthy figure for Slovenia. Anything above 60% on anything, except abolishing the taxes, would be hard to achieve.

So suddenly, the Pro NATO lobby caught unawares and disorganized, the NATO opposition managed to push down these figures 10 or more points in a few months. The Governments public awareness campaign on NATO has started but has not really shown results yet.

It is a small consolation if we observe the figures very carefully and find out that even in the case of a referendum today, more of the people actually voting would support than oppose membership.

What we know is that especially the political elite has to be loud and clear in support of our membership bid on a continuous basis so that the public gets the message. We have to find somewhat devious ways, like direct mailings to the households to bypass the generally unsympathetic media.

I believe there is no doubt we will win this campaign. We have prepared a game plan to tackle this major problem.

And what is more important, when the going gets tough, the tough get going. Or in other words, when Slovenia was a virtual Ally during the Allied Force campaign and our public understood well enough we were working with NATO against Milošević, the support for NATO membership never fell below 50%. Slovenians then understood well enough that they had to stand up and be counted and not hide behind unpopular decisions of a government. The Government now has to demonstrate to the Slovenians that the time to stand up and be counted is as valid now, in spite of Slovenia not facing any clearly identifiable threat, otherwise we will have to waive the invitation to join the Alliance goodbye.

The other big issue has to do with the share of the GDP for Defence. Slovenia has been criticized that it is not spending as high a percentage of the GDP on defense as the other aspirants. It is true.

According to the methodology we use we will be spending this year 1.5% of GDP on defence, while it is somehow expected that this share should be 2%.

In a way this is a moral requirement. If nations who are less wealthy spend 2%, why cannot Slovenia, which is relatively well off, spend as much? We used to answer that in actual Euros, or should I say dollars per capita, we are spending more than any other aspirant, and actually more per troop than 4 NATO members. But now we fully understand it is not so much the question of Capabilities as it is of Commitment.

Yes, Commitment has to be the word. This should be the C-word that we should concentrate on.

Slovenia has to use the rest of the time until Prague to show that it is fully Committed. By reversing the trend of public support we must unambigously show that the Slovenian electorate is with the NATO idea for the long haul. By raising the defense spending quicker than envisaged so far, we have to show that the political elite is also on board.

But we cannot revert to mere rhetoric and Potemkin's villages. Slovenians have always believed that their strength lay in Credibility, another C-word that is seldom used nowadays.

As far as public opinion polls are concerned we will probably still rely on the figures produced by the institutions which are led by Natoskeptics.

Our defense spending figures, which will be going up, will stay credible. We will not use any quick-fix methods.

Our defense planning, which has been assessed well by NATO, will have to stay credible. That is why we will be consulting already in June of this year on our new plans for achieving faster full professionalisation of the Slovenian Armed Forces.

The Slovenian Government adopted a formal decision 10 days ago to transfer from conscription service based armed forces to full professional force. The conscription service is to be abolished by mid 2004 with a view to conclude with a transitional process to full professional force by the end of 2010. The new ceiling for armed forces was set at 26.000 troops at the most with a planned downsizing to 18.000 troops if and when Slovenia becomes a full-fledged member of the Alliance.

The entire process will be supported by higher defense spending then originally envisaged and presented to NATO, with a final goal to reach 2% of GDP.

Since Slovenia wants to bring to the Alliance real military capabilities the decision to shift to full professional force was a logical step towards modern and flexible armed forces able to respond to new threats with new capabilities.

I have said I believed many of Slovenia's image problems stem from the fact that we behave perhaps in a too-European way.

That touches directly on the defense spending percentage, where all NATO EU member countries' ministers face similar problems when they face their finance, education and health ministers as does the Slovenian Defense Minister.

Also, you can never achieve 97% support for any single idea in a referendum in Slovenia, including getting rid of taxes.

I am not trying to say that Slovenia is a special case, far from it. But I believe that NATO candidacy is not a beauty contest. Each aspirant should be judged on its own merits.

If we look realistically at what Slovenia has done in the past few years in all the 5 chapters of MAP, then I believe we have not done worse than the rest.

There has been tremendous progress in the political and economic chapter. In the Defense chapter we have moved to realistic planning and have added new capability, especially in quickly deployable forces. We are ready to double at any moment the number of our troops in Bosnia, for instance.

As I have already indicated in the resources chapter the decision to raise the spending to 2% annually has been reached. It was not easy, but it is there to stay. Now we have to push for faster implementation.

In both security and legal chapters everything will be done by the time of Prague to allow Slovenia to become a full fledged member of the Alliance.

But are promises enough?

I believe that nations should be judged not so much in good times but especially when they are under duress.

As far as Slovenia is concerned I believe it is of importance that we were already Allies during World War II, with British and American military missions located at the Slovenian Resistance Headquarters. We did our bit to bring peace and security closer.

We were never true adversaries during the Cold War and Slovenia could remain a country of relatively liberal non-aligned Communism only because of the existence of NATO. Otherwise we would have probably been swallowed by the Communist Bloc. We are all very well aware of that.

One of the first acts of the first Democratic Parliament in Slovenia in the spring of 1990 was to support the Coalition in the Gulf War and even offer to send a medical station there. It was while we were still formally part of Communist Yugoslavia which clearly sided with Saddam.

Slovenia was attacked 11 years ago by one of the most powerful militaries of Europe. The expeditionary force had 22.000 troops and 800 armored vehicles, jet aircraft, helicopter fleets and so on. On the other hand Slovenia had its Territorial Defence forces, underarmed, undertrained, understaffed. The Yugoslavs believed they could take over Slovenia in a matter of hours.

When ten days later they were defeated, with only 9000 troops left, I guess they knew better. I believe when push comes to shove, you can count on Slovenia.

And I have mentioned the Allied Force Campaign. The decision to grant the use of air space to NATO, without any restrictions, was reached within 24 hours. No questions asked.

Or Counter-terrorism. I believe we have demonstrated that we can be trusted allies in this area. Within a few hours of the attack on the U.S., intelligence was provided and various forms of aid offered. All internal measures were swift and to the point. And what is most important: Slovenia joined the antiterorist Coalition with full public consensus.

I am glad my parents in the more removed past and I in the recent past have done our small bit to show that Slovenians can build Consensus and Coalitions and can be active in Countering terorism, three more C-words that are not out of place when the final judgment on Slovenia is made.

I hope that today I had managed to slightly change the view about Slovenia and its "Complacency."

We live with certain views that are hard to change.

However, I hope that in the future, when you think of Slovenia, you will not think of Complacency any longer, but of other C- words like:

- Capabilities, especially in South East Europe,
- Credible aspirant,
- Consensus builder,
- Coalition member,
- Countering terrorism,
- and most of all: Commitment.

Before I close and take eventual questions, I would like to touch upon the basic two questions that everyone who wants to keep the Alliance alive and well, meaning strong, would ask:

Firstly, will Slovenia be a provider or consumer of security?

And secondly, is democracy in Slovenia entrenched well enough so that it cannot be reversed?

Whatever we might think of Slovenia, it would be hard if not impossible to imagine that Slovenia would be a mere consumer of security or that it could go politically the wrong way. I hope we have established our credentials in these two areas well enough.

We are far far from perfect but we are here, as I have said, for the long haul.

We can do more until Prague and I hope we are given the opportunity to do even more after that.

Thank you.

224 DAYS TO PRAGUE

I hosted a lunch for the so-called V10 Ambassadors with Secretary General of NATO Lord Robertson on Thursday, April 11, 2002. The V10 referred not to a large internal combustion engine but to the 10 NATO Aspirant Countries that in May 2000 agreed in Vilnius, Lithuania's capital, to work together. In Slovenia the Vilnius group of countries is best known for the signing of the so-called (formally Latvia-proposed but actually Bruce-Jackson-penned) Vilnius Statement of 30 January 2003 that – in short – supported the U.S. invasion of Iraq. Slovenia's signing had and continues to have great ramifications in our country. As far as I am concerned, I am sure that without us signing it we would have been left on the sidelines and not have received in Prague the invitation to start accession talks. Perhaps this is the opportunity to bare my heart on the issue of the Vilnius Statement. I was in the meeting with our Minister of Foreign Affairs, a State Secretary and a few Ambassadors, deciding what Slovenia should do. Some people who supported the signing today claim that they did not. I was Ambassador to NATO; it was only natural for me to support it. In my short intervention, I said it was proper that we did not enthusiastically join the others right away, that we managed to include some of our ideas in the draft text and that we would only formally announce Slovenia's decision after Secretary Powell's televised speech on the suspected WMD's in Saddam's Iraq. I added, however, that I did not expect the speech to be a "silver bullet" but that we needed to join the group on account of our national interests if we actually wanted to enter NATO. Period.

Welcome, everyone, especially Lord Robertson,

I am sorry to have for the last time with us Konstantin Dimitrov. It was great to have you, Konstantin, as a colleague and as the most eloquent speaker in EAPC meetings.

Konstantin is such an easy name to pronounce. Mine is difficult. That's why my wine cellar is called Sheen-Coates, so people can properly prounce my last name, Šinkovec. I do hope it sounds Scottish enough so it will help Lord Robertson finally get it right.

And the wine is called 224 Days to Prague. If the wine is no good, it is because it is just an Aspirant, Aspiring wine, and it should only be judged after 224 Days. Quoting Lord Robertson: »There is still a lot of work to do - but there is still time to do it, « perhaps also applies to this wine.

I am glad to have Lord Robertson with us right after his meeting with President Bush.

Last week I received a call from a V10 mission: »What will the subject of the talk at the lunch be?"

I apologized and said that I just thought it might be interesting to hear from Lord Robertson eventually also about the thing called enlargement, or something like that.

Of course, if you can tell us anything, George? Quoting you again from your Washintong speech: »What I cannot say yet – and will not speak about until we meet in Prague – is exactly how many new members we will accept and which of the nine candidate countries will receive invitations.«

So, as I see it: the framework of this working lunch are the issues that the V10 are facing. We are in the midst of completing the third MAP cycle. It's been an extremely busy year for us. As it will be for the next 224 days.

One thing is clear: if it were up to the Ambassadors we would all be invited in Prague. However it is our Governments who have to deliver.

So, without further ado, let us raise glasses to our guest and to our governments for the success of all in Prague.

Cheers.

TO BUILD THE FUTURE TOGETHER

Former Director of the Private office of NATO Secretary General Manfred Wörner Claus-Peter Müller – who also ran the Manfred Wörner Circle – interviewed me for an issue of the magazine NATO's Nations and Partners for Peace, which was published late 2001 or early 2002.

Excellency, Slovenia will join NATO in the near future. What has been your greatest challenge for this decisive step?

I sincerely hope what you say is true. I have been involved in the process of Slovenia's emancipation and Euro-Atlantic integration for over a dozen years now. I believe I can vouch for the fact that our basic thinking has not changed in all this time. Slovenia's independence meant not an end to itself but also a chance for our nation to take a greater role, greater responsibility in international affairs. The inclusion of Slovenia into international organisations will on the one hand strengthen, not weaken those organisations. And on the other hand, we will be able to contribute more once inside than we could do outside. We have had experience in being Allies with NATO nations before, including World War II. We shouldered our part of the burden then. Also, we were never part of the Warsaw Pact, never adversaries. As the first Chairman of the Foreign affairs Committee in the first democratic parliament in Slovenia in 1990 I can tell you that one of the first resolutions of the parliament was to support the Western Coalition in the Gulf War. At that time we were formally still part of Yugoslavia which sided with the other side. In the

Allied Force campaign in 1998 we acted as Allies. However, it still remains a challenge to us to demonstrate clearly to the Allies that we have the will, the ability and the capabilities to be a true Ally. I hope that by the end of this year we will have achieved that.

In this process the Membership Action Plan (MAP) plays a vital role. Please explain its most important part for your country.

MAP, now in its third cycle, has proven to be a most useful tool for our preparations for membership in all the specified areas, in all the 5 chapters. It has helped us to organise ourselves and establish necessary discipline of all the Government bodies concerned. The well-structured consultations with the International Staff and the 19 member states have been most helpful; they are candid and constructive. I do not doubt that that is one of the reasons why we have been able to progress so far. It is important both for Slovenia and NATO that because of the results achieved in MAP and because of our experience in consultations (SPC(R), PMSC, NAC+1) our accession process should be easier than otherwise. Both Slovenia and NATO have learned how to work together.

How do you co-operate with the EAPC and the NAC?

Slovenia sees the EAPC as an important mechanism in the field of security, trust, confidence building and transparency in the Euro-Atlantic area. Its multi-layered structure enables us to choose those areas to which we can add value and also use it in a broader sense for our preparations for NATO membership. Besides its general Euro-Atlantic context it also enables us to participate in a narrower regional context. We participate in the EAPC from the very top to the bottom – from the Ambassadorial level to the very technical levels. EAPC has proven its value and significance. Actually you can hardly find anywhere else such a family of nations to work and consult together on common issues. It is important for Slovenia to participate in the decision-shaping process. The EAPC is a living mechanism that evolves every day to meet the new challenges and perspectives. I closely work with the permanent representatives on the North Atlantic Council on a regular basis. Slovenia meets once a year with the NAC in the framework of the

MAP process. This is an excellent opportunity to inform the Council about our work and progress.

During the Washington Summit Slovenia failed the accession to NATO. How was the reaction of the Slovenian people?

I would not agree that Slovenia failed the accession. The way I would put is that an opportunity was missed to invite Slovenia, as it had been a missed opportunity in 1997 in Madrid. However, in 1999 the Slovenian public understood that not enlargement but more the situation in the FRY was the priority of the Summit. I am not crying over spilt milk but I believe that Slovenia would have progressed even further, especially in the defence and military, if it had already been invited to join the Alliance. As a member of NATO, it could have already played a greater role in our common endeavours to increase security and stability of the Euro-Atlantic area. However, since then we have been everything but idle. Tremendous progress has been made and we will not show any slacking down before or after Prague. This fact should be recognised at the Prague Summit by issuing an invitation to Slovenia to join the Alliance. An invitation would signify a mandate that we can progress even faster.

How do you explain the NATO acceptance in the public opinion?

The Slovenian public opinion is too often judged on the basis of polls performed on very small samples. However, the latest authoritative poll performed in Slovenia showed there was more than a 2:1 ratio of the people supporting and opposing NATO membership, actually 53% in favour and 24% against. Or to be even more blunt, there are only 4% of Slovenians who do not believe Slovenia will become a member of NATO. Pretty impressive. However, this was the result taken before the Government's public awareness activities had actually started. I believe we can build upon this bedrock of staunch support for the membership, which has not failed us in the past years, even during the Allied Force campaign when Slovenians fully understood that we were already acting as Allies. You should also not forget that all the parliamentary parties, except for a small one, have supported membership in the Alliance for almost a decade now.

In which way can Slovenia demonstrate the readiness for NATO membership? Can Slovenia solve the deficits up to the Prague Summit?

The principles outlined in the "Study on NATO Enlargement", endorsed by Allies and published in 1995, still remain the basis for NATO's approach to inviting new members to join. Slovenia with its democratic political system, functioning and very successful market economy, clear record of human rights and minorities protection, and with a strong commitment to the peaceful settlement of any kind of disputes, be it internally or with other states, clearly meets the criteria set by the Study. Slovenian willingness and ability to meet commitments of the future membership in the Alliance in practice and not only on paper are in our view a critical factor which qualifies Slovenia as ready to join NATO. Our defence reform, which is proceeding in accordance with plans and timelines, agreed by Allies, plays a central role in achieving what constitutes "a readiness" for becoming a member of NATO. That is Slovenia's defence effort, which is strategically acceptable not only by the Alliance but also in the eyes of our public, and at the same time affordable by Slovenia. I do not like to think in terms of solving deficits up to the Prague Summit. We are not interested in some minor and easy "quick fixes" which would artificially create a better picture about our situation that in reality it is. We have unquestionably already achieved a lot but at the same time we would rather think in terms of a long term and sustainable commitment which has to rest on the sound defence planning for years to come. Slovenia continues to make significant progress in development of its armed forces with a focus on the development of capable and deployable reaction forces in accordance with NATO standards and strategy, so reflecting its strategic goal of Alliance membership". I am quoting the latest NATO's progress report on Slovenia and what it confirms is that we are on the right track but we have to keep the commitment. And I believe we are doing exactly that.

Please explain the geo-strategic situation of Slovenia. How are the relations to the neighbouring countries?

After September 11 the geo-strategic position, as that of other countries, has changed considerably. If we could have talked about Slovenia not facing any direct threat previous to the terrorist attacks in the United States, it is clear to all of us now that threats do not have recognisable faces or borders any longer. Contrary to what some »Natosklptics« say, there is even more reason now to be part of the Alliance. Only by working together can we face, and defeat, these new threats to the security of our nations. At the same time Slovenia, a Western Central European nation, bordering on South East Europe, is in a unique position to play an even greater role in our neighbourhood. We have developed excellent relations with our immediate neighbours, Alliance members Italy and Hungary being among them. We have invested a lot in helping stabilise the Western Balkans, both in defence, demining, humanitarian activities and, I would stress, in the economy. For instance, we are the largest foreign direct investors in Bosnia-Herzegovina. We have also shown to some of the troubled nations, by our example, that there is a "light at the end of the tunnel". Slovenia's inclusion in NATO would send a clear signal to them that the door to the Euro-Atlantic community is open to them once they fulfil the necessary criteria.

Slovenia's Armed Forces have up-graded the equipment to meet NATO standards. Where are the priorities?

Priorities are clearly given to the development of deployable and sustainable reaction forces, air defence and surveillance, Host Nation Support, C3I and deployable Combat Support and Combat Service Support elements. The entire modernisation programme is driven by the implementation of Partnership Goals agreed mutually by NATO and Slovenia, which is, much to our satisfaction, proceeding broadly according to our plan. The planned modernisation programme is very well in train with the financial projections and underpinned by a special Law (The Law on Basic Developments Programmes to 2007) which has provided additional US $259 million for equipping and modernisation of Armed Forces during this period. The funds will be used primarily in support of the implementation of those Partnership Goals that are indispensable for the obligations of future NATO membership. Those projects include the procurement of telecommunications and secure CIS equipment, connectivity with NATINEADS, new infantry and anti-tank weapons, acquisition of a tactical mobile communications network and hand-held combat radios, the purchase of additional Light Armoured Vehicles (Valuk, HMMWV), additional helicopters (Cougar), and modernisation of air defence assets.

What is your vision for the future?

We will be joining NATO, hopefully soon, the NATO as we know it now. Europe and the wider international community need NATO, a collective defence organisation that also is concerned with wider international security and stability. If there were no NATO it would have to be invented. The transatlantic link is irreplaceable. History has demonstrated that more than once. The role of the United States is vital. It is also clear that Europe needs to improve on its capabilities. And Russia needs to be as involved as possible. We are aware of the internal debates on NATO's future role and its internal mechanisms. We believe we can participate constructively in these debates. We want to build the future together.

THE NUMBERS GAME

My friend Manja Klemenčič who was working on her MPhil at the University of Cambridge got me an invitation to do my NATO song and dance – with the ingenious title "Slovenia and NATO" – at a Lunchtime Seminar at the Centre of International Studies of the University of Cambridge. It took place on Monday, 19 November 2001 at 1.00 pm at the Fitzwilliam House, 32 Trumpington Street. Yes, I kept the leaflet. I had known Manja from Brussels where she used to run a European student organization. I may have written a letter of recommendation for her MPhil application, so I guessed the invitation was a tit for tat. Later on she moved on to Harvard where she got her PhD and got stuck there. I spent the weekend before the speech roaming my very familiar town and the surroundings, which included some fine pubs with vicious apple ciders. But that's another story. I also had the time to read the student newspaper where I got the idea for a short story and had enough time to even write the first draft. It was published under the title "The Numbers Game" in my book of short stories "Love." Still in print, mind you. Mentioning so many numbers in my speech I can also use the title here.

Ladies and Gentlemen,

It is indeed a great pleasure for me to be able to address you today. I am awed by the atmosphere of the University of Cambridge, the institution of learning that I could only dream of attending.

Well, you may not believe everything I say, as you are all well aware that a diplomat is an honest man – oops, nowadays an honest *person* – who has to lie for his country. However, believe me, I am and have always been impressed by Cambridge.

May I thank Doctor Edwards and the Center for International Studies for the kind invitation. And Manja Klemenčič, who initiated this whole thing. She would, of course be much better at this as she is a top debater. I, unfortunately, still have to rely very much on my notes. However, I will never be Prime Minister. And I do not doubt that Manja has all the prerequisites to become one. Of course, worse things have happened to Fellows of her College – they became Archbishops of Canterbury.

Besides being honored and awed I am also slightly concerned. I am aware that "castigating with rods" – or in other words – "being beaten at the buttery hatch" used to be a regular punishment at the Corpus Christi College where I stayed over the weekend. I have read that one such beating occurred exactly 303 years before the day I was born. Well, I hope this only happens to undergraduates.

Cambridge is no foreign ground for me. At the time when I served as the first Slovenian Ambassador to the Court of St James's, half a dozen years from 1992 to 1997, I was often a visitor. I even spoke once on Slovenia at one of the Colleges, attended conferences and did things like unveiling a small Slovenian hayrack at the Botanical Gardens, working with a local charity called Friendship Link, attending parties at Madingley Hall and even initiated a town twinning.

Actually, just a couple of weeks ago the nearby St Ives got twinned with Medvode in Slovenia. It is not surprising that the Medvode municipality is exactly the place where I live in Slovenia. Slovenia being so small, it is not surprising either that the Mayor is a former party colleague of mine. We worked together both to make Slovenia independent from the former federation and Medvode to become independent of Ljubljana, Slovenia's capital.

Why am I telling you this? It is because the people in the democratic movement never saw dissociation from larger conglomerates as an end to itself. It meant emancipation, yes, but at the same time a basis for free opening up and eventual integration.

And I am glad to say that both my home municipality of Medvode and Slovenia are doing fine on their own and internationally. Slovenia not only opted for democracy and independence but also for wider Euro-Atlantic integration, opted for helping build Europe whole and free.

Today I would like to talk about Slovenia on its way towards future full-fledged NATO membership. May I first say a few things about Slovenia, then NATO, and then perhaps try to fuse them togetjher.

*

I am not going to go deep into the history of Slovenia. Let's forget the Big Bang and the Dinosaurs.

And there are certainly some scientific and not quite scientific disputes about where the Slovenians came from. I will not opt for one school of thought or another. I'll leave ancient history to historians.

What I want most of all to say at the outset is that the Slovenian people have been around in the same spot for at least 14 hundred years, ruled by themselves and others – just about everyone – until they reached full-fledged statehood ten years ago last June.

So Slovenia was not just a chip off the old block. Even before its independence and the victory of democracy it was a functioning state within another state. Actually, it was probably the only sort-of successful communist state in history. Liberal communism, open borders, liberal media, mixed economy, private property, you name it.

Do not despair; I am not harking back to the old days. I did my share to bring the old system down and help build a democratic one.

Throughout our history our territory was of interest to more or less distant neighbors. While this is good news in the times of peace for trade and tourism, there were times in history when we had our share of problems. In World War One hundreds of thousands of soldiers died on the Soča/Isonzo Front and in World War Two we were invaded and partitioned among our four neighbors.

We have learnt from this not only the importance of defense Alliances – we were Allies during World War Two, with U.S. and British military missions located at our Resistance headquarters – but also of building stability.

In the past ten years Slovenia has shaped up its economy. It is the only post-communist state, developed at the level of a couple of European Union member states (over 10,000 U.S. dollars GDP per capita). It is relatively well dealing with inflation, better than most similar countries (7%), and quite well with unemployment (expected below 7% next year), hard currency reserves (5.8 billion U.S. dollars) and is in the third place of EU applicants according to Foreign Direct Investments per capita (1200 U.S. dollars).

It is then no surprise at all that Slovenia is bound to close its EU membership negotiations by the end of next year. I expect it to be admitted into EU membership in the beginning of 2004.

We have achieved a very high level of respect for human and minority rights. I was especially glad of this at the time when I was negotiating our way into the Council of Europe about 10 years ago. Although it is true that the Council of Europe standards dropped later on and that countries with much lower credentials were admitted for political reasons.

I wish I could say that for Slovenia, but I cannot. Every time Slovenia enters an international organization it is on its own merits. Never because of any historical debts that anyone would feel should be repaid. It only happens after we fulfill the criteria. Not that there are no debts to be repaid…

But let me stop whining and get back to the subject.

When talking about the EU and NATO we do not have an either/ or but an and/and policy. Slovenia has no problem with this dilemma. Slovenia should be a member of both by 2004. We also very much see the importance of the Transatlantic Link and do not want the European Security and Defense Policy to be an instrument of separation, but of cooperation.

*

Let me say now something about NATO. Or let me start with a quote. These things usually work

The British 19th century libertarian, Jeremy Bentham, famously said that "the price of democracy is eternal vigilance." In the world we live in, especially after the 11th of September, this is very much evident.

Perhaps after the Fall of the Berlin Wall for a while this fact was not as evident. The continuing existence of the North Atlantic Treaty Organization was questioned by many. Especially by those, such as the Russians, that were only stumbling into the world of democracy.

I am surprised at mentioning Russia at all because I seldom do.

Slovenians are definitely *not* experts on Russia, but they are especially very much laid back about it. Well, we were never part of the Communist Bloc, the Warsaw Pact. Our concern with the eventual negative influence of Russia on further NATO enlargement is negligible.

It has been said that NATO was set up to keep Germany down, United States in and Russia out – well, I am not sure I got the order right. It is clear to all of us that NATO's present role has changed. There is no need to keep Germany down and we want to get Russia involved as much as possible. And yes, we want very much to keep the transatlantic relationship. History has shown the U.S. must stay involved in Europe.

There used to be a time that the justification for the existence of the Alliance was simply to be there. Security was about providing a counterweight to the Soviet Union in order to maintain the status quo in Europe.

As long as NATO was able to sustain adequate force levels to ensure deterrence and a minimal level of communication with its eastern adversary, not much more was required.

The end of the Cold War caused the absence of the traditional threat which gave NATO its *raison d'être*. But there is no such thing as the end of history. And the end of threats. Threats are and will be there.

The new security situation in Europe demands the shaping of the security environment as far to the east as possible, so that new threats are contained early or prevented from arising in the first place. Who is better placed than NATO to perform this job? There is no other organization with any serious capability and any serious defense planning.

If there was no NATO we would have to invent it.

It is true NATO cannot do everything. In the environment where we talk of interlocking institutions, the specific role of NATO is fuzzier than it was during the Cold War.

Security challenges have also become more diffuse. Some are latent, such as weapons of mass destruction. The threat cannot be conveniently quantified, as was the number of Soviet tanks or warheads. Terrorism is a similar problem. This is a conflict in which it is going to be difficult to measure our progress, let alone decide when to declare victory.

Neutrality does not provide the security it once did. Countries cannot opt out of the new security challenges in the way that they could declare themselves neutral or non-aligned (such as Slovenia as part of the former federation) in the confrontation between the Soviet Union and the West. Organized crime networks, weapons smugglers, terrorists and drug syndicates respect neither neutrality nor borders in deciding where to set up their networks. Refugees fleeing ethnic conflicts do not politely bypass neutral states. Weapons of mass destruction do not restrict their effect to NATO member states.

To be "out" means to have less influence on the shaping of international security.

NATO and the EU are the two institutional pillars of the Euro-Atlantic area. They have played a key role in the transition of new democracies and the integration of Europe. NATO will remain the core of transatlantic security and European stability, and the security dimension of the EU will serve to reinforce NATO's capability.

These complementary and mutually reinforcing institutions represent the foundation of the Euro-Atlantic community and constitute the security framework on which our nations rely.

The addition of three Central European states to NATO in 1999 has already contributed to the security, stability and cohesion of the new Europe, just as the EU's steps toward further enlargement have encouraged new democracies to embark upon important political and economic reforms.

These processes must continue. As they do, the integration of each new democracy into the Alliance and the European Union will be a major success towards the realization of the historic chance that the Fall of the Berlin Wall has given to us all.

*

Although Slovenia is under no imminent threat – but to ensure long term security – almost eight years ago the Slovenian Parliament agreed that Slovenia should pursue NATO membership.

I tried to initiate that even earlier. I spoke at the North Atlantic Assembly (now NATO Assembly) meeting just over ten years ago and bared my heart to the NATO parliamentarians by expressing my wish that Slovenia should join NATO. I admit that that was perhaps slightly premature. Slovenia still had not been generally recognized by then.

In the past years we have been actively involved in all the mechanisms developed for closer and closer cooperation with the Alliance within the Partnership for Peace and the Euro Atlantic Partnership Council. We have done a series of rounds of intensified dialogue with NATO.

We have just started our third annual cycle of the Membership Action Plan program introduced for nine aspirant countries at the Washington Summit in April 1999. After the last round of discussions with the Allies I can state that we are doing especially well in the Political, Economic, Security and Legal issues, while there is still room to improve on Defense and Resources issues.

In the area of military readiness we should further improve our defense planning in line with NATO and provide the necessary resources. Our Government plans to do its utmost to show further progress in these two areas, especially by downsizing the wartime strength, building up rapid reaction forces and increasing the defense budget as a percentage of the overall GDP.

Although Slovenia earmarked this year only 1.74% of the GDP for defense, this is an increase over last year's spending and we intend to keep raising the share over the next few years.

However, if we get down to nitty-gritty, in actual dollars spent on defense on the per capita basis, Slovenia is already at the top of the list of the Central European new democracies.

Slovenia also already spends more per troop than four NATO member states.

This is not the only way Slovenia has demonstrated its readiness for NATO membership. Two years ago in the NATO Allied Force campaign (against FRY) Slovenia acted like an Ally by granting NATO, within 24 hours of the request, the use of Slovenian air space. We also helped the effort in other ways that I cannot discuss here.

What we should also work on is to increase public support. Without any major information campaign by the Government we constantly have the bedrock of support of about half the public. While in July the support was at over 56% it dropped after September 11 to 49.7%. A month later it is back over 50%. To show that the support is real, let me mention that during the air campaign against targets in FRY, when Slovenians clearly knew we were acting as Allies and understood the danger, the support never dropped below 50%. However, I believe that the public support should rise to close to 60% and the share of people opposing should drop below 30%.

We can all rest assured that no eventual change of government can influence Slovenia's NATO policy. We have a continuing overall parliamentary consensus, with the opposition coming only from fringe groups.

I am convinced that Slovenia meets all the criteria for NATO membership: 1) it is a functioning democracy; 2) it has democratic civil-military relations; 3) very high treatment of minorities; 4) good relations with neighbors; and 5) can make a significant contribution to the Alliance.

This is not just rhetoric. We have also been sharing the burden of stabilizing South East Europe by providing troops, a third of our Air Force and a medical station to SFOR in Bosnia, officers and civilian police to KFOR in Kosovo, etc.

It is not just troops that we provide. Slovenia, a small country of two million, is, for instance, the largest investor in Bosnia. Our demining program in the Balkans represents 80% of all demining performed.

I believe we know how to take on Allied responsibilities. I always feel funny when I say this, but it is true: we are not asking what NATO can do for us but what *we* can do for NATO.

I am not the only one claiming this. I would like to quote the conclusions of a recent RAND Study on enlargement which in its final assessment on the "long list" of potential NATO members says the following:

"Of the MAP states, Slovenia is the most qualified and attractive candidate for membership from NATO's strategic perspective. The cost of Slovene integration will be virtually nil, and benefits, though small, will be potentially significant in view of NATO's focus on the Balkans."

Of course, the U.S. is not the only Ally. There are 19. We need the support of all of them.

I am always happy to point out that in 1997 at the Sintra ministerial meeting of the Alliance, which took place shortly before the Madrid Summit, the British Government supported the formula "3 plus Slovenia."

Unfortunately things did not turn out that way and in Madrid Slovenia was not invited. At the Washington Summit in 1999 no invitations were issued, in spite of our hope that at least one country could have been invited to demonstrate that there actually existed a credible Open Door Policy.

Now after President Bush's and NATO statements that zero option is off the table for the Prague Summit, we have more hope looking forward to the Summit which will take place in a year's time.

I do expect that candidates, such as Slovenia, will be issued invitations to join the Alliance.

Let me try and close here. I would be happy to answer any questions.

I am glad to see that Manja was not taking any notes. Perhaps I have said something that would have cost me my job.

You know how an ambassador finds out he has been recalled? It is when you get into the back of your car and it doesn't go anywhere!

Thank you.

FROM STAUNCH TO PAUNCH

The following is a toast at the lunch I organized on 15 September 2001 for ambassadors of Membership Action Plan countries with the United Kingdom Permanent Representative on the North Atlantic Council Emyr Jones-Parry. I had known Emyr since my London days where he was very supportive of Slovenia's ambitions. A scientist, he also claimed he had invented the Membership Action Plan. I never knew what the Allies' original intentions were with the MAP, either preparing aspirants for actual NATO membership, or giving them a toy that would put off their demands to receive invitations. God, I mean Emyr, only knew.

Colleagues,

May I just say a few words at the outset. Being the least eloquent of you all I have prepared a few speaking notes.

First of all I am extremely happy to have Ambassador Jones-Parry with us. Both him being an ambassador of an important NATO member country, as well as being a friend. Emyr and I go back a long time, especially if we look at our hair. I can vouch from personal experience Emyr is a friend of our countries.

As you might have noticed it is very hard for me to hide the good time I had in London. I am a convinced Britofile and perhaps there is no better time to demonstrate that then now when the UK clearly demonstrates staunch support for the antiterrorist action. And we are all also both staunch supporters of the action as well as staunch supporters of the transatlantic relationship.

But let me go from staunch to paunch.

Although this is supposed to be a working lunch, I have to admit I was desperately looking for an occasion to invite you here to officially open this room. So, firstly, I hope you will enjoy this lunch here, to where I tried to transplant a part of my residence.

Secondly, we have now, I believe all, produced our Annual National Programs and are faced with SPCR meetings ant the rest of the the annual tour. I hope you have received our executive summary and I look forward to receiving yours.

I sincerely hope that this is the last MAP and that we are invited next year at Prague. We have all progressed tremendously in all the five chapters if we consider the situation at the time of Washington. I hope the decision in Prague is clearcut and the process is identical to the one in Prague. There should be invitations for the countries deemed ready for membership and no »process« as a substitute.

I'm a sailor myself, but have never felt very good in a regatta. However I can always steer my boat from start to finish.

Thank you and bon apetit.

NINE TWELVE 2001

This was the day after 11 September 2001, after I had watched on CNN the World Trade Center Twin Towers in New York City burning. I had sent my staff home besieged with concerns that the NATO HQ, situated right next to the Brussels National Airport, could also be a target. On 9/12, we had an EAPC Ambassadorial meeting that followed the NAC meeting where the Allies had enacted Article 5 of the Washington Treaty. After we were informed of NAC's actions I had, among others, a brief intervention.

Secretary General,

May I just inform that the Government of Slovenia has offered to provide immediate assistance to the United States in the areas where it has significant material and human resources at its disposal, namely in the area of casualties' identification with medical forensic teams, as well as with blood supply.

Thank you.

WALL STREET JOURNAL SHUNNED

I wrote this article (with a little help from a friend who wanted to remain anonymous, but whose style of writing surpasses mine by light years, as evident below) for the Wall Street Journal Europe on the 10th anniversary of Slovenia's independence. It was supposed to be published on June 18, 2001 to mark the 10th Anniversary of Slovenian Independence. Unfortunately, I had to ask the editor, literally plead with him, not to publish it as I had found myself in an "untenable" position. It was either the article or, I believe, my job. There was another article written by my then boss, turned down by the newspaper, for being... well, let me not use the pejorative word. The editor acquiesced to my decision but later complained bitterly to the Prime Minister's Office. And I kept my job.

When George W. Bush met Vladimir Putin on Saturday, they put Slovenia at the top of the news agenda for all the right reasons. The contrast between this occasion and the last time Slovenia was the focus of international media during its independence war could not have been greater and indicates how far my country has come since leaving Yugoslavia almost ten years ago.

Today, Slovenia is a fully-fledged democracy, confident about the future with a growing economy and rising living standards at the level of some European Union member states. It is working hard towards membership of both NATO and the European Union, when these institutions next make it possible for aspiring members to join, and unintentionally acts as an example for other countries which threw off Communism in Eastern Europe, as well as other parts of the former Yugoslavia.

The presence of the world's two most powerful individuals in Ljubljana, the Slovenian capital, was no accident. Both men sought friendly territory for this, their first meeting, and Slovenia, which has excellent political, economic and cultural relations with both countries and no historical hang-ups about either, was a natural venue. Moreover, this summit illustrates how a small country can play an important role in the international arena and occasionally punch above its weight.

However, Slovenia is not neutral territory. The country has shown in the past, including its Resistance Movement against the Nazis during World War II, that it wants to be allied with the West. Slovenia was never part of the Warsaw Pact. One of the first acts of the new democratic Slovenian parliament in 1990 was to offer a medical station to the Coalition during the Gulf War. It was an early but crystal clear message where democratic Slovenia, then still part of the defunct federation, stood. Later, in 1999 in the Allied Force campaign over Kosovo Slovenia immediately granted NATO its air space and helped the Allies in other ways. For Slovenia, a Central European country, located "between Venice and Vienna," the idea of being part of "Europe whole and free" is much more than mere rhetoric.

Slovenia, which has a population of around 2 million, has had to punch consistently above its weight since leaving the former Yugoslavia. When last in the media spotlight ten years ago, the country was a battlefield. Two days after Slovenia declared independence from Yugoslavia, on 25 June 1991, the Yugoslav People's Army moved to crush this aspiration, which was shared by just about the entire population, and hold Yugoslavia together by force, thus triggering the first war in mainland Europe since 1945.

For ten days, as Slovene soldiers defended their country against their former compatriots and European Community foreign ministers and diplomats frantically attempted to mediate an end to hostilities, Slovenia's future hung in the balance. Perhaps inevitably, media images of the conflict portrayed Slovenia as a plucky, little nation determined to stand up for itself, a modern David ready to take on a modern Goliath.

Slovenia's decision to dissociate from Yugoslavia was not taken lightly. Moreover, it was not driven by selfishness or hostility towards the rest of the country to which it had belonged for more than 70 years or towards any of the other peoples of that country, but by the age long aspiration for national self-determination and to join the process of European integration. It was an aspiration which had no chance of being fulfilled as long as democratic Slovenia remained under the control of Communist Belgrade as a result of the rise to power of Slobodan Milošević in Serbia, his drive to create a Greater Serbia and the virtual inevitability of conflict in the country's ethnically mixed republics. By declaring independence Slovenia managed to distance itself from the devastation to come and, at the same time, to align itself politically and economically with Western Europe.

In the heady days following the breaching of the Berlin Wall, as the former Eastern bloc threw off the shackles of communism, the Soviet Union disintegrated and the European Community prepared for the single market of 1992, many Slovenes hoped, even expected, that their country would rapidly be embraced by the West and invited into the major EuroAtlantic institutions. It was not to be and, perhaps inevitably, the way forward has been paved with difficulty. However, every obstacle has proved an opportunity. The lengthy accession process for membership of NATO and the European Union forced Slovenia to go it alone, and has helped build a self-confident, modern national identity.

Formal international recognition came on 15 January 1992, almost seven months after the independence declaration. In the intervening period, Slovenia took charge of its destiny and launched a new currency, the *tolar,* whose value has held up in money markets during the past decade. As war engulfed Croatia and then Bosnia and Herzegovina, the traditional market for Slovene goods in the rest of Yugoslavia disappeared, forcing Slovene businessmen to look elsewhere to sell their wares.

Although Slovenia was able to join NATO's Partnership for Peace program right after its launch in March 1994, the country was unable to purchase the modern weaponry and communication systems necessary for building a modern military because, as part of the former Yugoslavia, it remained under an arms embargo until the Dayton Accord, the agreement ending the Bosnian war, came into force in December 1995. From then on and with special emphasis on it recently is has sought to develop military capabilities to become to an even larger extent a net contributor to Euroatlantic security.

Today, Slovenia is the largest foreign investor in Bosnia and, since the ouster of Slobodan Milošević, has been forging new links with the Federal Republic of Yugoslavia, especially with Serbia, while the democratic government of Montenegro all along had Slovenian support. Very active in the Stability Pact, Slovenia is coordinating mine clearance throughout war-torn regions of the rest of the former Yugoslavia via the Ljubljana-based International Demining Trust Fund, and has taken on a special role for examining and monitoring the rights of minorities. Moreover, Slovenia contributes personnel to both NATO-led operations in the Balkans, the SFOR in Bosnia-Herzegovina and the KFOR in Kosovo, an act of great political courage, given the potential impact of the return of body bags from conflicts which most Slovenes believed they had escaped a decade ago.

Slovenia participates because it believes, in its own way, it can help find and build durable solutions. Moreover, the challenges that confront the Euro-Atlantic area today are challenges that require joint action and it is the responsibility of countries with the relevant expertise and financial means to rise to meet them. Slovenia aspires to join NATO and the European Union to contribute to these communities, not to take from them. It seeks a transparent, level and open playing field for itself and other aspiring members, not subsidies nor assistance. And it wishes to make a habit of being in the news for all the right reasons.

Matjaž Šinkovec is Slovenia's ambassador to NATO. He was head of the Slovene Parliament's Foreign Relations Committee when Slovenia declared independence from Yugoslavia 10 years ago.

CALIFORNIA HIPPIE RETURNS

San Francisco was the last stop on the US speaking tour that I say a bit more about in the following chapter. On April 26 2001 Ambassadors Lazar Comanescu, Peter Burian and I participated in a public lecture at the World Affairs Council of Northern California titled "The Future of NATO: Reshaping a Post-Cold War Europe." The world is small: the lecture was recorded and broadcast on the National Public Radio on July 15, 2001, and heard, among others, by the daughter of my teacher and mentor in the 1970's San Francisco, Patrick Sweeney (check out my book The Magic Mr. Sweeney) – and we reconnected! What is more: A few years later, my friend Kerry King became the COO of the very same World Affairs Council of Northern California! There are actually photographs from the lecture, available on www. nato.int.

Mr Chairman, Ladies and Gentlemen,

It is a great privilege for me to be able to address you tonight. I am especially happy to be back in San Francisco, back in the City where I spent a number of my formative years in the early Seventies, and where I always love coming back to. A former California hippie, now Ambassador to NATO.

If JFK had the right to say what he said in Berlin four decades ago, I do have every right to proudly say: "I am a San Franciscan."

How things change. It was here in the City, in the Bay Area, that I learned a lot about pluralism, democracy, liberty, tolerance. It all served me well when I returned home to Slovenia and did my little bit for the emancipation of my country, a nation that only after 14 hundred years of subjugation reached its full-fledged statehood, ten years ago in June.

Throughout our history our territory was of interest to more or less distant neighbors. While this is good news in the times of peace for trade and tourism, there were times in history when we had our share of problems. In World War One hundreds of thousands of soldiers died on the Soča/Isonzo front and in World War Two we were invaded and partitioned among our neighbors.

We learnt from this not only the importance of defense Alliances – we were Allies during World War 2, with US and British military missions located at our Resistance headquarters – but also of building stability.

That is why when Slovenians finally had a chance to voice what sort of a country we wanted to build and what we wanted our immediate and wider neighborhood to look like, we not only opted for democracy and independence but also for wider Euro-Atlantic integration, building Europe whole and free.

While I lobbied abroad in the late Eighties and early Nineties, first for the understanding of what the Slovenian Democratic Opposition wanted to do and then after the first free elections and the successful popularly based move to independence, for the recognition of Slovenia, I was often asked by people abroad why Slovenia was separating from the former Federation while the rest of Europe was integrating.

I dared to point out the fact that you can only integrate if you are free to decide your destiny on your own and not be forcibly integrated by someone else. We have known totalitarian attempts in the past to integrate Europe by force. What we wanted was to freely integrate ourselves into democratic Alliances. There was a great difference for democratic Slovenians between democratic Brussels and communist Belgrade.

In the past ten years Slovenia has achieved remarkable progress. We have good relations with the neighbors and have fully entered the international community and its international organizations. Our negotiations on the membership in the European Union are proceeding so well that we should be ready to sign the Treaty by the end of next year.

Our economy, if you consider the per capita income, is on a par with EU member states such as Greece or Portugal. The economic outlook is optimistic, with low inflation for Central European standards, stable growth and falling unemployment.

When talking about the EU and NATO we do not have an either/or but an and/and policy. Slovenia has no problem with this dilemma. Slovenia should be a member of both by 2004. We also very much see the importance of the transatlantic connection and do not want the European Security and Defense Policy to be an instrument of separation, but of cooperation.

The EU and NATO are the two institutional pillars of the Euro-Atlantic area. They have played a key role in the transition of new democracies and the integration of Europe. NATO will remain the core of transatlantic security and European stability and the security dimension of the EU will serve to reinforce NATO's capability. These complementary and mutually reinforcing institutions represent the foundation of the Euro-Atlantic community and constitute the security framework on which our nations rely. The addition of three Central European states to NATO in 1999 has already contributed to the security, stability and cohesion of the new Europe, just as the EU's steps toward further enlargement have encouraged new democracies to embark on important political ad economic reforms.

These processes must continue. As they do, the integration of each new democracy into the Alliance and the European Union will be a major success towards the realisation of the historic chance that the Fall of the Berlin Wall has given to us all.

I am not sure how much the following view is understood here in the U.S., but I am sure that most if not all applicant countries are the best European friends of the U.S. and NATO. We have not forgotten that it was the transatlantic link that has made it possible for the captive nations of Europe to liberate themselves.

Although Slovenia is under no threat – but to ensure long term security, over seven years ago the Slovenian Parliament agreed to pursue NATO membership for Slovenia. Since then we have been actively involved in all the mechanisms developed for closer and closer cooperation with the Alliance.

Now we are close to completing our second annual cycle of the Membership Action Plan program introduced for nine aspirant countries at the Washington Summit two years ago. After the last round of discussions with the Allies I can state that we are doing especially well in the Political, Economic, Security and Legal issues, while there is still is room to improve on Defense and Resources issues.

Not to beat around the bush, this means that we should further improve our defense planning in line with NATO and provide the necessary resources. Our Government plans to do its utmost to show further progress in these two areas, especially by downsizing the war-time strength, building up rapid reaction forces and increasing the defense budget as a percentage of the overall GDP.

Although Slovenia earmarked this year only 1.45% of the GDP for defense, this is an increase over last year's spending and we intend to reach over 2% in a few years. However if we get down to nitty gritty, in actual dollars spent on defense on the per capita basis, Slovenia is at the top of the list off the Central European new democracies. Slovenia also already spends more per troop than 4 NATO member states.

This is not the only way Slovenia has shown its readiness for NATO membership. Two years ago in the NATO Allied Force campaign (against FRY) Slovenia acted like an Ally by granting NATO, within 24 hours of the request, the use of Slovenian air space.

The public support for NATO membership has been stable, between 50 & 60%, even during the air campaign. We have a continuing overall parliamentary consensus, with the opposition coming only from fringe groups.

We have clear evidence that the mere prospect of membership has moved us faster towards becoming a fully Western-style nation. We believe that Slovenia meets all the criteria for NATO membership: 1) it is a functioning democracy, 2) it has democratic civil-military relations, 3) very high treatment of minorities, 4) good relations with neighbors, and 5) can make a significant contribution to the Alliance.

This is not just rhetoric. We have also been sharing the burden of stabilizing South East Europe by providing troops, a third of our airforce and a medical station to SFOR in Bosnia, officers and civilian police to KFOR in Kosovo, etc. Slovenia, a country of 2 million, is also the largest investor in Bosnia.

I believe we know how to take on Allied responsibilities. It is corny but true when I say that we are asking what we can do for NATO, not what NATO can do for us.

- THE US Congress in 1996 in its NATO Enlargement Facilitation Act included Slovenia among the first four candidates to enter NATO, together with the Czech Republic, Hungary and Poland.
- Senator Roth in his Presidential Report to the North Atlantic Assembly stated in 1998: "That at the Washington Summit, Slovenia should be invited to begin negotiations aimed at accession to the North Atlantic Treaty."
- The same year the North Atlantic Assembly passed a resolution which urged the Allies to invite Slovenia and any other European democracies that have met the criteria for NATO membership.
- To cut this short I would just like to quote the conclusions of a recent RAND Study on enlargement which in its final assessment on the "long list" of potential NATO members says the following:
- Quote "Of the MAP states, Slovenia is the most qualified and attractive candidate for membership from NATO's strategic perspective. The cost of Slovene integration will be virtually nil, and benefits, though small, will be potentially significant in view of NATO's focus on the Balkans." End Quote.

As 17 US senators wrote in a letter to President Bush 3 weeks ago: It is in America's strategic interest that the process of NATO enlargement continues. They urged that NATO enlargement should become an early priority of the Administration.

I would like to close by saying that it is very important that the US starts the enlargement debate. The rest of NATO member states will follow.

And I do expect that at the Prague NATO Summit next year credible candidates, such as Slovenia, are issued invitations to join the Alliance.

Thank you.

WILSONIAN DOCRINE
AND SLOVENIA

While on a NATO organized and sponsored speakers' tour I had, together with the NATO ambassadors of the Czech Republic, Romania and Slovakia, the opportunity to present my song and dance at Princeton University on April 24 2001. It was done in the framework of the Woodrow Wilson School of Public and International Affairs panel discussion on "NATO Enlargement and the Future of Europe: Views from the Eastern Front." We also went to Washington, DC, New York City, Chicago, San Francisco and Stanford.

Mr Chairman, Ladies and Gentlemen,

It is a great privilege for me to be able to address you in the context of this public lecture together with my colleagues and friends from other Missions to NATO. Both the name of Princeton and Woodrow Wilson inspire awe.

Woodrow Wilson's name is not unrelated to the Slovenian history, a nation that after 14 hundred years of subjugation, only reached its full-fledged statehood ten years ago in June. Slovenia had a chance on the basis of Woodrow Wilson's 10th point (of 8 January, 1918) to achieve that much earlier, at the end of World War I, but our self-determination at the time slipped through our fingers.

This does not of course mean that we only got involved in the international life a decade ago. Slovenia in different shapes and under various forms of domination, as well as Slovenian individuals, played their part in shaping today's world, and especially Europe.

Being here in the States I should perhaps just mention that Thomas Jefferson when drafting the Declaration of Independence consulted among other studies a book on how Slovenians freely elected their dukes from the 7th century onward. While we might have inspired with our early democratic experience the Americans to some extent ages ago, you did definitely inspire us especially in the late Eighties in our movement to make Slovenia free – meaning both democratic and independent.

Being from a small and not well known country my presentation perhaps requires just a few titbits of otherwise superfluous information on where the heck Slovenia lies and what it's all about.

Slovenia is 8000 square miles large, or rather small (the size of a New England state) tucked away in between Italy, Austria, Hungary, Croatia and a bit of the Adriatic Sea. This makes it a mixture of Alpine, Mediterranean and Continental landscapes, climates and culture as well. It is a Central European State bordering on South East Europe.

While ten years ago we all heard a lot about Central Europe we now hear a lot about South East Europe. So life for Slovenians should not be boring. Also, throughout our history our territory was of interest to more or less distant neighbors. While this is good news in the times of peace for trade and tourism, there were times in history when we had our share of problems. In World War One a few hundred thousand soldiers died on the Soča/Isonzo front (with Ernest Hemingway observing) and in World War Two we were invaded and partitioned among the four neighbors.

We learnt from this not only the importance of defense Alliances – we were Allies during World War Two, with US and British military missions located at our Resistance headquarters – but also of building stability.

That is why when Slovenians finally had a chance to voice what sort of a country they wanted to build and what they wanted their closer and wider neighborhood to look like they not only opted for democracy and independence but also for wider Euro-Atlantic integration.

While I lobbied in the late Eighties and early Nineties – first for the understanding of what the Slovenian Democratic Opposition wanted to, do and then after the first free elections and the successful popularly based move to independence, for the recognition of Slovenia – I was often asked by people abroad why Slovenia was separating from the former Federation while the rest of Europe was integrating.

I dared to point to the fact that you can only integrate if you are free to decide your destiny on your own and not be forcibly integrated by someone else. We have known totalitarian attempts in the past to integrate Europe by force. What we wanted was to freely integrate ourselves into democratic Alliances. There was a great difference for democratic Slovenians between democratic Brussels and communist Belgrade.

It was just over 10 years ago, Slovenia still being part of the former Yugoslavia, when I proposed that Slovenia should join NATO. It was sheer madness, I guess, at the time, but I believe we all share the view that both Slovenia and NATO have changed to the point where this is not such a far fetched idea any longer.

In the past ten years Slovenia has achieved remarkable progress. We have good relations with the neighbors and fully entered the international community and its international organisations, even having served on the UN Security Council for two years. Our negotiations on the membership in the European Union are proceeding so well that we should be ready to sign the Treaty by the end of next year.

Our economy, if you consider the per capita income, is on a par with EU member states such as Greece or Portugal and higher than in the other EU or NATO Central European applicant countries. The economic outlook is optimistic, with low inflation for Central European standards, stable growth and falling unemployment.

When talking about the EU and NATO we don't have an either/or but an and/and policy. Slovenia has no problem with this dilemma and should be a member of both by the year 2004. We also very much see the importance of the transatlantic connection and do not want the European Common Security and Defense Policy to be an instrument of separation, but cooperation.

I am not sure how much the following view is understood here in the U.S., but I am positively sure that most if not all applicant countries, as well as the three least old member countries, are the best European friends of the U.S. and NATO. We have not forgotten that it was the transatlantic link that has made it possible for the captive nations of Europe to liberate themselves.

Over seven years ago the Slovenian Parliament agreed to pursue NATO membership for Slovenia. Since then we have been actively involved in all the mechanisms developed for closer and closer cooperation with the Alliance within the Partnership for Peace and the Euroatlantic Partnership Council. After the last round of discussions with the Allies I can state that we are doing especially well in the Political and Economic issues, Security issues and Legal issues, while there is still plenty of room to improve on Defense and Resources issues.

Not to beat around the bush this means that we should further improve our defense planning in line with NATO's and provide the necessary resources. Our Government will do its utmost to show further progress in these two areas, especially by down-sizing the war-time strenght, building up rapid reaction forces and increasing the defense budget as a percentage of the overall GDP.

Although Slovenia earmarked this year only 1.45% of the GDP for defense this is an increase over last year's spending and we intend to reach over 2% in a few years. However if we get down to nitty gritty, in actual dollars spent on defense on the per capita basis Slovenia is at the top of the list of all the Central European new democracies ($ 145). Slovenia also spends more per troop than 4 NATO member states and approximates Greek spending levels.

This is not the only way Slovenia has shown its readiness for NATO membership. Two years ago in the NATO Allied Force campaign (against FRY) Slovenia acted like an Ally by granting NATO, within 24 hours of the request, the use of its air space. We were the only partner country that did not put any conditions upon the use of its air space.

The public support for NATO membership has been stable, the only dip showed in the beginning of the year on account of the Depleted Uranium scare. Otherwise the support has been over 50%, even during the before mentioned air campaign. We have a continuing overall parliamentary consensus, with the opposition coming only from fringe groups.

The experience of the past two years' involvement in the Membership Action Plan has shown that Slovenia has managed to speed up a number of reforms not only in the defense area but also in the area of modernising legislation, speeding up the denationalisation process etc. We have clear evidence that the mere prospect of membership has moved us faster towards becoming a fully Western-style nation.

We believe that Slovenia meets all the criteria for NATO membership: 1) it is a functioning democracy, 2) it has democratic civil-military relations, 3) very high treatment of minorities, 4) good relations with neighbors, and 5) can make a significant contribution to the Alliance.

This is not just rhetoric. We have also been sharing the burden of stabilizing South East Europe by providing troops, a third of our airforce and a medical station to SFOR in Bosnia, officers and civilian police to KFOR in Kosovo. It is not just troops that we provide. Slovenia, a country of 2 million, is, for instance, the largest investor in Bosnia.

As I am just a diplomat, who supposedly has to lie for his country, perhaps I should just list a few undisputed facts here:

- The US Congress in 1996 in its NATO Enlargement Facilitation Act included Slovenia among the first four candidates to enter NATO, together with the Czech Republic, Hungary and Poland.
- Senator Roth in his Presidential Report to the North Atlantic Assembly stated in 1998: "That at the Washington Summit, Slovenia should be invited to begin negotiations aimed at accession to the North Atlantic Treaty."
- The same year the North Atlantic Assembly passed a resolution which urged the Allies to invite Slovenia and any other European democracies that have met the criteria for NATO membership.
- Slovenia has been mentioned both by the Madrid and Washington Summit Declarations as a leading NATO candidate.
- To cut this short I would just like to quote the conclusions of the recent RAND Study on enlargement which in its final assessment on the "long list" of potential NATO members says the following: "Of the MAP states, Slovenia is the most qualified and attractive candidate for membership from NATO's strategic perspective. The cost of Slovene integration will be virtually nil, and benefits, though small, will be potentially significant in view of NATO's focus on the Balkans."

I do not want to overdo this. But to me the best example of America's acceptance that a country has reached the right standards is when its citizens do not need visas to enter the U.S. any longer. I am glad Slovenia, as the only former communist country, reached that goal already a few years ago.

Thank you.

THE PERSISTENCE OF VISION

Keith Miles, Chair of the British Slovene Society in London, invited me to deliver a speech at their annual gathering to celebrate the greatest Slovenian Poet, France Prešeren. I have remained a patron of the Society since then. I drove up from Brussels with my wife, reminding myself of the wonders of driving on the left hand side of the road. I forget the exact date but it must have been a Saturday in early February 2001. The venue: my old stomping ground when I was Ambassador there 1992-1997: the Houses of Parliament. The title goes hand-in-hand with my story "The Persistence of Vision" in my alrerady mentioned collection of short stories "Love."

Chairman, John, Ambassador, dear friends,

It's nice to be back in London, nice to be among old friends, both from the UK as well as Slovenia.

And I'm proud to wear the PRO PATRIA medal presented to me on your behalf at the Foreign and Commonwealth Office by lord Howe, former Foreign Secretary.

I decided a while back nothing can keep me away from this celebration any longer. But I just wanted to see old friends, Keith and Slava Miles, Marjan and Shirley Keček, Željka and Ian Charles Jones, Borut Žunič and too many others to mention them all.

But Keith asked me to say a few words (actually he gave me 5 minutes) and so I have to do something. However I decided not to do my usual song and dance. I will talk about the persistence of vision. And my 5 minutes will drag on a little bit.

Last time I spoke to you was 4 years ago when I dedicated my address to our NATO ambitions. Funny that now I ended up in Brussels doing the NATO job for Slovenia.

Tonight I would like to say a few words about a subject that is not far removed from the phenomenon of Prešeren. It is about individuals whose dreams and persistence of vision result in common good.

Prešeren is a good example. One sole person who because of his own initiative did an enormous job for Slovenia, for all of our generations of the past two centuries. And I expect for centuries to come.

I've heard a lot of horse manure about how and why Slovenia became independent. Somehow it seems we listen more to people who know nothing about it, were never there, or if they were, they either opposed the whole process or did not lift a finger in favor.

I believe it all happened because of individuals who believed in democracy and freedom. They believed it was the natural right of Slovenes to be free as it was the right of any other people in the world.

As Prešeren would say it, *LESS FEARFUL THE LONG NIGHT OF LIFE's DENIAL/THAN LIVING 'NEATH THE SUN IN SUBJUGATION.*

I am glad many of these people are here tonight with us. They all contributed to this process because they believed in a dream and had a persistence of vision.

Of course in spite of all the vision and resolve we also had our doubts. In Prešeren's words: *IF A SEED WILL ONE DAY SPROUT, WHY, HE WHO SOWS IT DOES NOT KNOW.*

However, so many little, unknown people contributed so much and not just recently. For instance, my parents were imprisoned, sent for hard labour, faced death, survived, while both having a dream of a free Slovenia. They never saw it come, but I know they had the vision.

I did my little bit.

I first got in trouble with the police in 1968 when I protested – prematurely – before it was blessed at the top - against the occupation of Czechoslovakia. In 1970 when I was in high school I was caught red handed with a leaflet promoting political pluralism and turning the country into a confederation. I was questioned by the police. In 1988, with a few collegues, I was a founding member of a party that promoted democracy and independence. I was followed, my phone was tapped. In 1989 I proposed the formation of an opposition coalition, later also proposed a funny name for it, DEMOS, and it somehow won the first free elections.

And the rest is history.

Because of the persistence of vision of a great many little people.

And so many of them are gathered here tonight. You did your own bit in many ways.

It was not Milošević who caused Slovenia to become independent. It was not our selfishness. No deal was made with anyone. It was no great historical force. It was just you and me, people with dreams and the persistence of vision.

Perhaps I should end here but I would like to say one thing.

Lately, more than ever, not really outside of Slovenia, but especially inside, doubts about the events of 10 years ago have been raised. Doubts about the path we took. I will not elaborate too much, our foreign minister Dimitrij Rupel wrote an captivating article about that.

I've been following closely the utterings of these doubting Thomases. But it is the same people who opposed us a decade ago. The same people who laughed at you when you protested in Trafalgar Square.

I'm not particularly worried because they are just people without any vision. It is the people who are not comfortable living in a free society without their masters and puppeteers.

And these same people oppose Slovenia's entry into the EU and NATO. Well, I had to come to it. If people without vision oppose the choices Slovenians have made through their freely elected bodies, than I'm definitely not worried about our chances.

Of course, to achieve these goals which will ensure long term stable and safe future for Slovenia, it will take a lot more work, and, excuse me to say it one more time, persistence of vision.

Until, as Prešeren wrote, *ALL WILL BE/KINFOLK FREE/WITH NEIGHBOURS NONE IN ENMITY.*

Thank you.

PUT ENLARGEMENT
ON THE AGENDA!

This is one of my typical relatively short interventions at an EAPC Ambassadorial, delivered on 29 November 2000.

Secretary General,

I would just like to mention that we followed the NATO Parliamentary Assembly's Berlin session with great interest.

We welcome the draft resolution passed by the Political Committee on further NATO enlargement. We were encouraged by the bold language, proposing that the NATO Parliamentary Assembly calls upon the North Atlantic Council to issue no later than during its Summit meeeting in 2002 invitations to NATO accession negotiations to Slovenia, Slovakia and Lithuania, and any other European democracy that seeks membership in the Alliance and that has met the criteria for NATO membership as established in the Alliance's 1995 Study on NATO enlargement.

We hope that by next spring, after the Subcommittee on Enlargement visits the aspirant countries, the adoption of such a resolution by the Parliamentary Assembly itself is made possible. It will be high time that the question of Enlargement is put higher on NATO's agenda

Thank you.

MUSIC TO LORD ROBERTSON'S EARS

I wrote the text below to be used by Janez Janša, Slovenian Minister of Defense, and he delivered it at the EAPC In Defense Ministers' Session, June 9, 2000. It was his second stint as Slovenia's Defense Minister. I had been disgusted by the original speech written by the people at the MOD. Janša liked my version, but excluded the proposed fifth paragraph that said "We expect that by the time of the NATO Summit of 2002 the Allies will recognise this fact by inviting Slovenia to join its ranks." Before the session I "warned" Janša that the speech contained two issues (the contribution of a police platoon to UNMIK and Slovenia's announcement that it will contribute to the EU "Headline Goal") that needed to be decided by the Government. From my office he called Prime Minister Bajuk and "cleared" it with him (well, I knew who was actually in charge of the Government). Lord Robertson commented the offered UNMIK contribution as "music to my ears..." Janša skipped my proposed sentence: "My Government shall ensure that a high priority is given to them in our national force plans, and that resources are allocated as necessary," at the end of the penultimate paragraph. Both exclusions appear below in italics.

Lord Robertson, Ladies and Gentlemen,

It is a pleasure for me to join you this morning for this, my initial, Euro-Atlantic Partnership Council in Defense Ministers session, in my new capacity as the Defense Minister of the Republic of Slovenia.

May I use this opportunity to briefly stake out the policy of the new Government on Slovenia's accession to NATO. Membership in the Alliance is one of the two top priorities of the Government, based on a strong and binding cross-party parliamentary support. May I also underline that the parties forming the coalition have had a long track record of support for Slovenia's NATO membership.

While we have built a powerful partnership with the Alliance, which has contributed to Slovenia's growing role in conflict prevention and crisis management, that has been clearly demonstrated mostly in our neighbourhood to the South East, especially in Bosnia-Herzegovina and Kosovo, partnership as a long-term proposition is not enough to us. It is a pleasure that I can announce today that Slovenia will contribute a police platoon to UNMIK in Kosovo.

My Government will make an extra push, on the basis of what has already been done, to transform our armed forces so that they can play their full part in contributing to the collective defence of the Alliance. While Slovenia has already clearly shown by our concrete support for the Allied Force campaign that we understand how to take on Allied responsibilities in crisis management, the new Government will introduce a number of further initiatives to make Slovenia an even greater contributor to overall Euro-Atlantic security.

We expect that by the time of the NATO Summit of 2002 the Allies will recognise this fact by inviting Slovenia to join their ranks.

Let me now shortly address reports which are to be endorsed or noted today. We highly value the progress made since the Washington Summit in implementing initiatives regarding ways how to enhance Partnership for Peace and make it more operational. Given the importance of these initiatives and a potential payoff they could have on the overall interoperability of Partner forces with those of the Alliance in the ongoing operations, we support their further development to the point where detailed analysis of the resource implications becomes possible. It is at this point when we will be able to assess, plan, and commit national resources needed in support of more structured and more effective participation of our forces in NATO-led Peace Support Operations. I would like to mention in this framework, that Slovenia will also announce shortly its offer to contribute to the EU Headline Goal.

In this regard I would also like to support 2000 Partnership Goals Summary Report. For Slovenia, as an aspirant for full-fledged Alliance's membership, many of 2000 Partnership Goals represent demanding but achievable force planing targets which take account of the requirements implicit in future collective defence guarantees. *My Government shall ensure that a high priority is given to them in our national force plans, and that resources are allocated as necessary.*

Last but not least, I would also like to highlight the importance we attach to the full implementation of the Political Military Framework for NATO-led PfP operations. We think that the recent analysis proposed on increased Partner involvement is the right way ahead and we would like to encourage NATO to press ahead with the implementation of these proposals.

Thank you for your attention.

NO SUCH THING AS A FREE LUNCH

I first met George Robertson when he was Labor Party's Spokesman on Foreign Affairs. That was in March 1991, before Slovenia's independence. We kept in touch when I arrived in London in April 1992 as Slovenia's first Ambassador there and he was Shadow Secretary of State for Scotland. Then in 1997, the Labor Party won the elections and George became the Secretary of Defense. In 1999, after I had already arrived in Brussels, he became the new Secretary General of NATO, as a Baron, his title reading nowadays The Rt Hon. the Lord Robertson of Port Ellen, KT, GCMG, PC, FRSA, FRSE, I believe. We may not have agreed on everything in the past quarter of a century but I like him, he is a friend, and we keep in touch. Here are my "words of welcome" at the lunch I organized on 22 November 1999 in Brussels for NATO Aspirants' Ambassadors with George Robertson as the guest of honor.

Mylord,

It is an honor and pleasure to have you here with us. This is an informal setting and I have no intention to use it to present a common agenda.

Yet, we all represent countries that see themselves as future NATO Allies. Some of us have even had a chance to clearly demonstrate that we already feel and can act as Allies. That was in NATO's Allied Force operation where we showed clearly where we stood. We were definitely not neutral.

Just over two years ago, you and I met in a similar setting, where you as British Defense Secretary joined me and my Central European colleagues at a lunch in London. That was also an informal meeting but it is still remembered as I was reminded by some former colleagues of mine back in October in London at the Chatham House Conference on NATO.

I have no ambition to have everyone here remember this very lunch.

Yet one thing that I remember from the London lunch is that at the time we were a homogenous group, where all the countries had a similar international position. Today three of those countries have already joined NATO and five are negotiating EU membership. Perhaps when we look back in a few years, we will see how individual countries around this table achieved further progress in their Euro-Atlantic integration. Whoever it might be to join NATO first, it should be regarded as a success for everyone, just like we all welcomed the NATO accession of the latest three members.

Bon appétit.

CHATHAM HOUSE CALLING

I got invited during my tenure of Ambassador to NATO in Brussels by Chatham House, officially the Royal Institute of International Affairs, that I had once been a member of when ambassador to the Court of St James's, to a high level conference in London. The conference "NATO – Development in Partnership: Engagement and Advancement after 2000" meeting was attended, as far as I remember, both by former NATO SecGen Lord Carrington, who I knew very well from the times of the Conference on Yugoslavia in The Hague that he had chaired and I had been Slovenia's negotiator, as well as by George Robertson, who I first met a few months prior to Slovenia's Declaration of Independence, trying to sell to him the idea of Slovenia going on its own. Back in 1991, he did not quite accept my views, to say the least, but we remained in touch and eventually became friends during my long stint in London from 1992 to 1997. The following is the official version of my contribution, the *ad verbatim* probably was a bit less serious at some points.

Chairman, Mylord, Ladies and Gentlemen,

It is an honour to be invited to present Slovenia's and my own views on this occasion, especially following with my modest contribution the excellent presentations of Dr Karkoszka as well as Professors Pick and Pascu.

It is also a great pleasure to be back in London where I served for half a dozen years as Slovenia's first ambassador to the Court of St James's. I am glad to see that the Royal Institute of International Affairs is still very much a leading institution in the area of foreign and security policy.

I am especially happy that today we have at the conference Lord Carrington with whom I had the honour, among others, to negotiate on Slovenia's s recognition in the autumn of 91, and Lord Robertson, with whom I had the honour to discuss Slovenia's future Euroatlantic integration even before our independence in the spring of '91.

What I intend to do is to use a number of issues discussed by Dr Karkoszka as the starting point for presenting Slovenia's case, Slovenia being, as I see it, one of the front runners for NATO's next round of enlargement, if and when it will take place.

*

1. Dr Karkoszka first speaks about the ability or rather inability of the new NATO members to contribute to Alliance's common defence and joint Non Article 5 activities.

When Slovenia failed to be invited to join NATO back in Madrid in 1997, or perhaps I should say, when NATO failed to invite Slovenia, the Government, supported by the Parliament, decided that Slovenia would attempt to follow the 3 new members in their processes of fundamental restructuring and modernising of their armed forces in order to make the Slovenian armed forces as compatible with NATO requirements as those of the new members.

The basic difference that comes to mind first, in comparison with the new members, stems from the fact that Slovenia started building its armed forces from scratch and did not inherit any Soviet-style armed forces, having been formerly part of the non-aligned world.

However there seem to be more similarities than first meet the eye. That's why we also have to talk about stopping the technological decay of the weapons and equipment inherited, adopting Alliance standards and coping with the future tasks as an Alliance member.

As Lord Robertson said in Toronto: "The peace dividend has already been taken. That day is over. We don't live in a peaceful world anymore. Military cuts triggered by the end of the Cold War must stop because the world is still a very dangerous place." We should raise our military capabilities on an even higher level but with different, smaller and more efficient armed forces. That is even truer of NATO aspirant countries.

Our fundamental objective in the area of defence and military issues is to provide military capabilities for the execution of collective defence and the implementation of new NATO missions. In order to develop its defence system and armed forces, Slovenia is improving its military capabilities and will, as a NATO member state, contribute to the increase of its capabilities designated for mission accomplishment. Through the activities conducted in the areas of defence and the military, Slovenia is preparing for the implementation of NATO related missions, the taking on of risks in co-operation with other members, and assuming its share of responsibility as a NATO member state.

In the development of capabilities required by their participation within the Alliance the Slovenian Armed Forces are giving special emphasis to the provision of logistic support for rapid reaction forces, the training of logistic personnel for their participation in NATO-led PfP operations and the organisation of host nation support. Through preparations for the C4 system development and the procurement of modern communication equipment force command and control in terms of compliance with NATO standards has also seen tremendous improvement.

Slovenia is going to integrate the Defence Capabilities Initiative adopted in Washington into the process of establishing its own capabilities. Given the importance of efficient capabilities, especially in the implementation of Non-Article V missions and out-of-area operations, Slovenia is paying special attention to the attainment of interoperability levels for its own forces. The focus of preparations will be linked to NATO doctrine.

Through our active involvement in the PARP process, which resembles NATO Force Planning process, and our short, medium and long-term plans we are heading towards modern Armed Forces suitable for operating together with those of the Alliance.

Perhaps what I have just listed sounds at times as wishful thinking but it is soundly based on the Government's National Strategy for Slovenia's membership in NATO, adopted in February 98, and the MAP document which is supposed to be adopted this very day.

The National Strategy was a de facto Slovenian Membership Action Plan, even though it preceded the Washington Summit NATO decision, which required the »aspirant countries« to prepare such a plan, by over a year.

What is perhaps more important is that it is all based upon Slovenia's sound economy, Slovenia not only still being the most developed Central European country, but also an economy experiencing constant growth. That is why Slovenia is probably spending on the per capita basis more on defence than any other country of the region.

Slovenia enjoys a strong rate of growth of around 4% and the highest GDP per capita for Central Europe – of around 10.000 US$ with an inflation rate around 6% and unemployment of around 7%.

All of this adds up to a healthy economic outlook that will ensure that Slovenia will not be a financial burden for the Alliance, but on the contrary, will be a net contributor, if and when it is invited to accede.

In short, we can foot the bill.

Slovenia has a vested interest in the successful integration of the 3 new members in the Alliance. It is not only because of our goodwill, but because we see that their success is in direct relation to the Allies' willingness to extend membership to other qualified European democracies.

*

2. In the second topic of his paper Dr Karkoszka touches also upon the future of the Alliance, the validity of the defence functions and uncertainties and instabilities in South Eastern Europe.

This is in direct relation to the reasons why the aspirant countries are still lining up in front of NATO's door. Indeed, why join NATO?

For Slovenia it is definitely not due to any impending threat to our security or sovereignty, but rather, because we see joining NATO, as well as the European Union, as a means of consolidating our international position. Joining NATO will not only ensure Slovenia's national security, but will also provide us with the opportunity to contribute more substantially to security and stability regionally and in Europe as a whole.

Although Slovenia does not feel threatened, it lies close enough to an unstable region of the Western Balkans, to have concerns about the possible impact of continuing instability there. Although we have not been directly affected, and certainly do not envisage any spill-over, being well entrenched in Central Europe, there has been certain fallout – refugees, loss of business etc. from the continuing stream of crises in the area.

In our building relationship with the Alliance Slovenia is offering our knowledge, stemming from the historical experiences with the states of the area, as well as our energy and our resources.

In a similar way that the new member states can contribute greatly to the development of relations with Russia, Slovenia has all the assets to contribute substantially to the efforts of the international community in South Eastern Europe.

We have already shown our firm commitment to security and stability in the area. May I point out that Slovenia has fully supported NATO 's role in resolving the crisis in Kosovo. A year ago Slovenia granted its air space to NATO for air operations over FRY within 24 hours, without posing any conditions or limitations upon NATO. It was the first non-NATO member country to do so.

In the Allied Force air campaign Slovenia was not neutral and not just a partner. By contributing its air space and doing other things for NATO it was an Ally and it demonstrated it was ready to take on further allied responsibilities. The Slovenian population understood our role there, which is demonstrated by the fact that the most recent public opinion polls show an increase in public support for Slovenia's membership in the Alliance, which stands now at 57%. Even during the campaign itself the percentage never dropped below 50%.

That was definitely not the whole scope of Slovenia's involvement in South Eastern Europe. We have been and are active in the area in several ways. What especially counts is that we are present there with trade and investments. We do over 2 billion US dollars of business annually with the Western Balkans and have been in the past one of the major investors. We intend to continue playing such a role.

In the Stability Pact, as well as the Consultative Forum and the EAPC Ad-Hoc Working Group on South Eastern Europe, we intend to play an active, energetic role, starting in the areas of demining and regional reduction of small arms, and not just rhetoric. And we could play a role model for all those countries that want to proceed towards Euro-Atlantic integration. For instance, our high level of minority rights protection can hardly be surpassed anywhere in Europe or elsewhere.

At the time of the Washington Summit it was often said that the Kosovo issue dominated the meeting and prevented any serious discussion of invitations.

But the Kosovo issue could have worked in quite the opposite way.

The Alliance could have taken a bold position and realised that to show that it wants to project stability into the region it should invite Slovenia to join up. This would have shown to the troubled region, especially the FRY, that there is »light at the end of the tunnel« and that if they commit themselves to achieving Western values, they too, could one day join the Euro-Atlantic integration.

*

3. I agree with Dr Karkoszka's views of the future relationship and role of the new members towards Russia, as well as Ukraine. A number of aspirant countries, when they do become members will be in a similar position, while the whole process of the Baltic states' accession will be a litmus test of Russia's relations with Euro-Atlantic organizations.

In this sense Slovenia has a different position as it has experienced quite different history throughout a significant part of this century than the 3 new member states. While it cannot play a similar role towards Russia, at the same time Slovenia's accession should not put any further strains upon NATO's relations with her.

Russia has never publicly opposed Slovenia's membership. Also, Slovenia's inclusion would definitely not move NATO's borders towards Russia, but would rather enable its territorial contiguity and strengthen its southern flank.

*

4. On Dr Karkoszka's fourth point, the question of further enlargement, the aspirant countries do expect the new NATO members to keep the issue at the top of the agenda of the Alliance.

Increasing the Alliance's membership does represent widening the area of stability, but only if the new invitees fulfil the necessary standards in the political, economic and military fields. And this is in the direct interest of the future entrants. I do not believe that the aspirant countries would be interested in joining a weaker NATO, NATO with diminished efficiency, cohesion and credibility. At the same time NATO should not raise the entry criteria.

As far as Slovenia is concerned we have been assessed several times by the Allies as fulfilling the entry criteria. Slovenia's membership in NATO is not a divisive issue for the Alliance. No member country has ever opposed Slovenia's membership. It is indicative that the US Congress in its NATO Enlargement Facilitation Act, passed in 1996, included Slovenia among the first four entrants into NATO, together with the Czech Republic, Hungary and Poland.

Still, we intend to fully and energetically take part in the Membership Action Plan. We want to use it as a mechanism of improving even further and faster, and not as a set of new criteria for membership.

And as I see it, the MAP process has turned the accession process upside down, by requiring the aspirant countries to embark upon activities that the new members faced after having been invited.

By following this logic, set by the Alliance, the accession process for the future invitees should be quicker and perhaps less painful than for the three new members.

In Slovenia we believe that each country should be judged on its own merits.

NATO should pace, not pause, the process of its enlargement, as recently proposed by Senators Roth and Lugar, by extending an invitation of membership to those states able to meet the guidelines established by the 1995 NATO Study on Enlargement and should do so on a country-by-country basis. President Clinton said that Slovenia is an excellent candidate.

As I see it, perhaps we might not become an excellent member, but not a below average one either.

If the Alliance follows at its next opportunity its declared policies from the Washington Summit, then, I am sure, Slovenia will be invited to join up, as we believe, by slightly paraphrasing Washington, »the inclusion of Slovenia would serve the overall political and strategic interests of the Alliance, strengthen its effectiveness and cohesion, and enhance overall European security and stability.«

Being an Ally is nothing new to us. We were an Ally in World War II and were never a NATO adversary.

The mistake of not having invited Slovenia sooner, as put by Professor Pick today, should be rectified.

*

5. Point five. The Future members of NATO and the European Union want to participate fully in the integration process within Europe and are vitally interested in the development of the European Security and Defence Identity.

However, the present influence of the NATO non-member states is, at best, close to zero. In the whole process of changing European security architecture, which will deeply affect them in the aftermath, they are only allowed to stand on the sidelines. With the withering away of the Western European Union even the mirage-like influence of the associate partners could well be lost and there will be a hiatus of a few years until those countries become full fledged members of the EU and/or NATO.

I fully agree with Dr Karkoszka that a truly European security and defense policy can only be achieved with the participation of all states concerned.

In my opinion the actual area of EU's Common Foreign and Security Policy could be the area where the European Union could enlarge at a greater pace than elsewhere. This would also provide a boost for the whole debate of Europe's role in overall Euro-Atlantic security.

Slovenia, and I believe the other aspirant countries too, are staunch supporters of the transatlantic nature of the Alliance.

Let them be heard.

Thank you.

HELPING THE WESTERN BALKANS

There were attempts by some Allies and some NATO officials to pack Slovenia into a South East Europe grouping, mostly with the countries of the former Yugoslavia, east of Slovenia. I seemed to be a pain in the neck resisting such development and this was expressed well in some calls from Washington to Ljubljana in which I was called the "Brussels Problem." I had a bit of paranoia that there were forces trying to put us into some "Yugoslav" context again. With the support of the then Minister of Foreign Affairs Dr. Boris Frlec, I plodded on and in the end achieved the re-shaping and relabeling of the grouping. The following is my intervention at the meeting of the Consultative Forum on Security Matters on South Eastern Europe at NATO on 19 July 1999. Most of my surviving EAPC interventions are gathering dust, waiting for the eventual birth of the book "Putting Slovenia on the Map."

Secretary General,

May I first express our appreciation that since our first meeting on May 21ˢᵗ, the concerns Slovenia had had at the time, have been addressed and we are looking forward very much to cooperate constructively in the work of the Consultative Forum on South East Europe. The Forum has a clear concept now and we look forward to contribute to its contents.

It is in the interest of Slovenia – a Central European country bordering on the unstable region of South-Eastern Europe – that this area becomes, as soon as possible, stable and closely linked to the developed and democratic part of Europe.

To this intent, Slovenia has been since its establishment as an independent state over eight years ago engaged in the endeavours of the international community to ensure that the unstable parts of South-Eastern Europe, and in particular the territory of FRY, no longer represent a threat to peace in Europe. We are aware of our responsibility for the stability and progress of this region. We are willing to assume our share of the burden, and continue to make available our good offices, resources, knowledge and experience.

Slovenia has actively contributed in the past to the endeavours by the international community towards stabilisation in Albania, Bosnia and Herzegovina, Kosovo and Macedonia. I will not waste your time by listing them, but may I just mention at this point a few of our current efforts.

Slovenia proposed two years ago the setting up of a »mini Marshall Plan« for South Eastern Europe which should represent an inseparable part of stabilisation endeavours by the international community. Not surprisingly then, Slovenia is participating in the Stability Pact, which we consider a most important and comprehensive stabilisation project for the region.

Within the Stability Pact Slovenia has already offered to organise sub-tables on human and minority rights, as well as on small and medium-sized enterprises. We have a lot of experience in these areas. In addition we plan to organise several international meetings and conferences in the fall of 1999 to provide support to the Stability Pact.

One of the key prerequisites for reducing tensions and the possibilities of a renewed outburst of hostilities is arms control and the reduction of armament ceilings. There are definitely still too many arms in this region. In this vein, Slovenia is ready to resume negotiations on Article 5 of Annex 1-B of the Dayton Peace Agreement (on the basis of further consistent implementation of provisions under Article 4).

Slovenia is also joining international efforts for increased human security, mainly in the fields of demining, combat against illicit traffic in small arms and the protection of the rights of child in armed conflicts. Slovenia has established an International Trust Fund for Demining and Mine Victims Assistance in Bosnia and Herzegovina which has so far raised more than 18 million US dollars and is currently carrying out demining operations over an area of 1.5 million square meters and has assisted a large number of mine victims. We are also starting our demining operations in Croatia and have offered to follow suit in Kosovo to respond to an urgent humanitarian need.

The experience gained over the last ten years has shown that no institution could tackle alone the challenges in South Eastern Europe. Cooperation between NATO, the EU, WEU, UN, OSCE, the Council of Europe and other international organisations in the entire crisis span – from early warning to post-conflict rehabilitation - is of paramount importance. What we do not want to see is a duplication of efforts of the various international organisations (NATO should find its own *niche,* so to say.)

The solidarity and concrete assistance provided by the international community in the latest crisis clearly demonstrates the democratic character of the Euroatlantic community and its institutions. They have assumed the task of creating conditions for stabilisation, democracy, economic development and good neighbourly relations. These conditions will enable countries in this turbulent part of Europe to gradually integrate into Europe.

It is perhaps easy enough to talk about different iniatives. I hope we face the same situation when we tackle the question of the funds necessary to carry them out.

There is still a widely spread belief that the reasons for the outbreak of numerous crises in the so-called »territory of the former Yugoslavia« have arisen from the existing ethnic and religious differences. On the other hand, in Slovenia we believe that these crises are the consequence of intolerance and of the state policy of rabid nationalism pursued by the Serb regime for many years. The deficit of democracy in Serbia has been so severe that it could not be overcome by any dialogue.

The decisive intervention by NATO in Kosovo, in which Slovenia participated to the extent that it could, has brought the area closer to peace. Stability, however, cannot be anticipated without democratic rule in Serbia, which would provide a prospective for integration into Europe and international assistance for rehabilitation and development. This requires well-coordinated action by all international factors and organisations in support of democracy in Serbia.

Currently we see positive signs in Serbia but the opposition is not as yet strong enough to deliver quick changes. Also, an eventual departure of Milošević will not ensure an automatic democratic renewal of Serbia. What has happened in the recent past or in the past ten years was not only up to one man. The process of internal catharsis of the Serb people will not be a short-term affair.

The role of democratic media is of utmost importance in the entire present area of FRY, in Serbia, Montenegro, Kosovo and Vojvodina. Slovenia is willing to participate in the initiatives for democratisation of the media in Serbia as well as in re-establishing political contacts with the forward looking parties, groups and individuals.

In Montenegro, where the leadership is already committed to democratic change, the international community should play an active role to preserve and perhaps help enhance Montenegro's position. It is not inconceivable that the Montenegrin government could opt for a more radical political direction in the form of a referendum on independence and the full establishment of its statehood. The processes are very sensitive both externally and internally. Also, the public opinion has not backed yet these ideas outright. But the time seems to be working in Djukanović's favor.

Slovenia supports the democratic and reformist direction of the present government of Montenegro. It is not insignificant that the first Representative Office of the Government of Montenegro opened in Ljubljana. We have developed a continuous dialogue with this Government. To allay any eventual fears, I would like to stress that we have been advising the Montenegrin Government to tread carefully and not radicalize their relations with Serbia in a way which could result in the outbreak of a new war.

On the question of Kosovo, it is important to establish the rule of law and democratic institutions in Kosovo. It is necessary that there is full disarmament of KLA and other armed groups and that there is an agreement of all factions of Kosovar Albanians, including that of Rugova, on their inclusion in the new institutions. The autonomy of Kosovo must be ensured in order to establish the trust of the Albanian inhabitants of Kosovo in the authorities and in the state.

One more thing: ten years ago all the Slovenian political parties, both in Government and Opposition, united to condemn the Serb abuse of Kosovar Albanians human rights. What we are saying now is that the Serb minority in Kosovo must also be protected right away. Their treatment in Kosovo will represent a lithmus test for the new institutions and the majority population.

In Kosovo, Slovenia will not only participate in KFOR but will also take part in the civilian structures (for instance, UN administration, OSCE police instructors, ICTY experts), as well as building of economic ties, having been in the past a major investor in the Kosovo economy.

Thank you.

SLOVENIA AND NATO AFTER WASHINGTON

I spoke on NATO at every opportunity; hopefully also to people that mattered, as far as our drive for membership was concerned…. Yep, speeches definitely resembled each other, especially if I did not have enough time to tailor them to the audience. This one was delivered to the NATO Air Command and Control System Management Agency at the NATO HQ in Brussels on May 19, 1999 and was very much based on my earlier speech to the Dr. Manfred Wörner Circle. The major difference was disappointment with the Allies not having bothered to invite new aspirants for membership to join. I mention the impolite statement by the German Foreign Minister Joschka Fischer about the premature recognition of Slovenia (and Croatia). I could not hold my tongue in front of quite a number of Germans in the hall.

Ladies and Gentlemen,

It is a pleasure and an honor to address you on this occasion.

I always feel a bit funny when talking to people in the military or people closely connected with the military about Slovenia's foreign policy ambitions. On those occasions I feel I have to admit that I used to be a conscientious objector.

Before this turns you off I have to explain that that happened at the time when the military in Slovenia was directed from outside of Slovenia, when it spoke a foreign language, tried to implant an alien totaliaran ideology in the draftees' minds and prevented Slovenians from attempting to struggle for their emancipation. I managed to evade both the military service and jail as well, which was often the place where they put conscientious objectors.

This then is why I was a conscientious objector. I hope you share my view that I was doing the right thing. Today, when we have a modern, democratic, vibrant military of our own, I would serve, but they say I'm too old for it.

Not understanding the circumstances we lived in can also result in misunderstnding our process of independence.

I was so often asked why Slovenia was separating when all of Europe was uniting. My simple answer was that we had to be free first to choose our alliances and integrations. We did not want to be integrated by a totalitarian system. What sort of Europe and world would that be? Hitler wanted to integrate Europe. Would you want to live in a place like that? No thanks!

We are not simply replacing Belgrade by Brussels. There is a tiny difference between the two, and it is not the fine cuisine of this town. Serbian cuisine is fine enough but there are other things that are tasteless. It is the difference between democracy and totalitarianism.

I expect this should be understood by now because of Milošević's notoriety. It was not quite understood back in 1991.

I even negotiated once with Milošević. It was the time of the Conference on the Former Yugoslavia in The Hague when he was heading the Serbian delegation. I headed the Slovenian one. He was skilfull, he was persuasive. Everyone believed him. We did not.

But even now in some circles the »premature recognition of Slovenia and Croatia« is being mentioned. Not long ago we heard this from Joschka Fischer.

Well, let's talk about NATO. My only claim to fame on this subject matter might be something of which I have been reminded back home when I was leaving for my new job in Brussels back in January. Back in 1990, before Slovenia's independence, I wrote in an article that Slovenia had to become a member of NATO.

It was perhaps sheer insanity at that time. It was almost within our reach at the time of the Madrid Summit less than two years ago and it slipped through our fingers in Washington a few weeks ago. Next time it will not.

However, straightjackets for NATO visionaries have been laid away. I do not believe that there are many people in the know who doubt that Slovenia will - one day - become a full fledged NATO member.

A few years ago when I headed Slovenia's mission to the Court of St James's I had to pay attention – in my speeches – to spice up the matter with humor. I will try not to do that in these quite different - august - surrroundings of NATO HQ.

You should know that Slovenians are very serious people. And thrifty. I'm not sure you have heard about the Slovenian Kamikaze pilot who flew 25 successful missions.

*

At the time when Slovenia first started thinking seriously about NATO - NATO was still living in almost suspended animation. After having had fulfilled the historical role of keeping peace in Europe since the Forties - and at the same time had given the right international security environment for the existence of relative well being to Slovenia with its non-alignement, liberal communism and open borders - NATO was suspended at - sort of - Sweet Little Sixteen. The decision to grow up beyond 16 has given NATO new life. No one can stagnate and survive. That is clear in life, in business and it's clear in NATO.

While not invited in Madrid in July 1997 with the Czech Republic, Hungary and Poland to begin accession talks with NATO, Slovenia was, along with Romania, singled out for special recognition by the Alliance in the context of future membership. This was more or less repeated at the Washington Summit.

We were not happy, the dry language did not satisfy us, we should have achieved more. However, my country remains strongly committed to joining NATO and we will continue to work actively and agressively towards this goal.

Don't worry about the word agressively. Slovenia, not having any resources worth mentioning, except for the human resources, only knows how to be aggressive at work. We have shown this throughout our history and have never invaded our neighbours. Even our National Anthem, called

The Toast, written over 150 years ago, talks of neighbours as friends and about peace in the world. Strange people. At least it seemed so throughout our 14 hundred year recorded turbulent history in that corner of Europe between the Alps and the Adriatic. But perhaps our time has come. The time for peace and security throughout an undivided continent. We will do our best to contribute to it.

*

Why Join NATO? It's not due to any impending threat to our security or sovereignty, but rather, because we see joining NATO, as well as the European Union, as a means of consolidating our position within Europe. This is where our culture, history and geography place us. Joining NATO will not only ensure Slovenia's national security within the most effective system of collective defence in history, but will also provide us the opportunity to contribute more substantially to security and stability regionally and in Europe as a whole.

The past year and a half has been a particular period in our relations with NATO. A year ago we adopted the National Strategy for integration into NATO. This strategy stipulates Slovenia's engagement to promote increased cooperation, interoperability and harmonisation with NATO standards.

The Membership Action Plan (or MAP) introduced at the Washington Summit is nothing new to us; it encompasses all the areas of our own Strategy. Where MAP can be of use to us is to provide formal NATO's feedback on our fulfilment o the NATO accession criteria. So far we have heard from the Allies that we are ready for membership, now they will have to write this down and sign it.

We have also been conducting a high-level political dialogue with the Alliance through numerous visits, including NATO Secretary General Javier Solana's and NATO Supreme Allied Commander Europe General Wesley Clark's visits to Slovenia. Slovenian Foreign and Defence Ministers came to Brussels to address the NATO Council in March of last year and President Kučan visited NATO Headquarters last October. We also conducted an intensified dialogue with NATO at the expert level.

In addition, we have undertaken a number of practical activities and innovations, including hosting NATO's annual Economics Colloquium, the first time this has ever been held outside Brussels. We hosted a seminar on regional military cooperation and in October NATO's Science Committee held a workshop in Ljubljana. Last November, Slovenia hosted the NATO/PfP exercise Cooperative Adventure Exchange '98, the largest NATO "out of area" exercise to date.

All of this activity helps our preparations for eventual membership. We are closely observing the progress of the Czech Republic, Hungary and Poland as they have become full-fledged members of the Alliance and are taking actions in parallel, as if we were one of these countries. Their smooth integration into NATO will be an important factor in favour of further enlargement and not its postponement.

One of the ways in which Slovenia has demonstrated its readiness for NATO membership is through its active participation in both Partnership for Peace (PfP) and the Euro-Atlantic Partnership Council (EAPC). We have achieved transparency in defence planning and budgeting and ensured democratic control of the armed forces. We have also demonstrated our readiness to contribute to international peace support operations, to develop cooperative military relations with NATO, and to work towards achieving interoperability with NATO forces.

In this context, we have undertaken a number of cooperative agreements with the Allies and Partners, designed to improve the interoperability of our armed forces. We have made our Alpine Training Centre in Bohinjska Bela available for NATO and PfP training exercises and Allied vessels make regular port calls to the Slovenian port of Koper.

We are also developing a battalion-size specialised unit for participation in PfP training exercises and international peace support operations.

As an energetic participant in the European security architecture, Slovenia as a Central European country has demonstrated that it is a dependable partner and a force for stability in the region southeast of our borders. Among other activities, we are contributing forces to SFOR in Bosnia, including a military police platoon as part of the Multinational Specialised Unit (MSU). We are also contributing to the WEU-led MAPE in Albania, after having taken part in the Italian-led Alba operation. We have also created a fund for mine victims in Bosnia.

Slovenia, understanding Southeastern Europe better than many other Euroatlantic nations, has and will contribute a lot towards peace and security in the region. We have the knowledge, we have the energy and we have the resources.

Yet, Slovenia is a Central European country and will not agree to any eventual attempts to submerge it into any subregional Southeast European integration as a substitute for Euroatlantic integration. Sometimes Slovenia is being presented as a Southeast Europe or Balkan country. Slovenia lies between Vienna and Venice. If that makes it part of the Balkans then geograpgy should be rewritten.

We have especially demonstrated our responsibility towards helping securiy and stabiliy in supporting NATO's role in resolving the crisis in Kosovo by granting air space to NATO for air operations over FRY, contributed to the Kosovo Verification Mission and to KFOR and Allied Harbour.

When we granted air space to NATO last October, we did that within 24 hours, without posing any conditions or limitations upon NATO. We were the only non-NATO member country to do so. This quick and brave action of the Government later on received full backing of the opposition – just about the only area of support the Government has ever received from the Opposition. It is actually the opposition Social Democrats who have been and are the staunchest supporters of Slovenia's membership of NATO.

Speaking of staunch support - Slovenia is a staunch supporter of Allied Force.

In the Allied Force Slovenia is not neutral. And it is not just a partner. By contributing its air space and doing other things for NATO it is an Ally and is ready to take on further Allied responsibilities.

Being an Ally of the West is nothing new to us. The Slovenian Resistance movement was an Ally during World War II. We were also never part of the Warsaw Pact. Also, one of the first acts of the first democratically elected parliament in Slovenia in 1990 was to support the Western Coalition side in the Gulf War and we even offered to contribute a medical unit. This was still while we were part of Communist Serb dominated Yugoslav Federation which sided with Saddam. Who else?

When Slovenia was opting for democracy and independence it was opting at the same time for Euroatlantic integration. Our independence was not an end to itself. We did not want to create an insular Slovenia and live happily ever after.

A premature recognition of Slovenia? Common, Joschka (Mr. Fischer)!

In the broader regional context, we participate in the Italian-Hungarian-Slovenian multinational light land force, in the Central Europen Nations Cooperation in Peace Support Initiative (CENCOOP) and in the United Nations Peacekeeping Force in Cyprus (UNFICYP). Slovenia is also active in such regional initiatives as the Southeast European Cooperative Initiative (SECI), the Royaumont process and the Central European Initiative (CEI). In the process of creation of the Multinational Peace Force South Eastern Europe (MPF SEE), Slovenia and the U.S. participate as active observers.

*

How real is the Open Door Policy set up by NATO in Madrid? There is a feeling of some sort of **virtuality** of the Open Door Policy. Can we watch this "open" door for years and years and see no one go through? How will the candidate countries react to that?

How will the people in a candidate country observe NATO, if their country fulfills the criteria, contributes to regional and overall security, can foot the bill of its joining up and see, for instance, that all their neighbors have been allowed in while they are still waiting in front of this virtual open door.

How would - for instance - and this is purely speculative - Slovenians observe NATO if they one day realized that all their erstwhile adversaries - countries that occupied and partioned their country in World War 2 while Slovenians fought on the Allied side - were in NATO and they were not?

How would they see such an Alliance? I might be the only one asking this question. However, letting suitable candidate countries wait too long in front of NATO's door and not being allowed in could defeat the purpose of the Alliance.

Slovenia has established a stable system of parliamentary democracy with a high degree of protection of human and minority rights. We also have effective democratic civilian control over the armed forces and enjoy good-neighbourly relation with other countries in the region.

We have successfully implemented market reforms, with the process of privatisation in its final stage. Slovenia enjoys a strong rate of growth of around 4% and the highest GDP per capita for Central Europe – of around 10.000 US$ with an inflation rate around 6% and unemployment of around 7 % . Our defence spending will increase from the present 1.8 of GDP to 2.3% of GDP by the year 2003 as pledged by the government and agreed by the Parliament.

All of this adds up to a healthy economic outlook that will ensure that Slovenia will not be a financial burden for the Alliance, but on the contrary, will be a net contributor, if and when it is invited to accede.

How do we move ahead?

Enlargement is a building and not a dividing process. The prospect of joining NATO has had a positive effect on many countries in Central and Eastern Europe. It has contributed to providing the secure and stable environment necessary for building and strengthening democratic processes, a market economy, and protection of human rights and freedoms. It has fostered various forms of regional and subregional cooperation. The seven years of Slovenia's independence are a positive testament to NATO's effect on the region.

NATO has proved to be not merely a guarantor of democracy, stability and security for its member states, but it has also assumed responsibility for maintaining security and stability in the "out of area."

In Slovenia we welcomed the opportunity thus created for participation in evolving European security structures. We responded by deepening and enhancing our cooperation with NATO.

We are committed to becoming a credible and constructive NATO member. We expect that at the next opportunity our candidacy will finally result in an invitation.

Slovenia's early membership in NATO is not a divisive issue for the Alliance. No member country has ever opposed Slovenia's membership. It is indicative that the US Congress in its NATO Enlargement Facilitation Act passed in 1996, included Slovenia among the first four entrants into NATO, together with the Czech Republic, Hungary and Poland. In the same vein, in November 1998, Senator William V. Roth, Jr., in his Presidential Report to the North Atlantic Assembly stated, that "at the Washington Summit, Slovenia should be invited to begin negotiations aimed at accession to the North Atlantic Treaty."

At the time of the Washington Summit it was often said that the Kosovo issue dominated the meeting and prevented any serious discussion of invitations.

But the Kosovo issue could have worked in quite the opposite way.

The Alliance could have taken a bold position and realized that to show that it wants to project stability into the region it should invite Slovenia to join up. This would have shown to the troubled region, especially the FRY, that there is »light at the end of the tunnel« and that if they commit themselves to achieve Western values, they too could join the Euro-Atlantic integrations one day.

In my vision I see Slovenia as the 20th member of the Alliance.

Ladies and Gentlemen, I have tried to demonstrate today that Slovenia fulfills the accession criteria and that its membership should be in the direct interest of the Alliance.

May I thank you kindly for your patience.

SWALLOWING MY PRIDE

I wrote the following speech for Prime Minister Dr. Janez Drnovšek to be delivered at the meeting of the Euro Atlantic Partnership Council (EAPC) on 25 April 1999 in the framework of NATO's Washington Summit. I based it upon a draft supplied by one of the brightest young diplomats at the Slovenian MFA, Andrej Slapničar, later our ambassador in Paris and Strasbourg. I still keep his draft with my heavy corrections and additions in my terrible handwriting. I was sure I was the person who knew best what my Prime Minister should say. Anyway, he was the person who had decided the previous year to have me as Slovenia's first Ambassador to NATO, in spite of me being seen as someone from the other side of the political spectrum. However, after the delegation's arrival in Washington DC, I realized that the Prime Minister had brought with him a completely new "advisor," working hard on another draft. I swallowed my pride and dropped by her – a bit stale smelling – hotel room and managed to avert the most outrageous stupidities and atrocities in the text. She knew nothing about NATO or Slovenia's recent history. Her version was much weaker than mine (which was – as usually – a bit over the top). Perhaps her version has been published somewhere at some point. I have no recollection what Drnovšek actually said in the meeting. The whole Summit thing was pretty cool, including my first dinner at the White House, actually probably on the South Lawn; there were 500 guests if I remember correctly.

Mr. President, Mr. Chairman, Excellencies, Ladies and Gentlemen, dear Colleagues,

While we are celebrating two important anniversaries, the fiftieth anniversary of NATO and the fifth anniversary of the Partnership for Peace, here in Washington – a most appropriate place – we are also faced with a tragic situation in Kosovo.

NATO is for the first time in its fifty year history involved militarily in the turbulent region of South-eastern Europe. When deciding whether to launch air strikes against targets in the Federal Republic of Yugoslavia in order to stop the humanitarian catastrophe, NATO was taking into account the very basic values on which it firmly stands: democracy, human rights, the rule of law and the protection of human rights.

Thus the Summit is marked by very specific security-policy circumstances. The present moment dictates decisive, determined, and comprehensive decision-making of the Allied leaders to determine the future security image of an undivided Euro Atlantic area.

This is the moment to seize the opportunity and make a crucial impact on the future of the troubled region. It is not only the question of settling the Kosovo crisis but by giving the region a clear impetus towards stability and a vision of reconstruction, development and prosperity.

What can the Alliance do to project stability into the region? Firstly, it should issue invitation for membership to the country in the neighborhood that has clearly demonstrated that it has fulfilled the necessary criteria and is already contributing substantially to the strengthening of security and stability in South-eastern Europe, especially by taking on an Allied role in the Allied Force operation. Secondly, the Alliance should give clear perspective of PfP membership to the cooperative countries of the region, not yet members. And finally, by giving a vision to the FRY or its constituent parts that there is a "light at the end of the tunnel" if they accept what is demanded: reconstruction, development, prosperity and eventual Euro-Atlantic integration.

Slovenia is an unwavering, staunch supporter of Allied Force. We are providing our so much needed air space for air operations over FRY and are ready to do even more to assure the success of the operation.

We see that the thin line between membership and partnership is getting even thinner for the countries that are taking on Allied responsibilities, and in parallel receiving the Alliance's security guarantees. We appreciate it that our new role is recognized also by the Alliance.

Slovenia is not impatient, but we do believe that NATO should recognize our efforts and our progress and admit us into the Alliance. Slovenia belongs in NATO in a civilizational, geographical, cultural, sociological as well as geopolitical and geostrategic sense. A timely confirmation of the once again declared Open Door Policy will also avoid heightened expectations for every future round of NATO Enlargement and thus make those expectations more realistic.

While Slovenia welcomes the Membership Action Plan and the Enhanced and More Operational Partnership in which it will take an active part, we firmly believe that Article Ten of the Washington Treaty and Article 8 of the Madrid Summit Declaration, as well as the 1995 Study on NATO Enlargement remain the basis for further NATO Enlargement. A country, as well developed and prepared as Slovenia is, cannot envisage the MAP as its "road map" towards membership.

The continuation of the enlargement process is not only in the interest of the aspirant countries but I believe very much in the direct interest of the Alliance. NATO has proven that by its three new members. Their inclusion is not only important for them but also for the entire family of Euro-Atlantic nations and an important encouragement for NATO candidates.

Only an enlarged NATO can respond to the new security challenges in Europe. May I add that one must not forget that the enlargement process should be geographically balanced. That is why it is vital that the next round of enlargement moves the Alliance's borders towards South and South-East.

Thank you.

TRYING TO GET A WORD
TO CLINTON

I wrote a few letters to people who I thought could influence the thinking on inviting Slovenia to join NATO. I am including just three. This is one of the letters of 21 April 1999. I wrote to The Honorable Mel Carnahan, Governour of Missouri. He belonged to the high ranks of the Democratic Party. I have known the Carnahans since the time of the first democratic elections in post-communist Hungary in 1990 when I first met Robin and Tom. Later on my family and I stayed both at the Governor's Mansion in Jefferson City and – after the tragic airplane crash that killed the Governor and his son Randy – also at their Farm near Rolla. Both Tom and his brother Russ with their wives, as well as Robin, visited us at our home in Zgornje Pirniče that my boys nowadays call Kmetija, meaning Farm. As far as the Clintons are concerned, I did attend the NATO Summit Dinner at the White House in 1999 and a decade and a half later met and briefly talked to Hillary at the European External Action Service building, at a humorous reception hosted by Catherine Ashton.

Dear Governor,

You may remember my family's visit to Jefferson City almost 4 years ago during our long trip throughout the United States. We enjoyed very much your kind hospitality at the historic Governor's Mansion. Our boys, Boštjan and Aleš, still talk with fondness about their stay on the top floor.

May I just let you know that after my almost 6 year stint as Slovenia's first Ambassador to London (and Dublin) I returned to the Slovenian Foreign Ministry but was asked after a year to take over as Slovenia's first Ambassador to NATO in Brussels. I have been here just over two months now.

At the dinner that you and Mrs Carnahan kindly offered to Magdalena and me we also discussed, among other things, the progress that Slovenia has made since its independence in 1991 as well as its future Euro-Atlantic integration.

May I inform you that Slovenia, with the best developed economy in Central Europe, a country based on the rule of law, high respect of human and minority rights, and well on its way to European Union membership, is also a candidate for membership in NATO.

Slovenia was very close to being invited almost two years ago at the time of the Madrid Summit together with the Czech Republic, Hungary and Poland. Unfortunately, in spite of the general view of the Allies that Slovenia was fulfilling the entrance criteria as well as the three other Central European countries it was decided that its turn would come at the next occasion.

And we see the Washington Summit in a couple of days as that occasion. Since Madrid Slovenia has done a lot in all the areas that represent entrance criteria and is seen by the Allies, including the U.S., as a prime candidate. Unfortunately, once again, there is no consensus at this point on new invitations.

The United States plays a crucial, I think I can say, decisive role on this question. From all my soundings with my colleagues here, I understand that President Clinton's initiative to invite Slovenia would be accepted by the rest of the Allies. And it would also demonstrate to the other aspirants that the door remains open and that they too will be able to accede when they fulfil the criteria and when the Alliance decides that their accession would also strengthen the Alliance.

Knowing your close relationship with the President may I ask you to talk to him on this point. He is the one to make a change.

There is another reason why an invitation at this point to Slovenia would be timely.

It concerns the dark clouds of the Kosovo crisis hanging over the NATO Summit in Washington which is to mark the 50th Anniversary of the Atlantic Alliance. In spite of the serious and tragic situation in Kosovo, the Summit can result in a celebration, if bold, visionary steps are taken when the Heads of State or Government meet.

This is the moment to seize the opportunity and make a crucial impact on the future of the troubled region to the Southeast of Slovenia's borders. It is not only the question of settling the Kosovo crisis but of giving the region a powerful impetus towards stability and clear perspective of reconstruction, development, prosperity and reconciliation.

If the NATO leaders find the vision to project stability into the region they should issue an invitation to the country that has demonstrated time and time again that it has fulfilled the entry criteria and that it is able to take on Allied responsibilities. Slovenia has not only proven that it is a constructive and reliable partner of NATO, in the latest crisis it has not remained on the sidelines as a neutral observer but has taken on an important step forward.

Since last October my country has been, without preconditions, granting its air space to NATO, even though Slovenia does not border on the Federal Republic of Yugoslavia. Currently its air space is being heavily used for air operations over FRY. And Slovenia, an unwavering, staunch supporter of Allied Force, is ready to do more in its, as we see it, Allied role, hoping to contribute as much as it can to a successful operation.

By inviting Slovenia, formerly part of the defunct federation, a country which is not part of the problem but can contribute significantly towards a solution, the Alliance can demonstrate to the Balkan region that there is »light at the end of the tunnel« if the norms of Euro-Atlantic nations are respected. That, after the acceptance of the international community's demands and the end of hostilities, there is a realistic chance of moving FRY, or its constituent parts, towards Euro-Atlantic integration.

Slovenia can, with its knowledge of the region, stemming from its past decades long co-habitation, contribute even more substantially as a new, reliable member of the Alliance. Being, as I have mentioned, the most developed country of Central Europe, Slovenia also has its ample own resources to make this transition towards full-fledged membership smooth.

The opportunity to make this brave, visionary step should not be wasted.

Governor, I would appreciate highly your personal assistance in this.

Please convey Magdalena's and my best wishes also to Mrs Carnahan. I have lately talked both to Tom and Robin and treasure their friendship very much.

Sincerely Yours,

DEAR GEORGE

I wrote this letter to my friend The Rt. Hon George Robertson, MP, the British Secretary of State for Defense on 20 April 1999.

Dear George,

It was good to see you few weeks ago in London at the time of the RUSI Conference. It is interesting how our paths have been crossing since our initial meeting in London 8 years ago when I first tried to persuade you that future Slovenian independence would represent a bedrock of our future democratic Euro-Atlantic integration.

I admit, it sounded far-fetched at the time. However, we could both see at our later meetings during my (highly enjoyable) stay in London that Slovenia proved to be a viable example of a newly independent modern European state, based on the rule of law, high respect of human and minority rights as well as successful economic transformation.

I would like to thank you and the United Kingdom for continuous support given to this course of our development. I will never forget the times around the meeting at Sintra when the British Government supported the 3+Slovenia option for the Alliance's invitations at Madrid. Unfortunately, due to well-known reasons, it happened otherwise.

In a few days we will be meeting in Washington at the historic 50th Anniversary of the Atlantic Alliance. In spite of the serious and tragic situation in Kosovo, the event can result in a celebration, if bold, visionary steps are taken when the Heads of State or Government meet.

This is the moment to seize the opportunity and make a crucial impact on the future of the troubled region to the south-east of Slovenia's borders. It is not only the question of settling the Kosovo crisis but of giving the region a powerful impetus towards stability and clear perspective of reconstruction, development, prosperity and reconciliation.

If the leaders find the vision to project stability into the region they should issue an invitation to the country that has demonstrated time and time again that it has fulfilled the entry criteria and that it is able to take on Allied responsibilities. Slovenia has not only proven that it is a constructive and reliable partner of NATO, but in the latest crisis it has taken on an important step forward.

Since last October my country has been, without preconditions, granting its air space to NATO. Currently it is being heavily used for air operations over FRY. And Slovenia, an unwavering, staunch supporter of Allied Force, is ready to do more in its, as we see it, Allied role, hoping to contribute as much as it can to a successful operation.

By inviting Slovenia, formerly part of the defunct federation, a country which is not part of the problem but can contribute significantly towards a solution, the Alliance can demonstrate to the Balkan region that there is »light at the end of the tunnel« if the norms of Euro-Atlantic nations are respected. That, after the acceptance of the international community's demands and the end of hostilities, there is a realistic chance of moving FRY or its constituent parts towards Euro-Atlantic integration.

George, Slovenia can, with its knowledge of the region, stemming from its past decades long co-habitation, contribute even more substantially as a new, reliable member of the Alliance. You are also well aware that as the most developed country of Central Europe, well on its way towards EU membership, it also has its ample own resources to make this transition towards full-fledged membership smooth.

An invitation to Slovenia, which is widely seen by the Allies as a prime candidate for NATO membership, could also demonstrate to the other aspirants that the door remains open and that they too will be able to accede in time.

The opportunity to make this brave, visionary step should not be wasted. The British Government, knowing well Slovenia's credentials,

COMMAND AND CONTROL

The Speaking Notes I had for the meeting on 7 April 1999 at the NATO HQ with U.S. Secretary of Defense William Cohen are printed below. I definitely delivered the gist of it, but I cannot vouch that every single word was uttered. Anyway, I saw the matter discussed as my baby, as I had been, before leaving Ljubljana for Brussels, vitally involved in the decision to grant Slovenian air space to NATO. The proof that in the meeting I also mentioned Milošević's harmful command and control mechanism, would come later on when Prime Minister Drnovšek visited the Supreme Allied Commander Europe Gen. Wesley Clark at the SHAPE HQ in Mons, Belgium. At that meeting, after a few pleasantries exchanged, Gen. Clarke turned to me and said: "Ambassador, we did what you asked us for." He meant the bombing of the TV transmitter in Belgrade. My Prime Minister gave me a strange look but never commented. I am not sure the General participated in the meeting with Secretary Cohen. Perhaps he meant a personal talk I had with him in Mons when I mentioned the eventually harmful effect of the satellite TV transmission of the Serbian TV and suggested such broadcasts should be switched off. Be it as it may...

Secretary Cohen, Ambassador Vershbow, Gentlemen,

May I thank you very much for accepting the Slovenian initiative to meet the ambassadors of, may I say, "Frontline Countries," in the Allied Force campaign for a brief briefing, or "security consultations."

And I would just like to add at this point that Slovenia is a staunch supporter of Allied Force. We have been unwavering in our support of NATO's role since last October when we granted air space – without any preconditions – for NATO's activities over FRY.

Slovenia does not consider itself just a Partner within the PfP framework but an Ally in this "Anti-Milošević Alliance." We hope NATO recognizes our role. One way of demonstrating this would be through closer briefings and sharing of information. We would expect briefings following NAC meetings and before the Press briefings, their contents being also privileged information and not just a few crumbs from the Press briefings.

The Slovenian Government, supported by the Opposition, believes that NATO should not ease but intensify its military operations to force Milošević to agree to what has been demanded of him.

Slovenia appreciates NATO's security guarantees as stated in the letters of Secretary General Solana to our Prime Minister, even though we do not feel threatened by FRY at this point.

Actually our public opinion polls have over the past few days seen an important increase of support for Allied Force to over 60%, over 65% for granting air space and over 76% for accepting refugees.

Slovenians know Milošević perhaps better than the rest. When I first met him in 1991, as we were negotiating Slovenia's independence, he looked completely trustworthy, but I did not believe a word he said. I knew everything he did was in his own – short term – interest. It's sad that it has taken so long for the rest of the world to realize that.

One concrete point I would like to make: it is of importance to break the backbone of Serbia's propaganda machine, specifically by taking out Serbia's TV transmitters. They are not part of the Media; they are part of Command and Control. The Serbs watching Serbian TV have absolutely no idea what is going on in Kosovo.

May I say at the end that NATO has – at the Washington Summit – a great opportunity to project stability into this part of Europe by giving a clear impetus to the Open Door Policy.

Thank you.

WRITING TO NATO SECRETARY GENERAL

On 30 March 1999, I wrote this letter on Slovenia's position on the Kosovo crisis to Secretary General of NATO Javier Solana.

Dear Secretary General,

Slovenia has been for the past decade in the front ranks of countries warning of the abuse of human rights in Kosovo and of the consequences this might have on the political and security situation in the province and the region as a whole.

Slovenia, also being a prime candidate for full-fledged NATO membership, fully supports the Allied Force action over the Federal Republic of Yugoslavia.

In this operation Slovenia is not just a partner country within the context of PfP and EAPC. Having promptly reacted to NATO's request last October by granting its air space for NATO's air operations over the FRY, Slovenia has, may I say, taken on an Allied role. Slovenia is the only country which has granted its air space to NATO but does not border on the Federal Republic of Yugoslavia. We appreciated NATO's understanding of our role in this operation resulting in the security guarantees extended to Slovenia, as stated in your letters to Prime Minister Dr Drnovšek on 13 October 1998 and 24 March 1999.

Our »Allied« position is strengthened by the fact that Slovenia, since the start of the operation, has been unwavering in its staunch support for the action to help stop the humanitarian catastrophe in Kosovo and create the basis for a just and long lasting solution of the crisis. You are also aware that Slovenia was the first Partner country to offer its participation in KFOR. I also hope that the intelligence information on Kosovo provided by Slovenia has been of use to the Alliance.

Ready and willing to continue acting together with NATO Slovenia has great interest in being informed of the operation to the highest extent possible. Unfortunately until now we have only been briefed as Partners or within the SFOR framework which we find insufficient.

May I suggest, Secretary General, that countries which are taking on almost Allied roles in the operation be briefed alongside the NATO member countries, within the NAC Ambassadorial, 19 + n or some other appropriate formula of enhanced cooperation.

You may rest assured, Secretary General, that we would accept such a role with utmost seriousness.

Please accept, Secretary General, the assurances of my highest consideration.

SLOVENIA AND NATO: 20/20 VISION

This was my first "major" speech on Slovenia's NATO ambitions, after I had arrived at the HQ in January 1999. I was invited to speak already on 22 March at a luncheon of the "Dr. Manfred Wörner Circle," named after the late former Secretary General, by its driving force Peter Müller. I was asked to provide the speech to be published in their publication "NATO's Nations and Partners for Peace." I turned in just a slightly cleaned version (without subtitles like Sweet Little Sixteen or HATO) which joined the speeches of two U.S. ambassadors, as well as the ambassadors of Hungary, the Czech Republic, Italy and Romania. I adapted the text later on to use it at other occasions. Like the one to the AFCEA crowd that in this book precedes the original, on account of chapters going from the latest to the earliest.

Ladies and Gentlemen,

It is a pleasure and an honor to address you on this occasion. I feel humbled in front of so many people who know a lot more abot NATO than I do. I have spoken on Slovenia's ambitions to join the Alliance in front of other audiences before, but none as knowledgeable on the subject as you are.

My only claim to fame on this subject matter might be something of which I have just been reminded back home. Back in 1990, before Slovenia's independence, I wrote in an article that Slovenia had to become a member of NATO. It was perhaps sheer insanity at that time, almost within our reach at the time of the Madrid Summit less than two years ago and will be perhaps slipping through our fingers in the next few weeks.

However, straightjackets for NATO visionaries have been laid away. I do not believe that there are many doubting Thomases in the know who doubt that Slovenia will – one day – become a full-fledged NATO member.

A few years ago when I headed Slovenia's mission to the Court of St James's I had to pay attention - in my speeches - to spice up the matter with humour. I will try not to do that in these quite different – august – surrroundings, but I hope you will still allow me to use a lighter approach to this – serious – matter. I believe this approach is suitable - especially at this time when we hear from most sources that the issuing of new invitations at the Washington Summit is highly doubtable. You would not want me to get all depressed in front of you.

SWEET LITTLE SIXTEEN

At the time when Slovenia first started thinking seriously about NATO - NATO was still living in almost suspended animation. After having had fulfilled the historical role of keeping peace in Europe since teh Forties - and at the same time given the right environment for the existence of relative well being to Slovenia with its liberal communism and open borders – NATO was suspended at sort-of Sweet Little Sixteen. The decision to grow up beyond 16, beyond this age - has given NATO new life. No one can stagnate and survive. That is clear in life, in business and it's clear in NATO.

While not invited in Madrid in July 1997 with the Czech Republic, Hungary and Poland to begin accession talk with NATO, Slovenia was, along with Romania, singled out for special recognition by the Alliance in the context of future membership. My country remains strongly committed to joining NATO and we will continue to work towards this goal.

Why?

It's not due to any impending threat to our security or sovereignty, but rather, because we see joining NATO, as well as the European Union, as a means of consolidating our democratic system and position within Europe. This is where our culture, history and geography place us. Joining NATO will not only ensure Slovenia's national security within the most effective system of collective defence in history, but will also provide us the opportunity to contribute more substantially to security and stability regionally and in Europe as a whole.

This year has been a particular period in our relations with NATO. Last February we adopted a national strategy for integration into NATO. This strategy stipulates Slovenia's engagement to promote increased cooperation, interoperability and harmonisation with NATO standards. A concrete example of this commitment is legislation which mandates that all military equipment procured must meet NATO standards.

We have also been conducting a high-level political dialogue with the Alliance through numerous visits, including NATO Secretary General Javier Solana's and NATO Supreme Allied Commander Europe, General Wesley Clark's visits to Slovenia. Slovenian Foreign Minister Boris Frlec and the Minister of Defence Tit Turnšek went to Brussels to address the NATO Council in March of last year and President Milan Kučan visited NATO Headquarters last October. We have also been conducting an intensified dialogue with NATO at the expert level.

In addition, we have undertaken a number of practical activities and innovations, including hosting NATO's annual Economics Colloquium, the first time this has ever been held outside Brussels. We hosted a seminar on regional military cooperation and in October and NATO's Science Committee held a workshop in Ljubljana. Last November, Slovenia hosted the NATO/PfP exercise Cooperative Adventure Exchange '98, the largest NATO "out of area" exercise to date.

All of this activity helps our preparations for eventual membership. We are closely observing the progress of the Czech Republic, Hungary and Poland as they have become full-fledged members of the Alliance and are taking actions in parallel, as if we were one of these countries. Their smooth integration into NATO will be an important factor in favour of further enlargement and not its postponement.

One of the ways in which Slovenia has demonstrated its readiness for NATO membership is through its active participation in both Partnership for Peace (PfP) and the Euro-Atlantic Partnership Council (EAPC). We committed ourselves to achieving transparency in defence planning and budgeting and to ensuring democratic control of the armed forces. We also declared our readiness to contribute to international peace support operations, to develop cooperative military relations with NATO, and to work towards achieving interoperability with NATO forces.

In this context, we have undertaken a number of cooperative agreements with the allies and partners, designed to improve the interoperability of our armed forces. We have made our Alpine Training Centre in Bohinjska Bela available for NATO and PfP training exercises and Allied vessels make regular port calls to the Slovenian port of Koper. We are also developing a battalion-size specialised unit for participation in PfP training exercises and international peace support operations.

As an energetic participant in the European security architecture, Slovenia has demonstrated that it is a dependable partner and a force for stability in the region southeast of our borders. Among other activities, we are contributing forces to SFOR in Bosnia, including a military police platoon as part of the Multinational Specialised Unit (MSU). We are also contributing to the WEU-led MAPE in Albania, after having taken part in the Italian-led Alba operation.

We have also demonstrated our responsibility in supporting NATO's role in resolving the crisis in Kosovo by granting air space to NATO for operations over FRY, contributed to the Kosovo Verification Mission and offered to contribute to KFOR.

In addition, we have established an international trust fund in Slovenia for de-mining and mine victim assistance in Bosnia.

In the broader regional context, we participate in the Italian-Hungarian-Slovenian multinational light land force, in the Central Europen Nations Cooperation in Peace Support Initiative (CENCOOP) and in the United Nations Peacekeeping Force in Cyprus (UNFICYP). Slovenia is also active in such regional initiatives as the Southeast European Cooperative Initiative (SECI), the Royaumont process and the Central European Initiative (CEI). In the process of creation of the Multinational Peace Force South Eastern Europe (MPF SEE), Slovenia and the U.S. participate as active observers.

NATO

We have seen that not everyone is enthusiasic about the enlargement of the Alliance – within the Alliance and without. I remember the fierce opposition when I still served in the UK. Actually, a group of opponents there – mostly made up of former ambassadors to the USSR – even gave themselves a name – BONE - Britons Opposing NATO Expansion. When meeting people supporting or opposing NATO enlagement in the States a year ago I could immediately distinguish who was who. The supporters talked about NATO enlargement while the opponents spoke of NATO expansion.

And I believe NATO enlargement or expansion will remain a **bone** of contenion also in the future. A lot of the arguments against were quite valid, but valid arguments are so often proven wrong. And to a large extent they have been proven wrong in the case of the so-called first wave of NATO enlargement. And I expect the rest will be proven wrong in the future.

And to put it lightly – this is no joke – it is clear why Russians should not like NATO. In Russian they spell NATO H. A. T. O. HATO. How could they like it?

But what worries me more is the sort of virtuality of the Open Door Policy. Can we watch this "open" door for years and years and see no one go through? How will the candidate countries react to that?

How will the people in a candidate country observe NATO, if their country fulfills the criteria, contributes to regional and overall security, can foot the bill of its joining up and see, for instance, that all their neighbors have been allowed in while they are still waiting in front of this virtual open door.

How would - for instance - and this is purely speculative - Slovenians observe NATO if they one day realized that all their erstwhile adversaries - countries that occupied and partioned their country in World War 2 while Slovenians fought on the Allied side - were in NATO and they were not? How would they see such an Alliance? I may be the only one asking this question. However, letting suitable candidate countries wait too long in front of NATO's door and not being allowed in could defeat the purpose of the Alliance.

Slovenia has established a stable system of parliamentary democracy with a high degree of protection of human and minority rights. We also have effective democratic civilian control over the armed forces and enjoy good-neighbourly relation with other countries in the region.

We have successfully implemented market reforms, with the process of privatisation in its final stage. Slovenia enjoys a strong rate of growth of around 4% and a relatively high GDP per capita for Central Europe – of arround US$10,000 with an inflation rate around 8% and unemployment around 7%. Our defense spending will increase from the present 1.85 of GDP (US$365 million) to the level of 2.3% of GDP (US$544 million) by the year 2003, as pledged by the Government and agreed by the Parliament. All of this adds up to a healthy economic outlook that will ensure that Slovenia will not be a financial burden for the Alliance, but will, on the contrary, be a net contributor, if and when it is invited to accede.

20/20 VISION

How do we move ahead?

Enlargement is a building and not a dividing process. The prospect of joining NATO has had a positive effect on many countries in Central and Eastern Europe. It has contributed to providing the secure and stable environment necessary for building and strengthening democratic processes, a market economy, and protection of human rights and freedoms. It has fostered various forms of regional and subregional cooperation. The seven years of Slovenia's independence are a positive testament to NATO's effect on the region.

NATO has proven to be not merely a guarantor of democracy, stability and security for its member states, but it has also assumed responsibility for maintaining security and stability in the "out of area."

In Slovenia we welcomed the opportunity thus created for participation in evolving European security structures. We responded by deepening and enhancing our cooperation with NATO. We are committed to eventually becoming a credible and constructive NATO member. We hope and expect that our candidacy will be studied carefully.

Slovenia's early membership in NATO is not a divisive issue for the Alliance. No member country has ever opposed Slovenia's membership. It is indicative that the US Congress in its NATO Enlargement Facilitation Act passed in 1996, included Slovenia among the first four entrants into NATO, together with the Czech Republic, Hungary and Poland. In the same vein in November 1998 Senator William V. Roth, Jr. in his

Presidential Report to the North Atlantic Assembly stated, that "at the Washington Summit, Slovenia should be invited to begin negotiations aimed at accession to the North Atlantic Treaty."

I have titled today's address Slovenia & NATO: 20/20 Vision. It's an exopression which signifies perfect vision. It is important to see how the enlargement will jump from 19 member countries forward to 20, 21, 22.

In my vision – and perhaps it is faulty as I wear glasses to correct my nearsightedness – I see Slovenia as the 20th member of teh Alliance. I have tried to demonstrate today that it fulfills the accession criteria and that its membership should be in the direct interest of the Alliance.

Thank you.

FIRST TIME ON NATO

I went to Madrid in September 1991 to attend the North Atlantic Assembly, in 1999 renamed as NATO Parliamentary Assembly. The NAA was chaired at the time by its President, U.S. Senator Charles Rose. I was invited as a speaker from a country that had no international status whatsoever; it was right after our Declaration of Independence, the Yugoslav military invasion, and their defeat. I had the chance to present our, or rather *my* case at the, if I remember correctly, Political Committee session. There also was a Croatian representative, their National Assembly President Žarko Domljan, whose statement, following mine, basically was: "Like Slovenia, Croatia will…" Before leaving Ljubljana there had been a discussion in the Foreign Affairs Committee, that I chaired, whether I should go. The Socialist Party MP Jože Smole expressed his concern that I would enroll Slovenia in NATO. I answered that I would be very happy to do that if I could. He was not the only skeptic though. Those were the early days. When in Madrid, I realized those were early days for NATO too. No imagination. Everyone was still saying that they could never have imagined the Fall of the Wall 10 years previously… Anyway, I did clearly express my interest in Slovenia joining NATO. Like back at home, probably everyone thought I was a bit funny in the head. The following is the text I had prepared and, I believe, mostly delivered.

Mr Chairman, Colleagues,

It is indeed a great honor for me to participate in the work of the North Atlantic Assembly. It is also a privilege, as I come from a newly independent country that is on the way to being universally recognized. A country, that so far had no chance to voice its opinion on the world scene.

You may expect me to talk about the recent past when Slovenia was faced with a cowardly and bloody military attack by the federal government of the defunct Yugoslavia. But let me leave history to historians. I believe it is time to look forward, not back.

What counts is that Slovenia has been since June 25 of this year both *de-iure* and *de-facto* an independent country that has already been recognized by a number of countries. May I express my belief that your invitation to me to speak here, as a representative of the Slovenian Parliament, is also a sort of recognition by the North Atlantic Assembly of Slovenia as a subject of international law. Growing up as a kid in Communist Slovenia, not everything I heard about NATO was positive. Yet NATO was never perceived in the public as an adversary. Also, the official position of the federation was non-aligned; therefore not part of the Communist Bloc or Warsaw Pact.

Those of us who opposed the Communist system and were in favor of democracy understood well that we would never have a chance to topple the Communist regime without NATO's existence. NATO represented the bedrock of democracy, more than any other Western institution.

Slovenia has been from the outset of its pro-democracy movement turned towards wider, democratic integration. Not independence for its own sake. We do not want to be an island. We want to open up. Thus we have made it very clear that we want to join the European Community. Slovenia is now a state ruled by law, independent and democratic, with a high regard for human and minority rights.

I wish I could present today Slovenia's bid to join NATO. It is my personal hope that Slovenia could join this democratic defense organization. However, when I left Ljubljana I promised my parliamentary colleagues not to do so. I believe, however, that this can become soon also Slovenia's official policy. I will dedicate myself to this idea.

Slovenia does not need the protection of NATO's umbrella. Our Territorial Defense, our Army, demonstrated clearly that it is capable of defending the country against a much stronger and a devious adversary. We are also – as the economy is concerned – a viable country, as well developed as a couple of EC member states. But I believe only strong and stable countries can join NATO and it is my hope that, when the time comes, NATO will realize that and make it possible for such countries to join.

Thank you.

Printed in the United States
by Baker & Taylor Publisher Services